T0265219

Sitcommentary

Sitcommentary

Television Comedies That Changed America

MARK A. ROBINSON

ROWMAN & LITTLEFIELD
Lanham • Boulder • New York • London

Published by Rowman & Littlefield
An imprint of The Rowman & Littlefield Publishing Group, Inc.
4501 Forbes Boulevard, Suite 200, Lanham, Maryland 20706
www.rowman.com

86-90 Paul Street, London EC2A 4NE

British Library Cataloguing in Publication Information Available

Library of Congress Cataloging-in-Publication Data

Names: Robinson, Mark A., 1973– author.
Title: Sitcommentary : television comedies that changed America / Mark A. Robinson.
Description: Lanham : Rowman & Littlefield, [2019] | Includes bibliographical references and index.
Identifiers: LCCN 2019010047 (print) | LCCN 2019011170 (ebook) | ISBN 9781538114209 (electronic) | ISBN 9781538114193 (cloth : alk. paper) | ISBN 9781538190494 (paperback)
Subjects: LCSH: Situation comedies (Television programs)—United States. | Television broadcasting—Social aspects—United States.
Classification: LCC PN1992.8.C66 (ebook) | LCC PN1992.8.C66 R63 2019 (print) | DDC 791.45/617—dc23
LC record available at https://lccn.loc.gov/2019010047

For my mother,
Laureen Coleman,
who introduced me to *Maude*,
who let me stay up past my bedtime to watch *The Facts of Life*,
and who continually puts up with my quoting *The Golden Girls*.

Contents

Preface

I was an odd child . . .

As a little boy growing up in the 1970s and 1980s, I watched loads of television. Just like most of the kids my age, I needed my regular doses of cartoons, adventure programs, and situation comedies. Heck, I used to sneak out of my room on Friday nights and hide behind the chair, where I would watch *Dallas*. This love of television isn't what made me peculiar. If that were the case, every person I know would be off-the-beam. No, what did set me apart was my voracious appetite for collecting television.

"Collecting television? What does that mean?" would be your logical response to that statement. For as long as I can remember, I wanted to know every name of every performer and of every character they played on every television show that I encountered. Committing cast lists to memory was my passion. I can vividly remember at age five knowing that Carroll O'Connor played Archie Bunker, that Beatrice Arthur played Maude Findlay, that John Travolta played Vinnie Barbarino, and that Esther Rolle played Florida Evans. This is not an exaggeration. It was simply information that was relevant to my world.

When I was in third grade, I received a cassette recorder for Christmas. It was among the most cherished and probably most utilized presents to ever make its way under the tree. So what was the first thing that I sat down and preserved on my first Memorex tape? The theme song to *The Mary Tyler Moore Show*. I had always loved the ditty and the feeling it gave me, a notion of optimism and hope in an otherwise dreary world. I'd grab a winter hat, put it on my head, and toss it in the air when Mary did. Soon, I was combing cable television to find as many theme songs as I could locate to record just so that I could listen to them anytime that I wanted to. Many an afternoon and evening was spent crouched on our red pile carpet in front of the RCA television, pressing "Record."

Once you have a collection of theme songs, what exactly does one do with it? Like most kids (sarcasm implied), I committed every lyric of every song to memory. It is a hilarious side note to this story to admit that I was in a singing group in college where we sang nothing but TV theme songs, so listening to those cassettes was time well spent, chalked up to "rehearsal"—lots and lots of rehearsal.

As I got older, a wonderful thing came along called Nick at Nite, essentially the nighttime programming of the Nickelodeon children's network. On it, classic television (particularly sitcoms) played from the decades before I was born. I was introduced to generations of unwatched television, with shows like *The Munsters, Bewitched, I Dream of Jeannie, The Donna Reed Show, Dennis the Menace,* and *The Beverly Hillbillies* to explore. More cast lists to memorize, more theme songs to record and sing.

With time, the shows of my childhood eventually graduated into the classic television roster of Nick at Nite. An older and mature me was revisiting shows like *All in the Family, Maude, Good Times, One Day at a Time,* and *Soap* and discovering that they held hidden gems of social relevance, irony, and dark comedy. It was at this point that my interest grew in how comedy was capable of more than just laughs. It was at this point that I started to understand that some people were laughing *at* Archie Bunker and that some people were laughing *with* Archie Bunker. Moving forward, I sought out sitcoms that were more than just a string of jokes. Whether I could have articulated this exact thought at the time I am not sure, but I wanted to laugh and learn at the same time. I craved comedy that made me think, that made me face my biases and prejudices, and that presented me with people, places, and perspectives that I would have otherwise not encountered in a small rural town in upstate New York.

So my interest in television has been around as long as I can remember. It has stayed with me and propelled me to write about it whenever I can, though I do split my love of television with my passions for writing about film and Broadway musicals. It has inspired me to write a book about television theme songs and how those melodies and lyrics have lifted us and moved us. It was always the next logical step that I would write something about how the television sitcom reflected and facilitated social change in America. This book, hopefully, is a testament to the impact that television has had on shaping me and the world in which we all live.

When first deciding how to lay this book out, there were several approaches I realized I could choose from. Some people suggested that I group sitcoms by category, such as LGBTQ topics, women's issues, political, and so on. In many ways, that would have made for an easier book to write. However, I started thinking about the kind of book a television fan would want to read. Since I've spent a lot of time reading about television, its history, and its legacy, I concluded that the book I wanted to create was going to be one that best served a younger, curious version of myself.

When I pick up a book about television, I always thumb through it to see if my favorite shows are included. I immediately search for *The Golden Girls* (my favorite sitcom of all time), then move on to see what is written about the ones I admire, such as *All in the Family*, *Designing Women*, and *Good Times*. I wanted to create a book where the initiated, interested, and also the aficionados could quickly find the sitcom they were seeking without having to dig through the index to figure out what pages it is on. I expect that most people will not read this book cover to cover (although I certainly invite you to do so) but rather will jump around in a way that meets their needs and interests. I have, however, tried to link shows within chapters, tying titles to relevant sitcoms that came before with similar themes as well as to their heirs apparent. Where appropriate, I have also offered suggestions for additional reading about that program.

You will find that certain chapters discuss one aspect or theme of a show that made it stand out, while other chapters point to particular noteworthy episodes. For each show, I have tried to capture the essence of its popularity while also offering details about what made it groundbreaking or unconventional. Some series, such as *All in the Family* and *Roseanne*, had so many episodes that broke new ground. Those chapters are obviously much longer than those for sitcoms that may have had one special episode or one feature that made it a benchmark in our exploration of sitcoms that fostered and facilitated social change.

Acknowledgments

I would like to thank Thomas S. Hischak and Todd Stephen Schechter for their help and support with research and for assisting in assembling the book; Angelina Du Puy for patiently reading chapters and offering constructive criticism; Derek Davidson at Photofest for his invaluable assistance in finding the pictures for this publication; the ongoing input and encouragement of my editor Stephen Ryan at Rowman & Littlefield; and my undying gratitude to James Rice, Robin Duffy, Robbie Rozelle, Cathy Hischak, Tiffany Robinson, and the other supportive friends who pushed and prodded me to write this book.

Introduction

Television: It is the most accessible form of media entertainment, reaching millions of viewers every day, influencing lives and shaping minds, and providing a platform for us to learn and evolve both as individuals and as a collective. If you think about the impact that television has on our daily lives, how tethered so many of us are to its escapist magic and its information (not to mention its relative affordability), is there any other form of entertainment with the potential to reach the masses with its messages, both positive and negative?

There used to be a time in the United States (before cable and internet streaming sites) when almost every home had a television with an antenna harnessed to the roof for watching three networks. NBC, CBS, and ABC held the reigns of programming power for decades, with an occasional fourth, such as the DuMont network, also factoring into the equation. Families gathered around the television from its arrival on the scene in the 1940s, first convening in the homes of those who could afford the luxury and then in their own living rooms when "the tube," as television would be dubbed, became viable for all. The ritual of watching television established itself quickly.

Early in television's history, it became clear that programs providing humor were among the favorites of what it had to offer. People like to laugh, and people like to laugh together. Early shows, such as *Mary Kate and Johnny*, *The Ed Wynn Show*, *Texaco Star Theatre* (with Milton Berle), *Make Room for Daddy*, and *I Love Lucy* all played into our inherent need to laugh. Is it any surprise that sketch comedy and variety shows, as well as the television sitcom, have endured the test of time and remained a part of the television landscape for 70-plus years?

What is it about laughter that brings us together? As we wander about the day-to-day world, we encounter negativity at every turn. Our jobs can often get us down. Navigating the road rage on our commute to work can be a harrowing experience. We face all kinds of darkness, such as death and disease, money worries, and car troubles, not to mention the bigotry, racism, sexism, and homophobia that we encounter on our life's journey. We need to combat the negatives with a positive. There is a reason that the phrase "laughter is the best medicine" continues to endure. When we sit down to watch a rerun of *Seinfeld* or *The Carol Burnett Show*, we feel healed by taking the time to laugh at our foibles, failures, and societal idiosyncrasies. Comedy helps us look at each other and ourselves and, even for the briefest moment, not take life so seriously.

But humor can also inform and enlighten. A heavy-handed approach to exploring a touchy issue or one that is divisive can turn people off to having the discussion that works them through the conflict. Through humor, difficult-to-digest topics somehow become more palatable, the tension broken by laughter, the wounds easier to endure. This is how television situation comedy has managed (and continues to manage) to break down barriers, present new perspectives, and evolve our individual and collective consciousness. If you can break it up with laughter, you can explore just about anything.

Television comedy has long been the frontline offensive in how America evolves on social issues. From *I Love Lucy* exploring in relative detail a television pregnancy to *Will & Grace* normalizing a gay male character as the catalyst for a sitcom, it has been situation comedy that has challenged us to revisit our social mores and reshape how we think about the world in which we live. A long line of important (and beloved) sitcoms have had an enormous influence on our collective psyche, including *The Brady Bunch, Julia, That Girl, The Mary Tyler Moore Show, M*A*S*H, All in the Family, Maude, The Jeffersons, Good Times, One Day at a Time, Soap, The Facts of Life, Kate & Allie, The Hogan Family, The Golden Girls, The Cosby Show, Designing Women, Murphy Brown, A Different World, Roseanne, Ellen, All American Girl*, and *Modern Family*. Each has broken down barriers and facilitated discussion, debate, and social evolution in America. This book strives to take you on a journey through some of these sometimes controversial, often groundbreaking, television shows that dared to look at the world and the people who inhabit it in a new light.

Mary Kay and Johnny
PUTTING THE QUESTION TO BED

Aired: November 18, 1947–March 11, 1950
Networks: DuMont (1947–1948), CBS (1949), and NBC (1948–1949, 1949–
  1950)
Created by: Mary Kay Stearns and Johnny Stearns
Cast: Mary Kay Stearns (Herself), Johnny Stearns (Himself), Howard Thomas
  (Himself), Nydia Westman (Herself), Christopher William Stearns (Him-
  self), Jim Stevenson (Announcer)

It all comes down to sharing a bed—such a simple thing for a couple to do.
Here, in the early part of the 21st century, the idea of a duo of consenting adults
sharing a bed is so common that we hardly think twice about its implications.
Television of today represents a wide range of couple configurations in bed: heterosexual couples, homosexual couples, bisexual couples, transgender couples,
and all other variations imaginable. Television and its ever-influential and he-
licoptering censors were not always as freethinking about people sharing a bed
on the tube. In fact, actors who portrayed married couples were typically found
sleeping separately in twin beds. How was this even close to reality? How were
we to comprehend where their children came from? This aspect of early television storytelling lacked a verisimilitude that was starkly apparent and utterly
laughable. Was this an attempt to maintain decency? Did they think audiences
wouldn't understand that these were actors and actresses performing in front of a
camera crew? What kind of salacious goings-on would they think were going on?

Mary Kay and Johnny ran on the Dumont Network, then CBS, and finally
NBC, airing from 1947 to 1950, with approximately 300 episodes (the exact
number is unclear) made over a three-year period. The program starred the real-
life husband-and-wife duo of Mary Kay and Johnny Stearns. On the show, the

couple lived in a Greenwich Village apartment, and the plot followed the usual day-to-day trials and tribulations of a sitcom family. He was a bank employee, and she was his colorful and kooky wife. The couple also had a son on *Mary Kay and Johnny*, with their real-life son Christopher playing himself (Mary Kay was pregnant during the series, and the child was incorporated into the show). The series was well regarded at the time, with *Billboard* reviewing it in a positive light:

> This program comes close to being a model television show. In detailing the adventures, mainly domestic, of a young married couple, Johnny and Mary Kay Stearns have come up with charming and fresh material, which always takes into consideration that there are cameras taking everything in.[1]

One of the things that those cameras took in was a television couple who shared a bed. This was 1947, very early in the emergence of television as a form of entertainment, and there we have it: two adults sharing one sleeping space. Perhaps it was because they were a real-life married couple that it was acceptable, but that seems unlikely due to something called the "Hays Code."

The Hays Code was established in 1930, a series of censorship rules applied to filmmaking by a group calling themselves the Moral Guardians. In reality, the Hays Office had been established by the studio system of its own volition, fearful that if they didn't put a series of moral standards in place, the government would sweep in and do it for them. By 1934, the code was strictly enforced. One of the code's strictures was to avoid "any licentious or suggestive nudity" and that a man and woman in bed together was to be avoided. Moving forward, films were made with couples having separate beds, divided by a night table so that viewers couldn't even fathom their pushing the beds together to have relations. This was applied to characters who were married within the context of the story, but it extended to real-life married couples who were cast opposite each other in movies.

As television came more and more into play in the late 1940s and began to really boom in the 1950s, the Hays Code came along for the ride. In fact, it was in television where it was more strictly enforced, wielding a great deal of cautious censorship well into the late 1960s, when we still see shows like *The Dick Van Dyke Show* separating married couples for their nocturnal slumber. Eventually, the Hays Code would be replaced by the Motion Picture Association of America rating system in Hollywood. The first characters played by a non–husband-and-wife acting pair to share a bed was Samantha and Darrin on *Bewitched* (1964–1972), followed closely by Herman and Lily on *The Munsters* (1964–1966). So how did *Mary Kay and Johnny* slip through the cracks?

We can only speculate as to how *Mary Kay and Johnny* got away with such a daring stunt, if it was indeed that. Perhaps it had something to do with the timing. Television was still so new in 1947, and the rules and guidelines weren't

John and Mary Kay Stearns in *Mary Kay and Johnny*. CBS/Photofest © CBS

exactly written in stone yet, just guided by what had been considered appropriate for film. In its novelty and newness, it probably never occurred to the powers that be to consider that people might be offended by a real-life married couple sharing a bed. Also, the show initially aired on the DuMont Network, one of the early pioneers of network television, where *Mary Kay and Johnny* was the first situation comedy. The show was also recorded live in front of an audience, and each episode was only 15 minutes in length. How much trouble could one get into with that many people in the room and with only 15 minutes to make it happen?

There has never been any real explanation as to how *Mary Kay and Johnny* achieved this milestone so early in television's story, but it is true that all that followed for almost two decades was a conservative take on marital relations in the bedroom, falling just short of a Berlin Wall keeping everything respectable and properly divided. In the late 1960s and early 1970s, television was filming whole scenes with couples in bed, including *The Brady Bunch*, *The Bob Newhart Show*, and *Maude*. But it all started with *Mary Kay and Johnny*.

Amos 'n' Andy
ONE STEP FORWARD, TWO STEPS BACK

Aired: June 28, 1951–April 13, 1953

Network: CBS

Created by: Charles J. Correll and Freeman F. Gosden, based on their WMAQ radio program *Amos 'n' Andy*

Cast: Alvin Childress (Amos Jones), Spencer Williams (Andrew "Andy" Hogg Brown), Tim Moore (George "Kingfish" Stevens), Ernestine Wade (Sapphire Stevens), Amanda Randolph (Ramona Smith, Sapphire's Mama), Johnny Lee (Algonquin J. Calhoun), Nick Stewart (billed as "Nick O'Demus" [Lightnin']), Jane Adams (Ruby Jones)

Theme Song: "Angel's Serenade," by Gaetano Braga (performed by the Jeff Alexander Chorus)

What can sometimes seem like progress in telling the stories of minorities can, in retrospect, be defined as one step forward and two steps back. In film, this happened with the actress Hattie McDaniel, who played Mammy in the 1939 classic *Gone with the Wind*. On the one hand, McDaniel broke barriers in Hollywood with her portrayal of Scarlet O'Hara's stalwart black slave, winning an Oscar for Best Supporting Actress, the first African American to do so. On the other hand, McDaniel found herself cast in similar roles for the rest of her career, and some found this counterproductive to sought-after dignified opportunities for black performers. McDaniel would spend the years following *Gone with the Wind* playing similar roles of the dutiful "Mammy" type, never given an opportunity to step outside of the stereotype.

Amos 'n' Andy started out as a popular radio show that ran from 1928 to 1960. It was set in Harlem in New York City and was centered around a black community, particularly those close to the title characters. The show was created, written, and voiced by two white men: Freeman Gosden, who played

Tim Moore and Jester Hairston in *Amos 'n' Andy*. CBS/Photofest © CBS

Amos Jones, and Charles Correll, who played Andrew Hogg Brown. The radio program was so popular that it was eventually decided to turn it into a television sitcom. CBS ran the program on its network from 1951 to 1953. Unfortunately, *Amos 'n' Andy*, though groundbreaking for being the first African American–led sitcom, perpetuated more stereotypes than it overcame.

This was the 1950s, and minstrel shows were still popular in the United States. They depicted blacks as caricatures: uneducated, always cheerful, simple-minded, and singing and dancing wherever they went. There was no substance or depth to a minstrel show character, which featured white men (and occasionally women) in blackface lampooning the stereotypes of black culture. Mickey Rooney and Judy Garland had done it in the 1939 film musical *Babes in Arms*. Disney incorporated animated crows that acted in the manner of a thinly veiled minstrel show into their beloved classic *Dumbo* (1941). Even the 1954 film *White Christmas* celebrates the institution of the minstrel show in a musical sequence titled "Minstrel Number" with the songs "I'd Rather See a Minstrel Show," "Mister Bones," and "Mandy." In *White Christmas*, however, there was no attempt at blackface, but the film did depict it as a glorious, lost art form. Thus was the image painted of blacks in the Hollywood of the 1930s through 1950s.

Amos 'n' Andy was not a minstrel show, but its makeup was rooted in that kind of thinking. Starting with the radio show, it was apparent that two white men were spoofing the black community in a vulgar and unflattering way. When *Amos 'n' Andy* was turned into a television show, Gosden and Correll considered having black men act out and lip-synch the title characters while they provided their familiar vocal characterizations. Again, it would have white men imposing their cartoonish, stereotyped voices on the characters. Fortunately, Gosden and Correll came to the conclusion that it wouldn't be right to take this approach, and they embarked on a nationwide search to find the right black Americans to play the titular duo.

The casting of the *Amos 'n' Andy* television program became a nationally publicized event, with the likes of President Harry Truman and General Dwight D. Eisenhower weighing in on the possibilities. Fluornoy Miller, a black vaudevillian, was brought on board to assist in the search. Ultimately, Alvin Childress was chosen to play Amos Jones, and Spencer Williams was selected to play Andrew Hogg Brown. The former was described as a compliant Uncle Tom type, levelheaded, and without humor. The latter was a dim, lighthearted rube who was easily tricked and in constant pursuit of a pretty girl. The show also included George "Kingfish" Stevens a schemer who was always taking advantage of his fellow man. Wives on the program were depicted as shrewish, ugly, and loud. These character types were directly drawn from the classic minstrel show stereotypes.

Amos 'n' Andy premiered on CBS in June 1951. The first episode drew the ire of the National Association for the Advancement of Colored People (NAACP), which was not happy with the show, leading it to seek an injunction in federal court that would keep CBS from further airing it. For many organizations, including the Michigan Federation of Teachers, the Students for Democratic Action, the United Hatters, and the Cap and Millinery Workers Union, the show was caricature of the black American, a vulgar representation of a minority who were struggling to achieve civil rights and equality. A show of this ilk would only perpetuate stereotypes and hurt their cause.

Actor James Edwards, a gatekeeper for dignified roles for African Americans, was a vocal opponent of *Amos 'n' Andy*, concerned that the 142 jobs provided to black Americans by *Amos 'n' Andy* was not in balance with the damage that the program was doing to millions of minorities who would suffer from the caricature-laden stereotypes it was delivering.

In June and July 1951, the NAACP held its annual conference in Atlanta, Georgia. There, the organization passed a resolution on the show, encouraging its members to boycott it:

> The new television show, *Amos 'n' Andy*, depicts Negroes in a stereotyped and derogatory manner, and the practice of manufacturers, distributors, retailers, persons, or firms sponsoring or promoting this show, the *Beulah* show, or others of this type is condemned.[1]

The NAACP's lawsuit against CBS detailed, with a great deal of specificity, the objections brought about by a show like *Amos 'n' Andy*:

- It tends to strengthen the conclusion among uninformed and prejudiced people that Negroes are inferior, lazy, dumb and dishonest.
- Every character in this one and only show with an all-Negro cast is either a clown or a crook.
- Negro doctors are shown as quacks and thieves.
- Negro lawyers are shown as slippery cowards, ignorant of their profession and without ethics.
- Negro women are shown as cackling, screaming shrews, in big-mouth close-ups using street slang, just short of vulgarity.
- All Negroes are shown as dodging work of any kind.
- Millions of white Americans see this *Amos 'n' Andy* picture and think the entire race is the same.[2]

Interestingly, the actors in the show defended *Amos 'n' Andy*, speaking out against NAACP representatives, citing the opportunities that it offered black performers. Their support of the program may have had more to do with the opportunities the show was offering them individually and not as a collective. Even within the parameters of a seemingly "black" show, *Amos 'n' Andy* had no producers, directors, or writers of color. It was the story of a fictional black America as seen through the lens of white creators. There was little that was authentic about the picture that they painted.

Not every African American was opposed to *Amos 'n' Andy*, and not everything about the show was palpably offensive. The setting, for one, did nothing to perpetuate stereotypes and preconceived notions of a poverty-stricken Harlem ghetto. Like all sitcoms of the day, apartments looked clean and livable and were outfitted with comfortable (if sparse) furniture. Clothing was rarely ragtag (unless it was specific to a role), and a wide array of characters on the show represented all walks of life, including doctors, lawyers, and politicians. It was seldom conveyed that these professions and successes were unachievable, but the show often suggested that a black person must be manipulative and devious to reach such heights. This is arguably where *Amos 'n' Andy* did the most damage in its depiction of an underrepresented and misrepresented minority.

Another area where *Amos 'n' Andy* was both careful and conscientious was in how the occasional white characters interacted with the central characters on the program. Remembering that the show premiered in 1951, when segregation was a regular practice in America, the show nevertheless presented whites as tolerant of race differences. One particular episode featured "Kingfish" and his family eating at a restaurant operated by whites, and they had no issues in being served. White characters were never demeaning toward the black characters, nor did they discriminate. This, however, did little to bolster the positive messages the show was extolling because the larger picture was still a black experience seen through rose-colored glasses.

The *Pittsburgh Courier*, an influential black newspaper of the time, found much to admire in *Amos 'n' Andy*. It offered its praise: "It provides for the first time lucrative and continuous employment for many talented troupers who have waited a long time for this kind of an open-door opportunity into the great and rapidly expanding television industry."[3]

Amos 'n' Andy lasted for only two seasons, with a total of 52 episodes created. The relatively short tenure for the television show did not mean that the show and its effects merely went away. The show entered into syndication, where it continued to play until 1966, when CBS finally agreed to take the show out of circulation. The 1960s brought an evolving representation of black America in entertainment (particularly onstage and in film), though it is important to note that very few programs centered around African Americans were produced during this decade. It would not be until Norman Lear produced the sitcom *Good Times* in 1974 that television audiences would be given a more authentic perspective of the black experience (and even that was not without its stereotypes).

I Love Lucy

AS HAPPY AS TWO CAN BE

Aired: October 15, 1951–May 6, 1957
Network: CBS
Created by: Desi Arnaz, Madelyn Pugh, Jess Oppenheimer, and Bob Carroll Jr.
Cast: Lucille Ball (Lucy Ricardo), Desi Arnaz (Ricky Ricardo), Vivian Vance (Ethel Mertz), William Frawley (Fred Mertz), Richard Keith (Ricky Ricardo Jr.), Mike Mayer and Joe Mayer ("Little Ricky")
Theme Song: "I Love Lucy," by Eliot Daniel, lyrics by Harold Adamson (performed by Desi Arnaz in one episode of season 3)

Perhaps no situation comedy is more beloved than the iconic *I Love Lucy*, which played on CBS from 1951 to 1957. Indeed, the antics of the show's star, Lucille Ball, from physical humor to a screwball comedy of errors, provided some of television's most revered moments of laughter. Whether she was wrapping candies moving down an ever-increasingly sped-up conveyer belt, pitching a bottle of Vitameatavegamin (unknowingly getting drunk in the process), or stalking a celebrity with some ridiculous disguise, there are so many moments of *I Love Lucy* that have become legend. What few people stop to consider is how this seemingly innocuous comedy was breaking ground both on-screen and behind the scenes.

Actress Lucille Ball had been one of the contract players of Hollywood's Golden Age, a glamorous type whose film career was never as top ranking as that of, say, Greta Garbo, Norma Shearer, Myrna Loy, or Judy Garland. Still, she had found some success in pictures, but it wouldn't be until she took hold of the reins that her untapped potential would be revealed. The lady was a comic genius and would soon find a level of stardom and influence in the relatively new medium of television that all but eclipsed her career on the silver screen.

In 1950, Lucille Ball and her then husband Desi Arnaz formed Desilu Productions, an effort to bring her popular radio show *My Favorite Husband* to television. "Desilu" was, of course, the splicing together of their two names, "Desi" and "Lucille." What they came together to create was one of television's most successful independent producing organizations of the day. *My Favorite Husband* would eventually see the light of day when it was renamed and pitched to CBS as *I Love Lucy*. Desilu Productions would also be the money and creative

Lucille Ball in *I Love Lucy*. *CBS/Photofest © CBS*

support behind such shows as *The Untouchables* and the pioneering sci-fi drama *Star Trek*. However, it was *I Love Lucy* that was the raison d'être for Desilu, and it would prove to be a smart investment for the pair.

I Love Lucy starred Lucille Ball as Lucy Ricardo, the housewife of popular New York City nightclub owner, band leader, and performer Ricky Ricardo. Ricky was the practical one, well respected in show business, and careful with family finances. Lucy was starstruck, always trying to get into Ricky's act at the club (or movies, theater, or television) and would stop at nothing short of ludicrous shenanigans to achieve that coveted place in the spotlight. Ricky, who felt she had little talent or ability, wanted her to stay at home and follow the prescribed duties of wifedom, cooking and cleaning and such. In the same building lived Lucy and Ricky's landlords, Fred and Ethel Mertz. Fred was known as cheap, and he exhibited a curmudgeonly demeanor that was masking a kind heart. He was Ricky's best friend and was often confided in when Ricky was trying to conceal something from Lucy. Ethel, who was opinionated but personable, was Lucy's best friend and partner in crime. She could always be talked into whatever harebrained scheme Lucy was concocting. The Mertzes were like family to the Ricardos, coming and going from the apartment with great frequency and always there for all major holidays and milestones.

I Love Lucy was immensely popular, ranking number 1 in the Nielsen ratings for four of its six seasons on the air. People literally loved Lucy, and the sitcom's success put Ms. Ball in position to become one of television's most powerful women. For the 1950s, this was a groundbreaking achievement, as the studio system was almost entirely owned and run by men. Lucy's role in Desilu was relegated mainly to creative control of projects, but in 1962, on their divorce, Lucy bought out Desi's portion of the company and assumed full responsibility of the company until she sold it in 1967 to Gulf + Western, which would in turn transform the company into Paramount Television (the television branch of Paramount Pictures). This made Lucille Ball one of the earliest female movers and shakers of television.

In season 2, episode 10, which originally aired on December 12, 1952, *I Love Lucy* would have its first controversial episode. Titled "Lucy Is Enceinte," the installment could not seem more innocuous by today's standards but in the early 1950s was an eyebrow-raising reason for everyone to panic. In the episode, Lucy would announce to her husband that she was pregnant, though it would include a hilarious lead-up to telling him as our favorite redhead tried to find the courage. That was it, though: a simple announcement of one of life's most treasured moments was enough to turn television on its ear. It wasn't the first time that television had featured a pregnancy. Going back to 1947 with the first sitcom, *Mary Kay and Johnny*, the titular actress had become pregnant, and this point was included as part of her character's story line. With *Mary Kay and*

Johnny, however, the pregnancy was neither overt nor a recurring part of the story. With *I Love Lucy*, that would be different.

Lucille Ball was pregnant with her first child, and it was decided that this would be written into her character's story line. Television audiences would be privy to Lucy's pregnancy and the ups and downs of being with child, building toward the climactic event of going to the hospital to give birth. No television show had ever spent this kind of time on a woman in what was considered a "delicate condition." Through the better part of the fall of 1952, audiences saw Lucy experience cravings (pickles dipped in papaya milkshakes), don maternity clothing, and make preparations for the child's imminent arrival. However, Lucille Ball was not allowed to call herself "pregnant." To CBS executives, the idea of its star appearing with child on television bordered on being scandalous. The mention of pregnancy hinted that sex had occurred, and Lucy and Desi slept in twin beds separated by a nightstand. She couldn't possibly be pregnant if a piece of furniture was in the way. In reality, "pregnant" was considered a vulgar word to say on television in the day, so euphemisms like "expecting" were used to hint at her condition.

The episode of the birth titled "Lucy Goes to the Hospital" was filmed on November 14, 1952, but was held in reserve until January 19, 1953, 12 hours after Ball and Arnaz welcomed Desi Arnaz Jr. into the world. To make sure that the episode would not be deemed offensive or too controversial, a rabbi, a priest, and a minister were asked to review the teleplay before it was recorded; 71.9 percent of all American homes tuned in to the episode to meet the newborn (fictional) "Little Ricky" with an estimated audience of 44 million viewers.

I Love Lucy may be remembered for a host of zany moments of iconic hilarity, but it was also a show that dared to take the time to explore one of humanity's most natural experiences: childbirth. After *I Love Lucy*, it wouldn't seem so taboo for a woman to be "pregnant," and eventually we, as a collective, would get over our hang-ups about something so simple and beautiful.

The Dick Van Dyke Show

WEARING THE PANTS IN THE FAMILY

Aired: October 3, 1961–June 1, 1966

Network: CBS

Created by: Carl Reiner

Cast: Dick Van Dyke (Robert Simpson "Rob" Petrie), Mary Tyler Moore (Laura Petrie), Rose Marie (Sally Rogers), Morey Amsterdam (Maurice "Buddy" Sorrell), Larry Mathews (Ritchie Petrie), Richard Deacon (Melvin "Mel" Cooley)

Theme Song: "Theme to *The Dick Van Dyke Show*," by Earle Hagen (lyrics by Morey Amsterdam, never aired)

How women were depicted on early television was rarely truthful and often demonstrated centuries of a patriarchal assumptions—stereotypes that bore little resemblance to who women were individually and collectively. From television's beginnings, rules about how women were to be portrayed and seen seemed to be an immediate concern. This even extended into what fashions were deemed acceptable. Women just weren't supposed to wear anything but a dress, particularly on television, where full skirts in the Donna Reed/June Cleaver vein were de rigueur in the 1950s and early 1960s. For a woman to don a pair of pants was considered unthinkable. Pants might just reveal too much of her shape, and, even though many women felt pants to be more comfortable, the wearing of them might make everyone uncomfortable.

The Dick Van Dyke Show was hardly a progressive situation comedy. In many ways, it harkened back to *Father Knows Best* and *Make Room for Daddy*, where the man of the house made the big decisions, went to work every day, and came home expecting a clean house and a meal on the table. *The Dick Van Dyke Show* was created by Carl Reiner and starred Dick Van Dyke, Rose Marie,

Morey Amsterdam, and Larry Mathews. Reiner had based the character of Rob Petrie on himself, loosely capturing his years as a television comedy writer.

Despite the exhausted "husband rules the roost" trope, the show had one thing going for it that propelled it into the realm of forward thinking about a practical depiction of women. This came at the insistence of *The Dick Van Dyke Show* costar and future television groundbreaker with her own series, Mary Tyler Moore.

Mary Tyler Moore insisted that women who clean house do not do so wearing dresses and pearls all of the time. Many women wore pants at home and then dressed up in dresses and skirts when going out into the world. Moore wanted her character of Laura Petrie to wear pants in the scenes where she was at home. The show's producers and the network (CBS) were uncomfortable with the request, worried that censors would find them too revealing of Moore's curvaceous figure. Ultimately, Moore had her way, and it was agreed that she could wear one pair of capri pants (also known as pedal pushers or clam diggers at the time) in one scene per episode.

The next concern was over how those pants were going to fit the actress, who had a dancer's body (from her work in musical theater and film). Would

Dick Van Dyke and Mary Tyler Moore in *The Dick Van Dyke Show*. CBS/ Photofest © CBS

there be too much cupping around her buttocks and crotch? The costume department was tasked with making sure that the pants that were secured for these at-home scenes remained loose and didn't create any panty lines or noticeable crevices or creases in the wrong places. As the series progressed from season to season, the concerns seemed to lessen; Laura wore pants in more than one scene per episode, and their fit became snugger and snugger.

Mary Tyler Moore wasn't the first actress to wear pants on television (Lucille Ball occasionally wore them, particularly during the episodes of her pregnancy on *I Love Lucy*). Moore was, however, the one who wore them most consistently, setting a fashion trend that soon saw women wearing pedal pushers both on television and in the real world. It seems like such a small thing, women wearing pants on television that most already wore (at least at home), but women have always been bound by stricter codes than men. When has television ever worried about a tight-fitting pair of trousers on a man or the cupping that occurred around the groin area? It is the age-old industry (and society) double standard that continues to be a part of how Hollywood treats men and women differently.

That Girl

A NEW KIND OF SITCOM FEMALE

Aired: September 8, 1966–March 19, 1971
Network: ABC
Created by: Bill Persky and Sam Denoff
Cast: Marlo Thomas (Ann Marie), Ted Bessell (Donald Hollinger), Lew Parker (Lew Marie) Bernie Kopell (Jerry Bauman), Rosemary DeCamp (Helen Marie)
Theme Song: "Theme to *That Girl*," composed by Sam Denoff and Earle Hagen

Predating *The Mary Tyler Moore Show* by four years, *That Girl* is considered by many to be the first "independent woman making a life of her own" sitcom of consequence. Created by Bill Persky and Sam Denoff, the series starred actress Marlo Thomas as "Ann Marie," an aspiring actor who leaves her small-town home in Brewster, New York, for the bright lights of Manhattan. *That Girl* ran on ABC for five seasons between 1966 and 1971.

Ann Marie was concerned with her career first. Like most struggling actors, she would take a variety of temporary positions to pay the bills as she waited for her star to rise. She did have a boyfriend, *Newsweek* writer Donald Hollinger, but he was not seen as either meal ticket nor her ultimate destination. Ann Marie's parents were played by Lew Parker and Rosemary DeCamp, and her friends were played by Ruth Buzzi, Reva Rose, and Bernie Kopell.

Marlo Thomas wanted to leave the show after four seasons, having grown tired of the premise and feeling as though she had exhausted all the possibilities of a young, single woman surviving in the big city. The producers convinced her to do a fifth season in which Ann Marie and Donald Hollinger would become engaged. Thomas, however, insisted that they end the series without an actual wedding. She felt that having Ann Marie get married would undercut the show's

Marlo Thomas in *That Girl*. ABC/Photofest © ABC

initial message that a woman could make it on her own. The ultimate goal for every female should not be to get married and start churning out babies.

In an article by Herbie J. Pilato, "*That Girl*: The One Who Changed Everything," written for the Television Academy website, the author speaks of Thomas's impact both on- and off-screen:

It was a perilous era for any comedy show, as the 1960s were dominated by chaos—political assassinations, race riots, recreational drug
use and the sexual revolution. Through it all, however, Thomas and
company successfully delivered an uplifting half-hour of escapism
that rode to the top of the ratings in each year of its five-year run.
Viewers quickly embraced the independent and lively character of
Ann Marie, particularly her relationship with Bessell's Donald Hollinger, which was portrayed as innocent and serious; pure, kind, loyal
and loving. Fans of the series grew to appreciate their respect for one
another. They adored how supportive Donald was of Ann's dreams,
and they loved their electrifying on-screen chemistry.[1]

Pilato also suggests that

> off-screen, [Thomas's] role influenced millions of women to take
> charge of their own lives, this at a time when the country was feeling
> the first jolts of the new feminist movement. Indeed, Ann Marie be-
> came one of the medium's first "emotionally intelligent" characters,
> female or otherwise, bursting with a unique blend of vivaciousness,
> innocence and smarts, and seizing control whenever she faced ad-
> versity.[2]

That Girl was never a ratings bonanza. During its five-season run, it remained in the middle of the Nielsen statistics. It always did just well enough to
be renewed for another season. Its long-term impact was where it would have
a longer, deeper hold on America. *That Girl* ushered in a parade of female-
centered situation comedies about strong, independent women. Series such as
Julia, *The Mary Tyler Moore Show*, *Designing Women*, *Murphy Brown*, and *Ellen*
all owe a debt of gratitude to *That Girl* for opening the doors that would lead
to their stories being told.

Julia
PRESENTING THE WHITE NEGRO

Aired: September 17, 1968–March 23, 1971
Network: NBC
Created by: Hal Kanter
Cast: Diahann Carroll (Julia Baker), Lloyd Nolan (Dr. Morton Chegley), Marc
    Copage (Corey Baker), Betty Beaird (Marie Waggedorn), Hank Brandt
    (Leonard Waggedorn), Michael Link (Earl J. Waggedorn), Lurene Tuttle
    (Nurse Hannah Yarby), Alison Susan Mills (Carol Deering), Mary Wickes
    (Melba Chegley), Eddie Quillan (Eddie Edson)
Theme Song: "Theme to *Julia*," composed by Elmer Bernstein

The year is 1968, and America has gone through a decade of change, evolution, turmoil, and tribulation. Both African Americans and women have made
enormous strides toward having a voice and achieving an equality that had
been historically kept from them through white male oppression and general
attitudes that asserted they should remain quietly in their place. Television occasionally reflected the times, with most series opting to maintain a patriarchal
white man's perspective. The idea of creating a sitcom that centered around a
black widowed female who juggled parenthood and a career was an awfully big
step that would be a hard sell to a television audience. And yet the arrival of the
program *Julia* was exactly what America needed at the time, a show that, along
with its contemporary *That Girl*, would open the doors for telling stories about
strong, independent women.

Julia told the story of Julia Baker, a woman of color who had been widowed
when her husband, Army captain Baker—an O-1 Bird Dog artillery spotter
pilot—had been killed in Vietnam. Julia had a little boy named Corey, a grade
schooler who had little memory of his father. The two of them lived in a small
apartment. Julia worked as a nurse for Dr. Morton Chegley in his office at a

Diahann Carroll, Lloyd Nolan, and Marc Copage in *Julia.* ***NBC/Photofest***
© *NBC*

large aerospace company. Julia dated, finding ongoing romance with Paul Cameron (Paul Winfield) and Steve Bruce (Fred Williamson). Corey's best friend, Earl J. Waggadorn, whose full name was used to address him, lived in the same building as the Bakers, with his parents Len and Marie and his baby brother. At work, Julia also had a friend in Nurse Hannah Yarby.

Although *Julia* had broken some barriers in its depiction of a single, black woman raising a child on her own, many were quick to criticize the show for not being all that realistic or for not offering much by way of educating viewers on the challenges that most African Americans were facing in the turbulent 1960s. Even the series star, Diahann Carroll, wasn't always pleased with the show's direction, but she also defended the strides the show was making. In December 1968, Carroll told *TV Guide*,

> For a hundred years we have been prevented from seeing accurate images of ourselves and we're all overconcerned and overreacting. . . . The needs of the white writer go to the superhuman being. At the moment, we are presenting the white Negro. And he has very little Negro-ness.[1]

In a later interview with PBS, the actress also had this to say about *Julia* and the time frame of when it appeared on television:

> The racial involvement was very minuscule on all television shows, and yet, [I] felt pressure to justify the dialog, the characters and even the costumes.[2]

Shows that broke barriers and presented minorities in a new light have always been under scrutiny by those who seek more accurate representation and by those who oppose representing minorities altogether. Was *Julia* walking a careful line to not upset either group but in doing so diluting the show's potential to be truly progressive? It is hard to argue that *Julia* was telling a story about a group, but then the show was about an individual.

Writers, however, did not entirely shirk their responsibility to give an accurate account of how blacks were treated in the United States in the late 1960s. Occasionally, *Julia* would delve into racially charged events of the day and make commentary on the egregious actions and laws that treated a large faction of society as second-class citizens. In one episode, the manager of the clinic where Julia was employed ordered downsizing, particularly the excising, of minorities. Dr. Chegley let one of the nurses go but insisted on keeping Julia in their employ. Chegley had to remind the manager that his edict was in violation of the Civil Rights Act, which had been passed five years earlier. But this was one of the rare occurrences that *Julia* aggressively took on racial inequities. In all other ways, it was a sitcom about a single mom raising a kid. The color of her skin was irrelevant.

In an article for Smithsonian.com, "Was the 1968 TV Show *Julia* a Milestone or a Millstone for Diversity?," writer Alice George tells how the show's writers were making it hard for Carroll to be true to herself and her heritage while walking the high-wire act of starring in a sitcom that was based on the story of one African American woman but simultaneously and symbolically representing them all:

> Carroll opposed a scene in which Julia reported that her first experience of racism was as late as her high school prom, and to show how strongly she felt, the actress left the TV lot on the day of the taping. However, with a white male power structure above her, she won mostly small victories. She wanted Julia to wear an Afro, and even that plea was rejected. Between scenes, she met in her dressing room with journalists, psychologists and leaders of organizations who were concerned about the show's impact. The pressure took a toll. "I cannot spend every weekend studying each word, writing an analysis of everything I think may possibly be insulting, then presenting it to you in the hope that we might come to an understanding," she told the show's creator, Hal Kanter. "You can see it—I'm falling apart."[3]

In 1970, Carroll had had enough. The stress was taking a physical toll on her, landing her in the hospital on a handful of occasions. She asked to be released from her contract at the end of the series' third season, and so *Julia* came to a conclusion.

The Courtship of Eddie's Father
A WARMHEARTED PERSON WHO'LL LOVE ME 'TIL THE END

Aired: September 17, 1969–March 1, 1972
Network: ABC
Created by: James Komack, based on the book (by Mark Toby) and the 1963 film (screenplay by John Gay), both of the same name
Cast: Bill Bixby (Tom Corbett), Brandon Cruz (Eddie Corbett), Miyoshi Umeki (Mrs. Livingston), Kristina Holland (Tina Rickles), James Komack (Norman Tinker)
Theme Song: "Best Friend," written and performed by Harry Nilsson

The Courtship of Eddie's Father is a sitcom based on the 1963 movie of the same name, itself adapted from the novel by Mark Toby. The story concerns a widower named Tom Corbett, whose little boy, Eddie, thinks it is time for his dad to remarry. In an effort to speed things along, little Eddie hatches schemes and orchestrates coincidences regarding the women in Tom's life. Eddie is sometimes aided and abetted in his manipulations by the Corbetts' well-meaning Japanese housekeeper Mrs. Livingston.

What set *The Courtship of Eddie's Father* apart from other sitcoms of its day was that it was directly addressing, for the first time, a sitcom family moving on after death. The series was not a barrel of laughs. It was a reflective television series with humorous overtones. Little Eddie was without a mother, and he saw his father aching from the loss of his beloved wife. He wanted to fix the problem and took on the enormous responsibility of negotiating a woman to fill his mother's void.

What also made *The Courtship of Eddie's Father* special was the relationship between father and son. Each of the show's episodes began with a gentle conversation between Eddie and Tom wherein the little boy would pose a question about life and his father would give him a thoughtful answer. One episode in

24

Bill Bixby, Brandon Cruz, and Miyoshi Umeki in *The Courtship of Eddie's Father*. ABC/Photofest © ABC

particular found Eddie wondering about equal rights for women and what that meant. Tom explained it beautifully, helping his child understand how women had been treated differently than men over the centuries. These exchanges were always simple and unassuming, so much being said with so little turmoil.

Asian Americans had seldom been central to television programs of the 1940s to 1960s. The inclusion of Mrs. Livingston on *The Courtship of Eddie's Father* marked one of the first Asian characters to be a recurring member of a television show. Japanese-born actress Miyoshi Umeki was already an established performer after immigrating to the United States. She was Tony nominated for her leading role as Mei Li in the Rodgers and Hammerstein Broadway musical *Flower Drum Song*, a role she would repeat in the screen adaptation. She had won an Academy Award in 1957 for her work on the film *Sayonara*. To date, she remains the only Asian actress to win an Oscar for acting. Her presence in *The Courtship of Eddie's Father* was a warm and welcome one but also groundbreaking in the inclusion of a minority and an Asian who was given "costar" status in the show's opening credits.

The Courtship of Eddie's Father ran on ABC between 1969 and 1972. Although many people may not be aware of the show itself, its theme song has gained iconic status. "Best Friend," written and performed by singer-songwriter Harry Nilsson, has been used in a handful of commercials and is sometimes used in film and television to underscore moments of father–son bonding. *The Courtship of Eddie's Father* was canceled after three seasons, not due to a lack of popularity but because star Bill Bixby had a falling out with the show's creator, James Komack. Bixby did not like the direction the series was taking, feeling that the story lines were straying too much from the original father–son premise.

The Brady Bunch

THIS GROUP MUST SOMEHOW FORM A FAMILY

Aired: September 26, 1969–March 8, 1974

Network: ABC

Created by: Sherwood Schwartz

Cast: Robert Reed (Mike Brady), Florence Henderson (Carol Brady), Ann B. Davis (Alice Nelson), Barry Williams (Greg Brady), Maureen McCormick (Marcia Brady), Christopher Knight (Peter Brady), Eve Plumb (Jan Brady), Mike Lookinland (Bobby Brady), Susan Olsen (Cindy Brady)

Theme Song: "Theme to *The Brady Bunch*," by Frank DeVol and Sherwood Schwartz (performed by the Peppermint Trolley Company [Paul Parrish, Lois Fletcher, and John Beland] in season 1 and by the Brady Bunch Kids in seasons 2 to 5)

In the past three or four decades, there have been a plethora of sitcoms that have challenged the definition of family and how it is portrayed on television. *The Golden Girls*, *The New Normal*, *Kate & Allie*, *Punky Brewster*, *The Facts of Life*, *Diff'rent Strokes*, *Will & Grace*, *Who's the Boss?*, *On Our Own*, *Full House*, *My Two Dads*, and *The Courtship of Eddie's Father* (to name a few) each offer a different dynamic that erased the boundaries society had created around the norms of how family was depicted. What these shows did, in fact, was represent what had always been there in the first place: a spectrum of family stories and people who came together to share not only their living arrangements but also their lives. This was not always the case.

Historically, television in its early days took a more traditional approach to its drawing the picture of the family unit. Sitcoms in the 1940s, 1950s, and even early 1960s were typically representative of one vanilla-type family: Dad, Mom, and kids. But this was hardly the only configuration out there. Divorce rates were climbing throughout the 20th century, and so were the number of blended families. Women with kids from their first marriage married men with children from their first. This could happen in other configurations as well—widows and widowers, a divorcée and a single man, and so on—but the reality was that the family unit and what was considered the "norm" was changing and

Christopher Knight, Barry Williams, Ann B. Davis, Eve Plumb, Florence Henderson, Robert Reed, Maureen McCormick, Susan Olsen, and Mike Lookinland in *The Brady Bunch*. ABC/Photofest © ABC

evolving at an exponential rate. Early television, however, was reluctant to reflect these nontraditional families in its programming despite the fact that they had always been there. It had been done before in the case of the 1957 sitcom *The Danny Thomas Show* (aka *Make Room for Daddy*) when actress Jean Hagen, who played the mother, Margaret, left the show. The writers killed her character off and gave her husband, Danny, a new love interest, a young widow named Kathy (Marjorie Lord), who had a little girl. Eventually, they married, and two families were melded into one. However, there was minimal adjustment to the new arrangement, and *The Danny Thomas Show* moved on with traditional plotlines, essentially glossing over a golden opportunity for a more compelling scenario. Television had presented a blended family, but it hadn't explored its possibilities. That all changed in 1969.

Television producer Sherwood Schwartz, who had been a writer for the 1950s comedies *I Married Joan* and *The Red Skelton Show* and was the creator and writer of the beloved *Gilligan's Island* (1964–1967) and the all-but-forgotten *It's about Time* (1966–1967), had an idea for a television sitcom that addressed blended families in a more direct way and that was an intrinsic part of the program's themes. The show was, of course, *The Brady Bunch*.

The Brady Bunch was the story of two single parents: the widowed Mike Brady, an architect with three boys of his own, and the inexplicably (or never explained) single Carol Martin, the mother of three girls. Schwartz had wanted Carol to be a divorcée, but that was considered too risqué in 1969. The other half of Carol's daughters' parentage remained a mystery within the context of the show, but the three girls adopted the Brady surname as their own. Also a regular part of the Brady family was their housekeeper, Alice, who had been Mike's domestic help before he married Carol. Alice offered sage advice and a grandmotherly-like love to all the Bradys, and they treated her with love and respect in return.

Then there were the kids. For the girls, there was the boy-crazy and popular Marcia, the neurotic Jan, and the tattletale moppet Cindy. On the boys' side was the super-groovy Greg, the curious and questioning Peter, and the incorrigible Bobby. Rounding out the household, at least in the beginning, was the boys' dog, Tiger, and the girls' cat, Fluffy, both of which disappeared early in the show's run. The three boys shared a bedroom, and the three girls shared a bedroom, but all six were relegated to one bathroom between them. It also had no visible toilet, which has led to ongoing jokes about where the children relieved themselves.

In the pilot episode of *The Brady Bunch* (filmed in 1968), all the main characters were introduced, each family in their former households and preparing for the wedding of Mike and Carol. Some discussion is exchanged about the fears of the new things ahead. The wedding is to be held in the backyard of the Martin home, and everything seems to be on its way to a pleasant day. However, things go awry when Tiger and Fluffy can't seem to get along, leading to their running through the reception, the boys and the girls in tow and each defending their respective pet. Things are not off to a good start for the new Brady clan, and Mike and Carol admonish the kids for their lack of effort in embracing their new siblings. The family moves into their new house that Mike has designed (how did an architect knowingly create a home with one bathroom for six kids?). The episode foreshadows the clash and conflict ahead, a television show finally addressing the challenges that most families face when two groups come together as one.

In season 1, episode 6, titled "A Clubhouse Is Not a Home," the Brady kids are at odds over the clubhouse, which the boys feel is their personal territory. The girls wants to use it as well, and after much squabbling, they try to build their own, which turns out to be poorly made and collapses. In an effort to be reasonable, the boys help the girls build their own. But things were not always as amicable where conflict resolution was concerned. In season 1, episode 7, "Kitty Karry-All Is Missing," Cindy's favorite doll cannot be found, and she blames Bobby for the theft since he was the only one nearby when it disappeared. Not long after, Bobby's harmonica is seemingly stolen, and he believes that Cindy has done it as retribution for the Kitty-Karry-All incident. Soon, the girls and the boys are squaring off against each other, taking sides and verbally attacking one another. It's boys from one family against girls from another, a mounting tension that shows that families do not meld quite as easily as past sitcoms had suggested. It turns out that the dog, Tiger, had stolen both items and hidden them in his doghouse.

In episode 8 of the first season, Mike prepares to take the boys on an annual camping trip that had always been a tradition in their former household. In "A-Camping We Will Go," Carol and Mike decide to continue the tradition with everyone attending (even Alice). The boys are immediately opposed to the girls horning in on their outing, and the girls are just as disgusted at the thought of spending time in the wilderness. Carol and Mike insist that everyone go and that everyone start acting like one family. Much of the trip is a disaster, exacerbated by the negative attitudes, but they soon begin to find common ground and begrudgingly come together.

Let's not forget about that age-old fairy-tale stereotype about stepmothers and stepsisters being wicked. When Bobby watches a television adaptation of *Cinderella*, he is teased by Marcia and Jan. This is followed by Carol asking for his help cleaning the chimney. Unable to reconcile what he has just watched on television with his new family members seemingly filling the roles of the story's villains, Bobby becomes alarmed that he will be abused in the way that Cinderella has. He plans to run away from home. In the episode (titled "Every Boy

Does It Once"), Carol learns of Bobby's plan and realizes that she has to make a more concerted effort to show Bobby that he is loved.

It wasn't just the kids who had to adjust. The adults had to make accommodations for their roles in the new family. Mike had to give the girls as much of a voice as he had always given his boys, often enforcing a compromise that felt like a betrayal to Greg, Peter, and Bobby. Carol had to navigate mothering boys, which was proving to be very different than what she knew about raising girls. Even poor Alice, who had always been used to the boys coming to her for help, advice, and attention, had to cede some of that responsibility to Carol despite feeling like she was no longer needed. These were real problems that blended families encounter, and kudos to *The Brady Bunch* for finally exploring them.

As the years passed, *The Brady Bunch* settled in for a more traditional sitcom narrative. With the adjustment period over, plots turned toward the ridiculous (some of them iconic for their over-the-top nonsense), so much so that actor Robert Reed often objected to the show's writing. It is, perhaps, due to his voice that the show retained some integrity and remained tethered to its concept of family relationships. In the final season, a new character was introduced in Cousin Oliver (Robbie Rist), who moved in with the Bradys, a clear sign that the show had exhausted its purpose and was winding to a close. There just wasn't anything new to tell about the Bradys, as the story of their coming together and becoming a close-knit, blended family was over. The "bunch" mentioned in the theme song was truly much more than that. The experiment had worked.

It would be wrong to disregard the impact that *The Brady Bunch* had on the television-watching audience. The show holds an iconic status in television that few other programs have enjoyed. Only *The Flintstones*, *Leave It to Beaver*, and *Gilligan's Island* can come close to holding a candle to it. Generations had the show's theme song (written by Schwartz and Frank De Vol) engrained in their psyches. All you had to do was sing "Here's the story, of a lovely lady . . ." and a room full of people would chime in and sing along, every lyric remembered by heart. The show's opening sequence, featuring the characters introduced in bright blue squares, was in and of itself iconic, a clever way of mapping out the story of how two families came together.

Through syndication, the show has never really gone away. It just continues to play for generations to come. Several made-for-TV reunion films and spin-off series resulted from the show's ever-present popularity: *The Brady Bunch Hour* (1976–1977), *The Brady Girls Get Married* (1981), *The Brady Brides* (1981), *A Very Brady Christmas* (1988), and *The Bradys* (1990). The show's cultural impact is probably best demonstrated by the two hit comedy films *The Brady Bunch Movie* (1995) and *A Very Brady Sequel* (1996), which outright spoofed many of the show's most memorable moments in a way that didn't require explanation. Audiences just knew *The Brady Bunch* so well that it simply wasn't necessary. They were already in on the joke.

The Brady Bunch, particularly in the first of its five seasons, was always lighthearted but conscientious about telling the story of a blended family. The show is seldom given its due for taking this giant step in how families are represented on television. It is easy to look at *The Brady Bunch* as escapist fun, colorful, corny, and too precious for words. It is all of these things, but lying underneath that sugary sitcom idealism, there is a show that was both thoughtful and progressive, moving closer to a more realistic representation of how a family operates. Sure, each episode ended with a "happily-ever-after" sitcom feel-good, but we knew that there would be new chaos and conflict to explore in that world of the extended family.

The Mary Tyler Moore Show
YOU'RE GONNA MAKE IT AFTER ALL

Aired: September 19, 1970–March 19, 1977
Network: CBS
Created by: James L. Brooks and Allan Burns
Cast: Mary Tyler Moore (Mary Richards), Edward Asner (Lou Grant), Valerie
   Harper (Rhoda Morgenstern), Gavin MacLeod (Murray Slaughter), Ted
   Knight (Ted Baxter), Cloris Leachman (Phyllis Lindstrom), Georgia Engel
   (Georgette Franklin Baxter), Betty White (Sue Ann Nivens), Lisa Gerritsen
   (Beth Lindstrom)
Theme Song: "Love Is All Around," by Sonny Curtis (performed by Sonny
   Curtis)

The 1960s brought a growing movement that sought to free women from oppression and male supremacy. Females were relegated mostly to staying in the
home under the thumb of their husbands who controlled the purse strings.
Women were the ongoing victims of centuries of societal mores prescribing
their fates, facilitated by a combination of religious attitudes toward a woman's
duty before God and her husband and a patriarchal society that assured that a
brethren of men would enjoy the opportunities while the ladies looked on with
a minimal voice. The women's liberation movement provided a platform for
solidarity and empowerment. Women began to flex their collective muscle, vo-
cally demonstrating their needs and wants and taking the stand that these were
part of their inherent rights. A woman, if she chose to, could survive and excel
outside of the parameters set for her by a male-governed society.
   Feminist writers who were the voices of the women's liberation movement
were concerned with how society could eliminate unfair sex roles and shape
a future for women that was full of possibility rather than mired in limita-
tions. Among these pioneering revolutionaries were Frances M. Beal, Simone

de Beauvoir, Shulamith Firestone, Carol Hanisch, Audre Lorde, Kate Millett, Robin Morgan, Marge Piercy, Adrienne Rich, and Gloria Steinem. In her essay "Liberation Ethic and the Equality Ethic," Jo Freeman strove to map out the purpose of the movement:

> To seek only equality, given the current male bias of the social values, is to assume that women want to be like men or that men are worth emulating. . . . It is just as dangerous to fall into the trap of seeking liberation without due concern for equality.[1]

The women's liberation movement wanted more than just equality with men, it was fighting for a world where women's unique sensibilities were an influential part of the changing landscape.

By the late 1960s, television had begun to embrace story lines that represented women in a wider range of capacities beyond doting mother and devoted wife. Programs such as *That Girl* and *Julia* ushered in a new wave of television that depicted women as wanting more: independent, career minded, intellectual, and captains of their own fate. Gone were the days of *The Donna Reed Show* and *The Adventures of Ozzie and Harriett*. There was a world of untold stories

Betty White, Gavin MacLeod, Edward Asner, Georgia Engel, Ted Knight, and Mary Tyler Moore in *The Mary Tyler Moore Show*. CBS/Photofest © CBS

about women who broke the mold, who had aspirations and drive outside of baking apple pies and watching soap operas (an unfair stereotype of the equally challenging career of the housewife). These women had always been there, but their numbers were growing as they found and employed that collective voice. Television eventually stepped up and provided a TV show that reflected the changing America and that empowered the American woman. The arrival of *The Mary Tyler Moore Show* brought the most daring portrait of a female character in a sitcom to date.

The year is 1970. A single woman, 30 years of age, having broken off an engagement, makes her way to the city of Minneapolis, Minnesota, to explore a single life and career. She lives in a small apartment, applies for a secretary position at a local news station, and ends up landing a job as associate producer of the six o'clock news. She must navigate the male-dominated profession, prove her mettle, and find a way to succeed on her own terms. She enjoys an independent life, balancing friendships and career, gaining confidence as a strong and independent woman, and touching the lives of everyone she encounters with her warmth and her strength. This is the basic premise, of course, for the revolutionary sitcom *The Mary Tyler Moore Show.*

The Mary Tyler Moore Show was created by James L. Brooks and Allan Burns and starred popular sitcom star Mary Tyler Moore, who had endeared herself to television audiences playing the unconventional housewife Laura Petrie on *The Dick Van Dyke Show*. The show premiered on September 19, 1970, and from the opening credits, audiences were made to understand that this would not be a sitcom like they were used to watching. The opening montage (set to the now legendary Sonny Curtis song "Love Is All Around") immediately painted a character who was new to us. Mary Richards was seen packing up her old life in a seemingly small town and driving to the city of Minneapolis, where she would start life anew. This opening sequence would change down the line, offering a glimpse of Mary enjoying the trials and tribulations of her success, but one thing remained a constant. In the final seconds of the opening, we saw Mary walking down the street, stopping, spinning around, and taking her hat off and launching it into the air, where it froze in the final frame. This moment would visually (and instantly) become the show's metaphor. With exuberant joy, Mary literally threw off that hat as if it were the past, letting her hair down, releasing herself from an oppressive world, exhibiting a courage and optimism that kept it suspended and that foreshadowed her success. So much was summed up in this five-second moment that it is not surprising that it became one of the most iconic moments of television.

Mary Richards worked at WJM studios, where she was surrounded by men: her lovable but crotchety boss Lou Grant, amiable news writer Murray Slaughter, and the narcissistic newscaster Ted Baxter. At home, she was good friends with her landlady, the flamboyant and opinionated Phyllis Lindstrom, and her neighbor, the sarcastic and eccentric Rhoda Morgenstern. As the show progressed, both Rhoda and Phyllis received spin-offs, requiring new characters to be introduced to fill the void. Sue Ann Nivens was a man-hungry woman who had her own cooking show on WJM, always cutting people down with a bright smile on her face. Georgette Franklin was Ted Baxter's ditzy, devoted girlfriend (and ultimately his wife). These were the recurring characters that made *The Mary Tyler Moore Show*, despite its star taking top and titular billing, one of the finest ensembles in television sitcom history.

So how did *The Mary Tyler Moore Show* deviate from the sitcoms of the past? One of its most groundbreaking achievements came in how the writers treated the characters. The show featured characters who actually evolved. Most sitcoms up to this point had characters who remained static. From episode to episode, little changed about who they were and where they were going. On *The Mary Tyler Moore Show*, fully realized characters had story arcs that played into their foibles and their goals. Mary was always too agreeable, and her need to keep everyone happy often led to her own comical problems. Lou Grant dealt with alcoholism, which ultimately led to a separation (and divorce) from his wife, Edie. Ted, despite being the show's pompous clown, revealed an underbelly of insecurities as he and Georgette grew serious. Phyllis and Rhoda had a tentative relationship at best, often bickering, Mary being the tug-of-war rope in the middle. Murray had challenges at home with his wife and family, was a recovering compulsive gambler, and could sometimes become frustrated at work. Even the difficult-to-navigate Sue Ann could prove to be a friend despite her sex drive and the people she would climb over to get what she wanted. Character-based story lines gave audiences a deeper connection to these people. Typical sitcoms of the 1950s and 1960s were plot driven, and the characters just went along for the ride. *The Mary Tyler Moore Show* provided a far more compelling scenario that was closer to real-life interpersonal relationships and how people transform over time.

The Mary Tyler Moore Show was also groundbreaking in its subject matter. The show was one of the first sitcoms to really begin to probe the change in America that had been incited by the 1960s. The show braved some uncharted territory for the television sitcom, paving the way for programs like *All in the Family, Maude, Good Times,* and *M*A*S*H,* all of which would owe to *The Mary Tyler Moore Show* the evolution of the character-driven, poignant, thought-provoking look at society filtered through humor.

In the opening of season 2, in an episode called "The Birds . . . and . . . um . . . Bees," Mary produces a documentary for WJM called "What's Your Sexual I.Q.?," and the station is inundated with phone calls from viewers who were uncomfortable with the subject matter. Phyllis, however, is raising a daughter named Beth and is uncomfortable broaching the birds and the bees with her, so asks Mary if she will do it (which she tactfully does). In 1971, TV sitcoms were not talking about sex, let alone addressing how parents talk to their kids about where babies come from. Although the episode is innocuous by today's standards, it certainly opened the eyes of viewers as to how the national dialogue on sex was changing. In episode 8 of the same season, Mary is forced to cross a picket line when the television news writers' union and other guilds go on strike in an episode titled "Thoroughly Unmilitant Mary." This scenario forced Mary and Lou to handle all aspects of producing the news (writing, technical, and anchoring), giving them a new perspective on how the station's labor deserved better treatment.

Rhoda Morgenstern as a character gave the show an opportunity to explore body image. Rhoda (and the actress who played her) was neither unattractive nor particularly overweight, but the character was constantly concerned about her size and appearance. In season 3, episode 6, titled "Rhoda the Beautiful," Rhoda loses 20 pounds, only to have her insecurities heighten when she enters a beauty pageant at a local department store. *The Mary Tyler Moore Show* was one of the first shows to really delve into character insecurities and recognize the struggles that women go through to maintain an image that is desirable to men. Insecurities, however, were not limited to the ladies. In "Operation Lou" (season 3, episode 13), Lou Grant goes into the hospital to have some shrapnel removed from his leg. While he is out of commission, he chooses Mary over Murray to run things at the office, leading to a divide between the usually close friends. The episode gave audiences a glimpse of a female character in a power position and offered subtle commentary about how the men in her charge would respond and the insecurities they felt when their masculinity is challenged by a strong, assertive female.

In the finale of season 6, the now-married Ted Baxter and his wife, Georgette, are having trouble conceiving. Again, this was relatively new territory for television. The option of adoption comes up, and the couple bring the 12-year-old boy David (Robbie Rist) into their fold. Just as the new family begins to settle in together, Georgette announces that she is pregnant after all. "Ted and the Kid" was an indication that television was embracing a wider range of family makeups, that the stereotypical convention of birth parents—mother and father with son and daughter—was not the only situation in which people found family. Insignificant as this may seem in this day and age, in the 1970s there was a stigma around adoption and anyone who could not produce children of their own biological makeup.

The Mary Tyler Moore Show was never overbearing in its presentation of topical issues. In fact, the show remained lighthearted throughout its seven-season run. There was very little the writers and producers would do that would offend audiences. The show's most celebrated episode dealt with how we handle death. In season 6, episode 7, called "Chuckles Bites the Dust," WJM's beloved children's show performer Chuckles the Clown is killed in a hilariously dark way. Chuckles was chosen to be the grand marshal of a circus parade and dressed as a character named "Peter Peanut." Unfortunately, an elephant that is part of the festivities can't resist the giant peanut, and poor Chuckles is trampled to death. The gang in the newsroom indulge in callous and corny jokes about the absurd turn of events, much to the mortification of Mary, who thinks they should be grieving his loss in a serious way. At the funeral, the minister performs a eulogy that attempts to sum up Chuckles's spirit, but his monologue refers to much of what made the clown hilarious. Mary is the only guest who cannot refrain from bursting into the very laughter that she had chided her coworkers for.

It was not hard to recognize the impact that *The Mary Tyler Moore Show* had on the direction of television. Audiences loved the show. It faired relatively well in the ratings, with it ranking (by each passing season) at numbers 22, 10, 7, 9, 11, and 19. The show was an Emmy juggernaut throughout the 1970s, winning Outstanding Comedy Series in 1975, 1976, and 1977. Mary Tyler Moore also took home three statuettes in 1973, 1974, and 1976 for Best Actress in a Comedy Series. The supporting cast was also well rewarded with Asner, Knight, Harper, White, and Leachman taking home Emmys for their supporting roles. It also won five Emmys for Outstanding Writing in a Comedy Series, and Jay Sandrich was honored twice for directing. *The Mary Tyler Moore Show* also produced three spin-off series: The sitcoms *Rhoda* and *Phyllis* and, after the show wrapped up, the hour-long drama *Lou Grant*, which took Ed Asner's character and placed him in more serious situations.

When the show came to its conclusion, it found the characters faced with losing their jobs when WJM changed ownership. In the end, the new owner fired Mary, Lou, Murray, and Sue Ann but decided to retain the bumbling Ted Baxter. The show ended on an emotional note as friends and coworkers said good-bye and faced having to move on with their lives. Although it was leaving the air, the long-term effects of *The Mary Tyler Moore Show* would be felt for decades to come, from every workplace comedy to every television show that dared to create women characters who shattered the barriers of societal expectations. In 1977, the series was given a Peabody Award with the committee citing what best sums up the show's legacy:

> *The Mary Tyler Moore Show* has established the benchmark by which all situation comedies must be judged . . . [recognizing it] for a consistent standard of excellence—and for a sympathetic portrayal of a career woman in today's changing society.[2]

All in the Family
THOSE WERE THE DAYS

Aired: January 12, 1971–April 8, 1979
Network: CBS
Created by: Norman Lear and Bud Yorkin, based on the British series *Till Death Us Do Part*, by Johnny Speight
Cast: Carroll O'Connor (Archie Bunker), Jean Stapleton (Edith Bunker), Sally Struthers (Gloria Bunker Stivic), Rob Reiner (Michael Stivic), Danielle Brisebois (Stephanie Mills)
Theme Song: "Those Were the Days," by Charles Strouse and Lee Adams (performed by Carroll O'Connor and Jean Stapleton)

In the early 1970s, America was hurting, healing, and evolving from a decade that had left the country in an identity crisis. The turbulence of the 1960s had led to a cynicism in the early 1970s as Americans faced myriad casualties of the Vietnam War, growing unemployment, and an icy divide between the majority and minority groups. Despite major strides throughout the 1960s with the vocal rise of the civil rights and feminist movements, society was nursing its wounds while facing an uncertain future. Assassinations of movement leaders such as John F. Kennedy, Martin Luther King Jr., Robert Kennedy, and Malcolm X; the rise of Richard Nixon; the Stonewall riots; the emergence of Gloria Steinem and Betty Friedan (the latter the author of *The Feminine Mystique*); and the plight of the working man all seemed to come to a head, paving the way for a decade where America was forced to take a hard look at itself and determine where it wanted to go next. Television in the late 1960s reflected very little of the growing tempest, offering mainly an escape from reality. Most programs distracted (as entertainment strives to do in tough times), skewing toward westerns (*Bonanza* and *Gunsmoke*), silly escapism (*Gilligan's Island* and *It's about Time*), magic (*Bewitched* and *I Dream of Jeannie*), rural sitcoms (*Green Acres* and *The Beverly Hill-*

39

billies), and upbeat family programming (*The Brady Bunch* and *Here's Lucy*). By the early 1970s, a few shows came on the scene that challenged audiences with thought-provoking, socially relevant plotlines, such as *The Mary Tyler Moore Show*, *Julia*, *That Girl*, *The Bob Newhart Show*, *The Courtship of Eddie's Father*, and *Star Trek*. The overall landscape, however, wasn't ideal for a television show that faced our country's demons head-on, that exercised humor in exploring our current and evolving situation, warts and all. Could such a program exist without creating an even larger divide in our nation? Ready for it or not, one of the most controversial, game-changing, thought-provoking, and influential television shows was about to enter that landscape, and the result would transform television from an entertainment box to a conduit for political discussion and societal debate. That show would be *All in the Family*.

Produced by Norman Lear and Bud Yorkin, *All in the Family* was inspired by the British sitcom *Till Death Us Do Part* (1965–1975) about a working-class man named Alf Garnett who holds racist, prejudiced, and antisocialist views. Living with his addled but kindly wife Else, as well as his daughter Rita and her socialist husband Mike, Alf often found himself at odds with the ever-changing world that, in his perception, was crumbling around him thanks to progressive

Carroll O'Connor and Sammy Davis Jr. in *All in the Family*. CBS/Photofest © CBS

and counterculture movements. Norman Lear had seen the show while living in the United Kingdom and decided that the basic premise was rife for reinterpreting for an American sitcom that addressed societal conflict and the litany of concerns facing the American people.

Initially, *All in the Family* was given a pilot in 1968 titled "Justice for All," which starred Carroll O'Connor and Jean Stapleton as Archie and Edith Justice, with Kelly Jean Peters playing Gloria and Tim McIntire playing her husband, Richard. Producers at ABC (where the show was being developed) decided to fund a second pilot titled "Those Were the Days," which swapped out Peters and McIntire for Candice Azzara and Chip Oliver to play Gloria and Richard, respectively. ABC, however, became nervous about producing a show with a loudmouthed bigot as its central character and decided not to move forward with *All in the Family*. Their loss was CBS's gain. Executives at CBS were rebranding their image, bringing to an end their string of rural sitcoms like *The Beverly Hillbillies*, *Green Acres*, and *Mayberry R.F.D.* in lieu of a more urban-set, sophisticated programming. *All in the Family* fit the bill, and the sitcom, with a few cast changes and a new last name for the family, found a home.

All in the Family premiered on CBS on January 12, 1971, and introduced television audiences to the Bunker clan of 704 Hauser Street, Queens, New York. The patriarch of the family was Archie Bunker, a blue-collar worker with regularly vocalized prejudices, seemingly in explosive disagreement with anyone who didn't think like him. Archie was outspoken and often quick to temper. If Archie seemed all bombast and bigotry, there was a tender side to the character, often showing his love and decency in surprising ways. In contrast with Archie's rough-edged and bristly persona was his counterpart, Edith, the often confused, always nervous, but extremely soft and lovable wife and mother. Edith was concerned about keeping the peace, often catering to Archie's whims but also questioning his logic in an innocent way that reflected a hidden person who wanted to emerge. Just as Archie had a gentle side, Edith had a feisty one that would occasionally reveal itself when she was pushed too hard or too far. Living with Archie and Edith was their grown daughter, Gloria Stivic, and her husband, Michael. Michael was a college student, caught up in the social change and movements of the time, coming in direct opposition to Archie, often inciting his wrath with his counterculture ideals. Gloria, who financially supported Michael while he attended college (during the show's first five years), was generally a friendly young woman but was capable of exhibiting her father's temper. Michael was an outspoken, opinionated liberal who was in a constant clash with his father-in-law. This quartet made up the Bunker household and was the recipe for nine seasons of comedic conflict and unyielding discussion of social change.

From *All in the Family*'s opening credits through the final credits, audiences were given a heaping dose of satire and irony. Archie and Edith sat down at a spinet piano and sang the show's (now iconic) theme song "Those Were the Days." With music by Charles Strouse and lyrics by Lee Adams (who had written scores for Broadway musicals such as *Bye Bye Birdie, Golden Boy,* and *Applause*), the song was a nostalgic look at the better times of yesteryear, pining for the likes of Glenn Miller and Herbert Hoover:

> Boy the way Glenn Miller played
> Songs that made the Hit Parade
> Guys like us we had it made
> Those were the days
>
> And you knew where you were then
> Girls were girls and men were men
> Mister, we could use a man like Herbert Hoover again
>
> Didn't need no welfare state
> Everybody pulled his weight
> Gee, our old LaSalle ran great
> Those were the days

The song not only made for a catchy theme but also adeptly established the world of Archie and Edith Bunker, an existence that was fading and that would be encroached on, episode after episode, with an ever-changing world brought about by social evolution and a progressive way of thinking. Bookending each episode on the rear was the piano instrumental "Remembering You" by Cecil Kellaway, a nostalgic piece that also recalled simpler times. This final stretch of music seemed to evoke a daydream, perhaps a fantasy, of an America whose time had passed.

In its maiden season, *All in the Family* was not shy about tackling topical issues that challenged the viewer. In season 1, episode 4, titled "Archie Gives Blood," Archie's ignorance is explored when he is giving blood at the local blood bank and has concerns about who might receive his donation. Archie is under the impression that different races have different types of blood.

The season 1, episode 5, issue was no less controversial when the topic of homosexuality is brought up in the Bunker household. In "Judging Books by Covers," a friend of Gloria and Michael—an intellectual and sensitive man named Roger (Anthony Geary)—comes to the house. Archie is convinced that the man is gay and has plenty to say with regard to how he could never be friends with a "fruit." As it turns out, Roger is straight. The tables are then turned on Archie when his friend Steve (Philip Carey), a drinking buddy and an ex-NFL athlete, turns out to be homosexual. The discussion of homosexuality was revolutionary for television at the time, but the show's unyielding approach to breaking down gay stereotypes put *All in the Family* ahead of the pack in dealing with the topic, confronting the preconceived notions of many Americans. Philip Carey, who played Steve in this episode, was well known for his macho characterizations in western films and television shows, adding a touch of shock value when his character turned out to be gay.

Season 1, episode 6, found Gloria and Mike expecting. "Gloria's Pregnancy" was arguably the show's most dramatic to date, with Gloria suffering a miscarriage at its conclusion. Archie is angry when he finds out that the couple, who are still in college, are having a child. When Mike and Gloria go looking for a new place to live, the pregnancy goes bad, and Gloria loses the child. Miscarriage, as sad and prevalent as it was at the time (and still can be), was not considered a topic for television, let alone a situation comedy. But *All in the Family* made the issues of women one of its salient subjects. Gloria would eventually bring a child to term on the program: a little boy named Joey.

An explosive issue for Archie Bunker was his inherent distrust of black people and how their presence was going to influence his life. In season 1, episode 8, "Lionel Moves into the Neighborhood," Archie's greatest fears were set in motion. Gloria and Mike have a good friend named Lionel Jefferson (Mike Evans), who happens to be black, and it is unhappy news for Archie when it is announced that Lionel and his parents are moving into the neighborhood (next door to the Bunkers). In fact, the television show would return to this topic in the season finale, with Archie campaigning to keep black families from moving into the neighborhood. For more than a century, New York City (and most neighborhoods in urban areas) consisted of communities defined by ethnicity and religion. The Irish lived on their streets, the Italians on theirs, and each minority group was confined to its prescribed zone. This was a product of a combination of reasons: immigrants clustering with their own for safety and cultural preservation, economic disparity between classes, employment opportunities (or lack thereof, depending on your race or ethnicity), and a fear of the unknown outside of the familiar. By the 1970s, the lines that separated these communities began to blur, with distinct communities bleeding into one another. The episode titled "The First and Last Supper" was a hot-button way to end a first season, demonstrating how the 1960s had changed America, suggesting a world where we had the potential to cohabitate as equals if only the closed-minded could be overcome. In true *All in the Family* fashion, the tide turned on Archie when Edith, who had made friends with Louise Jefferson (Isabel Sanford), accepted her invitation for the Bunkers to come to dinner. Now Archie would be forced to face the very family who had ignited this bigoted antithesis to the Welcome Wagon.

Archie Bunker was not the villain of the piece, and he was never intended to be construed as such. He was simply a hardworking, minimally educated man who was a product of his situation and upbringing. If his construction made him seem like a villain, it was O'Connor's portrayal of Archie that allowed him to retain his humanity. Archie had real concerns, and the possibility of losing his job was one of his ongoing worries. In season 1, episode 10, "Archie Is Worried about His Job," *All in the Family* touched on the fears of many Americans, using Archie as the conduit for expressing how layoffs and the rising unemployment rate of the 1970s were growing concerns that would get far worse before they would get better. Archie was industrious, trying to provide for his family in a world that was starting to look like a place that was both unrecognizable and threatening to his beliefs. O'Connor created that palpable fear in Archie, and though much of what came out of the character's mouth could be despicable to many viewers, it was just as relatable to others. It is important to note that O'Connor was the complete antithesis of his character in real life, a vocal liberal who was adamantly concerned about tapping into his character's truth and letting him exist not merely as a foil for a liberal platform but also as a means for discussion.

All the episodes that have been mentioned thus far occurred in *All in the Family*'s first season, 13 in all, as the sitcom was a mid-season replacement. Still, it is daunting to consider all that this show endeavored to plunge into during that baker's dozen of episodes. For a show that was breaking new ground, it was also taking a lot of risks, perhaps to the detriment of its long-term success. Indeed, *All in the Family* incited much response for dealing with its controversial issues—some of it negative but most of it positive. But it demonstrated that television audiences were up to the challenge of thinking and watching and, most important, invited them to laugh at society's foibles and differences. The next eight seasons would be no less probing and ambitious.

Season 2 would bring several of *All in the Family*'s signature episodes of distinction. Topics such as impotence, Catholicism, street violence, and art versus pornography are all given the Archie Bunker treatment. However, season 2 gave Edith more opportunities to shine. In season 2, episode 28, known as "Edith's Problem," the story has Mrs. Bunker experiencing menopause, another topic that had been pretty much unexplored as part of television's depiction of women. The once-resolutely-kind Edith finds herself going through a series of mood swings, blowing her temper one minute and an emotional puddle the next, all, of course, to the irritation and confusion of Archie.

Another episode of prominence in season 2 was titled "Cousin Maude's Visit," which brought Edith's cousin Maude Findlay (Beatrice Arthur) into the picture. Episode 11 found the Bunkers suffering from a debilitating flu and Cousin Maude, a formidable woman with ultraliberal leanings, coming into the household to take care of the family. Of course, Maude is continually at odds with Archie; she is just as stubborn in her progressive beliefs as he is in his conservative ones. More important, the episode introduced a character who would eventually lead to *All in the Family*'s first spin-off, the highly controversial and just as timely *Maude*. It is a shame that the character didn't return to *All in the Family* more often, as the dynamic between O'Connor and Arthur was comedic gold, a battle of the wills that saw two extremist political ideologies, each on the opposite end of the spectrum, juxtaposed in a battle royale of satire and cutting wit. Producers, however, once enlightened to Arthur's comedic ability, were anxious to give her a program of her own, so Maude appeared in only one more episode of *All in the Family*, the season 2 finale called "Maude," which set up the basic premise for and served as the backdoor pilot of the spin-off that would debut that fall (1972).

Arguably, the most well-known episode of *All in the Family* came in season 2, episode 21. Titled "Sammy's Visit," the installment holds the record for the longest laugh from a live studio audience. What could inspire such an achievement? Archie Bunker had taken up work as a cab driver, and one of his customers happens to be star of stage and screen Sammy Davis Jr. (playing himself), who was both black and Jewish. Either of these attributes would be enough to fire up the bigot in Archie Bunker, so the combination of the two should have served as high-octane fuel. Remarkably, Archie is starstruck by Sammy, so when the entertainer accidentally leaves his briefcase in the cab, Archie is thrilled to have him stop by the house to retrieve it. Archie, however, eventually reveals his true colors and offends his guest with some ignorant comments. Before Sammy leaves, however, Archie has the audacity to ask Mr. Davis to pose for a photo with him. Sammy complies, but just as the flash goes off, Sammy plants a kiss on Archie's cheek, leaving behind a souvenir of the bigot being smooched by a black Jewish man.

An area where *All in the Family* was prescient regarding issues that would escalate over the coming decades was on the topic of gun control. Thanks mostly to the Vietnam War and concerns around America's participation in it, as well as the rise of gang violence in urban populations, certain factions of society had grown increasingly in favor of gun control and gun elimination altogether. In season 3, episode 1, "Archie and the Editorial," Archie goes on a local news station to offer a public rebuttal to a recent editorial that called for the elimination of handguns. Espousing his Second Amendment rights, Archie gives his verbal monologue in favor of handguns only to be held at gunpoint and robbed while drinking at his favorite tavern, Kelcy's Bar. That was the kind of one-two punch that *All in the Family* endeavored to deliver, setting up Archie's logic and argument only to have it ironically turn on him in the end.

All in the Family was not just about Archie Bunker, though he was the dominant voice that propelled the program. In many ways, however, his wife Edith was the beating heart of the show, and when she was face-to-face with the issues of the day, it was often heart-wrenching to watch this kindly, frequently abused woman suffer at the experiences that came her way. In what may well be the most startling and haunting episode of *All in the Family*, a two-part episode (season 8, episodes 4 and 5) titled "Edith's 50th Birthday," the matriarch of the Bunker household is sexually assaulted by a stranger who is posing as a police detective (David Dukes). As the rest of the family is next door preparing a surprise party for Edith, the man comes to the door and Edith lets him in. The subsequent scene of the attempted rape was, to date, the most harrowing ever attempted in sitcom television, with Edith escaping when she uses a burned cake to attack the rapist. That singular moment resulted in the loudest cheers and applause ever received during the series' nine-year tenure on television. The series writers were careful to give Edith's postassault reactions and aftermath a viscerally honest truth, leading to the New York City Police Department and rape crisis centers utilizing the episode as part of their training to give professionals an understanding of what an assault survivor goes through.

Throughout its nine seasons, *All in the Family* went through many changes. Mike and Gloria went through a litany of marital travails, including a split-up, reconciliation, taking their son and moving to California, and ultimately ending things in divorce. In the beginning of season 8, Archie mortgages the house in order to buy Kelcy's Bar, turning it into Archie Bunker's Place, the first indication of the show winding down and transforming into what will eventually become its spin-off series. In its final season, it was clear that the show had exhausted almost any socially relevant topic it could. In an effort to breathe new life into the story lines, Archie and Edith are given a second chance at parenting. The couple take in Edith's cousin Floyd's daughter Stephanie, and much of season 9 took a cutesy turn toward wrapping plots around the moppet. The series concluded rather unceremoniously but with the powers that be planning to continue the series under the title *Archie Bunker's Place*. Perhaps it was understood that this wasn't really an end.

Less of a spin-off but more of a continuation of *All in the Family*, *Archie Bunker's Place* premiered in the fall of 1979, and O'Connor, Stapleton, and Brisebois came along for the ride. The new show centered more around Archie's tavern and his interactions with its regular patrons. Stapleton soon decided it was time to leave the show and appeared in only five of the series' first 14 episodes. With the focus on Archie establishing a rapport with his new business partner, a Jewish man named Murray Klein (Martin Balsam), who buys in when Archie's former partner decides he wants out, it was easy for the writers to cover for Stapleton's departure in the short term. But at the start of season 2 of *Archie Bunker's Place*, it was explained that Edith had died from a stroke. Archie mourned his wife, and the next year was spent with him moving past the loss of his beloved Edith. Eventually, he moved on and started dating, but the show was never quite the same without Edith Bunker. Her big heart balanced his big mouth, and, without it, the show's dynamic would never be the same.

Initially, *Archie Bunker's Place* held its own in the ratings, proving that the iconic character had not grown tiresome to television audiences. However, *Archie Bunker's Place* never held the wide appeal that *All in the Family* had enjoyed. Occasionally, Sally Struthers returned to the program to reprise her character of Gloria, which helped to maintain a connection between the new show and its predecessor. The magic, however, was just not there, and though the show ran for a total of four seasons, it was canceled before it could be given a conclusion that respectably culminated 14 years with the Bunkers.

All in the Family remains one of the most influential television series of all time, breaking down barriers and delving into topics that, until its premiere, television had been reluctant to address. The show inspired a handful of spin-offs, including *Maude*, *The Jeffersons*, *Archie Bunker's Place*, and *Gloria*, the first two iconic in their own right. From 1971 to 1976, *All in the Family* held the number 1 place in the Nielsen ratings and remained high on that chart for the duration of its time on television. Only three shows in history have held the number 1 spot for five years running (the other two are *The Cosby Show* and *American Idol*). *All in the Family* won multiple Emmy Awards, including wins for all four of the show's original cast members and four trophies for Outstanding Comedy Series. The show has enjoyed a healthy life in syndication, where new generations continue to be treated to a show that exhibits an audacity and wit that far surpasses contemporary programs. What Norman Lear and Bud Yorkin and their team of writers had envisioned for the television audience turned out to be a heartfelt, hilarious, poignant lesson in civics, current events, debate, and discussion. No television show, before or since, has provided such an opportunity.

Sanford and Son
THE BLACK ARCHIE BUNKER

Aired: January 14, 1972–March 25, 1977

Network: NBC

Created by: Norman Lear (uncredited) and Bud Yorkin, based on the BBC program *Steptoe and Son*, created by Ray Galton and Alan Simpson

Cast: Redd Foxx (Fred G. Sanford), Demond Wilson (Lamont Sanford), Beah Richards (Aunt Ethel), LaWanda Page (Aunt Esther Anderson), Whitman Mayo (Grady Wilson), Don Bexley (Bubba Bexley), Nathaniel Taylor (Rollo Lawson)

Theme Song: "The Streetbeater: Theme to *Sanford and Son*," composed by Quincy Jones

All in the Family was one of TV's most influential sitcoms, particularly due to the character of Archie Bunker, the loudmouthed, unrestrained bigot who occasionally showed a lovable side. Networks were hoping to recapture this magic that CBS had turned into a ratings juggernaut. NBC found its version of Archie Bunker in the cantankerous, irascible Fred Sanford, who would be the black counterpart to *All in the Family*'s antihero on TV's *Sanford and Son*. CBS had, in fact, passed on the show, a decision it would rue for seasons to come.

Developed by Norman Lear (who was the force behind *All in the Family*), *Sanford and Son* premiered on January 24, 1972, and remained a highly rated sitcom for its six-season run. It was loosely based on the BBC program *Steptoe and Son*. The story explored the relationship of a black junk dealer and his adult son who share a business and live together, the elder an opinionated, often bigoted grouch who was regularly at odds with his conscientious and concerned son. Living in near poverty and rarely able to pay their bills, the father–son duo would scrimp and scrape to make ends meet, hatching harebrained schemes to make quick money.

But *Sanford and Son* was not just a laugh-a-minute sitcom. Sure, it was consistently funny, but it also offered commentary on racial inequality and poverty and even explored aspects of the black man's frustration with the white man (Fred wasn't a fan of most whites and would disparage their treatment of minorities with a reverse bigotry that had rarely been depicted on television).

Fred Sanford lived and operated his business on 9114 South Central Avenue in the Watts neighborhood of Los Angeles, California. His son Lamont felt responsible for his old man. Despite wanting his independence and constantly considering leaving, Lamont worried about his aging father's ability to take care of himself. Fred, who was a widower, could be manipulative. When he didn't get his way, he'd grab his chest and call out to his dead wife, "Elizabeth! This is the big one! I'm on my way!" Lamont rarely fell for these dramatic monologues.

Also in the Sanford's world were Aunt Esther, the sister of Fred's late wife. A Bible thumper who was regularly frustrated with Fred's antics, the two would antagonize each other with a barrage of insults. Aunt Esther replaced Aunt Ethel, who was Fred's original antagonist on the show but nowhere near as memorable or as feisty as the pocketbook-swinging Aunt Esther. Grady Wilson was Fred's best friend. Grady, who was not too bright, was easily swayed by Fred to participate in whatever get-rich scheme was the flavor of the week. Fred's other close friend was Bubba Bexley, a jovial and good-natured layabout who hung around

Redd Foxx, Demond Wilson, and LaWanda Page in *Sanford and Son*. CBS/ Photofest © CBS

the shop. Lamont also had a close friend in Rollo Lawson, an ex-convict and someone Fred did not particularly like.

Sanford and Son was not as edgy as many of the Norman Lear sitcoms of the day. It traded in slapstick comedy and exaggerated scenarios that gave Redd Foxx a chance to do what he did best: make people laugh. Where the show is remembered for being controversial is for its flipping of the equation, depicting a character (Fred) who had endured bigotry and, born of his experiences, developed his own bigoted stance on the world, his character in constant judgment of everyone.

The series was also revolutionary in that it was an enormous hit. In 1972, a series with an all-black leading cast was pretty revolutionary. We hadn't quite come to a time where *The Jeffersons* were "moving on up to the East Side" or the Evans family was "not getting hassled, not getting hustled." *Sanford and Son* is what paved the way for more serious sitcoms about the plight of the African American family and for their representation in television altogether to come along. Sitcoms of this ilk would ultimately become a big part of the landscape in 1970s television.

Although *Sanford and Son* was a hit, it was not without its problems. For the show's first five seasons, it was in the top 10 of the Nielsen ratings, cresting at number 2 during its second and fourth seasons. However, Redd Foxx, frustrated over contract negotiations, walked off the set and left the show for a while. He was absent from the third season's final six episodes and the first three episodes of the fourth season until producers and network caved in to Foxx's per-episode request of higher pay. In his absence, the character of Grady took over the business for a while, but the show was just not the same without Foxx's Fred delivering his signature histrionics and beloved personality.

Maude

LADY GODIVA WAS A FREEDOM RIDER

Aired: September 12, 1972–April 22, 1978
Network: CBS
Created by: Norman Lear and Bud Yorkin
Cast: Beatrice Arthur (Maude Findlay), Bill Macy (Walter Findlay), Adrienne
  Barbeau, then Marcia Rodd (Carol Traynor), Conrad Bain (Dr. Arthur
  Harmon), Rue McClanahan (Vivian Harmon), Esther Rolle (Florida Ev-
  ans), Hermione Baddeley (Mrs. Nell Naugatuck), J. Pat O'Malley (Bert
  Beasley), Marlene Warfield (Victoria Butterfield), Brian Morrison, then
  Kraig Metzinger (Phillip Traynor)
Theme Song: "And Then There's Maude," by Marilyn and Alan Bergman and
  Dave Grusin (performed by Donny Hathaway)

The 1970s was arguably the most revolutionary decade in sitcom storytelling.
TV shows, particularly those under the influence of producer Norman Lear,
were cutting edge in their willingness to delve into societal issues and current
events, reflecting a cynicism that had fallen over America in reaction, largely, to
the turbulence of the 1960s. Financial recession, unemployment, the Watergate
scandal, the divisiveness of the Vietnam War, and minority groups still pressing
on to gain equal rights had created an America that was disillusioned with itself.
As the country marched toward its bicentennial, it found itself in the greatest
identity crisis of its 200 years. What was America going to be now? How did it
solve its problems? How could such polarized viewpoints of the left and right
find common ground? The answers may not have been clear, but the television
sitcom proved to be the ideal medium for reasoning it out. *All in the Family* was
the guiding star of these groundbreakers, followed closely by its equally audacious spin-off *Maude*.

Maude Findlay was the cousin of Edith Bunker. The character debuted in *All in the Family* on December 11, 1971, in an episode called "Cousin Maude's Visit." When the entire Bunker clan is suffering from the flu, the liberal-minded relative made the journey from her Tuckahoe, New York, residence to 704 Hauser Street, Queens, to take care of the family. Maude was the perfect foil for Archie Bunker, her inflexible, progressive voice an equal match for his conservative, bullheaded one. The character of Maude resonated with audiences, and producer Norman Lear was quick to initiate a spin-off. The result would be a sitcom that took its cue from its parent show, probing some of the most challenging issues of the day and shaping how America felt about them.

Any TV show that features a theme song celebrating the progress brought about by the likes of Lady Godiva and Joan of Arc is already promising something radical. The Dave Grusin/Alan and Marilyn Bergman ditty that opened each episode of *Maude*, with its rapid-fire, tongue-twisting conclusion, grouped the show's title character in with the female movers and shakers of world history: "that uncompromisin' enterprisin' anything but traqulizin' Right on Maude!"[1] This was telling us something, foreshadowing that we were in for something different where *Maude* was concerned.

Adrienne Barbeau, Beatrice Arthur, Bill Macy, and Esther Rolle in *Maude*.
CBS/Photofest © CBS

Maude premiered on CBS on September 12, 1972. Played by the indelible Beatrice Arthur, the show's title character was unlike any seen before on television. Maude had been married three times (once widowed, twice divorced) before her latest husband, Walter. Walter was an appliance salesman and an alcoholic, deeply in love with Maude but also frustrated by her antics. The couple had taken in Maude's adult daughter Carol, a divorcée with a son, Phillip. Maude employed three maids over the show's six seasons. The first was Florida Evans, a no-nonsense black woman who was regularly at odds with Maude's ultraliberal beliefs. Florida exited the show when the popular character was given her own spin-off, *Good Times*. The second domestic was Mrs. Nell Naugatuck, an elderly British woman who enjoyed more than the occasional cocktail. Mrs. Naugatuck also found herself squabbling with Maude. The character eventually met and married an Irish security guard. Together, they departed the Findlay household to move to Ireland. The final maid was the West Indian–born Victoria Butterfield, a character who was never quite as popular as Maude's two previous housekeepers but was just as spunky. Next door to the Findlay's lived Dr. Arthur Harmon, a conservative doctor who was Walter's best friend from the war. Arthur and Maude would regularly spar over political issues, each representing the polar extreme of conservatism and liberalism, respectively. Dr. Harmon eventually met and married Maude's college friend, the ditzy Vivian Harmon.

Maude's character, though completely earnest in her political and societal convictions, was what many at the time referred to as a "limousine liberal" or "knee-jerk liberal." A fierce but often uninformed advocate of racial and gender equality, Maude was a staunch Democrat and always voted the party line. She could be off-putting with her domineering and bombastic approach to conveying her passion for supporting the marginalized and the oppressed. Still, she always worked from a place of good intentions, even if she had to bulldoze people (particularly her husband) to make her point. Anytime her spouse even remotely shot back at her, she'd have the final word, proclaiming, "God'll get you for that, Walter!" Much of her appeal was achieved through Bea Arthur's carefully measured portrayal of Maude, warts and all.

Early in the show's first season, Maude and Walter were in the process of hiring a maid. In hiring Florida Evans, Maude finds herself conflicted about being a liberal employing a black domestic. What kind of message would that send? This was how Maude's conscience worked. Maude decides to treat Florida like a member of the family, something that the woman found hindered her ability to do her job. Maude insisted that Florida use the front door instead of the back door when buying groceries, even though the back door led directly into the kitchen. Maude couldn't have Florida think she was being treated differently for the color of her skin. Fortunately, Florida, who was always a witty and outspoken match for Maude, spoke up for herself, pointing out how Maude's condescension on racial issues was insulting, something she didn't understand and had never lived. She asserted that her employer's position on which door to use was actually making her job harder. Florida tried to quit but finally agreed to stay—but only if things were done on her own terms. Maude agreed, realizing, perhaps, that maybe she didn't understand racial disparity, that the civil rights movement of the 1960s had not been her fight.

But Maude was much more than just a mouthpiece for liberal thinking. She was a middle-aged woman, bright and articulate, a mother who enjoyed having sex, something that really hadn't been conveyed before on television. Sex was barely ever addressed on the tube, period. All of a sudden, here was a TV show about a libidinous 47-year-old woman who regularly copulated with her equally horny husband. They drank together. They partied together. They fought violently together, often smashing plates and other bric-a-brac in their battles. This was not Carol and Mike Brady. This was not June and Ward Cleaver. There was something refreshing about Maude's authenticity as both feminine and aggressive, no longer the Donna Reed, baking pies and acquiescing to her husband's judgment. In part, *Maude* changed how female characters would be imagined and written for television.

Maude also searched for a life outside of being a housewife, getting involved in charities and politics. She wasn't content to just sit at home and wait for Walter to come home from the appliance store. In "The Split," Maude had an opportunity to run for the New York state senate. An old-fashioned Walter, unyielding in his opposition to his wife assaying a political career, issued an ultimatum if she pursued the candidacy. Maude chose to run, and Walter left, albeit for a short period of time that eventually ended in their reconciliation when Maude lost the race. Even for all its revolutionary messages on women standing strong and asserting independence, *Maude* sometimes took two steps backward, particularly where the title character's relationship with her husband was concerned, but this also helped to demonstrate the distance women still had to go to be considered capable of autonomy from men.

An episode of controversy surrounded the topic of marijuana, a hot-button issue for the 1970s, when a rise in the use of the easy-to-acquire drug was a concern to many Americans. "The Grass Story" found the title character protesting the sentencing of a 19-year-old (Maude's grocery delivery boy) who had been arrested for possession. She and her other middle-aged housewife friends attempt to get arrested themselves for the same crime and then plan to stage a protest in the police station. Problems arise when Maude, who is in charge of acquiring the pot they will need for their plan to ignite, cannot find anyone from whom she can buy marijuana. The episode was in direct reaction to the impending Rockefeller Drug Laws, which assigned equal punishment (a minimum of 15 years in prison) for possession of marijuana, heroin, morphine, and cocaine. "The Grass Story" aired on December 5, 1972. The Rockefeller Drug Laws would be signed into effect by New York governor Nelson Rockefeller on May 8, 1973. The section of the law pertaining to marijuana was repealed in 1977 by Governor Hugh Carey.

Where *Maude* may have been its boldest and most groundbreaking was in its frank discussion and treatment of the subject of depression. Maude herself dealt with anxiety and depression. Her character regularly took tranquilizers, such as Miltown and Valium, in order to function. In an episode titled "The Analyst," Maude visits a psychiatrist and reveals a catalog of emotional issues, ranging from feelings about her dead father and her resentment toward her mother to her crisis over turning 50 and her complicated relationship with Walter. Walter Findlay, in turn, has to come to terms with his own alcoholism in the two-parter "Walter's Problem." Losing control during a bender, he strikes Maude, giving her a black eye. In his journey toward sobriety, Walter suffers a nervous breakdown. Later in the series, Walter attempts suicide when his business goes bankrupt. The 1970s had brought an open discussion of life's demons, and *Maude* was one of the first sitcoms to tackle topics of mental illness and alcoholism with brutal, unrelenting truth.

The most controversial episode of *Maude* was a two-parter referred to as "Maude's Dilemma," which aired during the show's first season in November 1972. The title character, who is going through menopause, finds out that she is pregnant with a change-of-life baby. Maude was uncertain about raising another child at this point in her life and was conflicted about what to do. Her daughter Carol offered the suggestion that abortion had been recently legalized in New York State and that it was an option. This episode aired just months before the landmark Supreme Court case *Roe v. Wade*, which made abortion legal in all 50 states. When Maude chose to abort the baby, thousands of antiabortion protestors wrote letters to CBS in opposition to the episode. Surprisingly, CBS reran "Maude's Dilemma" in August 1973 despite the controversy surrounding its initial airing. The episode was written by Susan Harris, who would later work with Bea Arthur on the sitcom *The Golden Girls*.

Maude was an extremely popular sitcom, ranking numbers 4, 6, 9, and 4 during its first four seasons. During its final two seasons, the show was moved from time slot to time slot, losing audience in the process and forcing the show below the top 30 when people no longer knew where to look for it. *Maude* was, in fact, renewed for another season, the story having progressed to Maude being appointed by the fictional New York governor to fill a congressional seat vacated by a deceased congressman. The show was to start over in Washington, with a new cast surrounding *Maude* as her aides and assistants. At the last minute,

Arthur decided that the show had run its course and chose to depart the program. Without Maude, the show could no longer move forward.

Beatrice Arthur did win an Emmy Award in 1977 for Best Leading Actress in a Comedy Series. It was surprisingly the only Emmy the series won despite being nominated 11 other times in various categories (including Best Comedy Series). The lack of recognition, however, does not undermine the influence the sitcom had. *Maude* marked a distinctive evolution in how comedy was portrayed on television. The show was hilarious in many ways, but it braved waters that were dark, murky, and often bordering on intense drama. Like its contemporary *M*A*S*H*, it was a sitcom that was most effective when it wrapped its troubling issues in a veil of humor, taking the time to shed light on the human condition while simultaneously inviting us to laugh at our humanity and inherent failings.

Bridget Loves Bernie

LOVE IS CRAZY

Aired: September 16, 1972–March 3, 1973
Network: CBS
Created by: Bernard Slade
Cast: David Birney (Bernie Steinberg), Bibi Osterwald (Sophie Steinberg), Meredith Baxter (Bridget Fitzgerald Steinberg), Harold J. Stone (Sam Steinberg), Audra Lindley (Amy Fitzgerald), David Doyle (Walter Fitzgerald), Ned Glass (Moe Plotnik), Robert Sampson (Father Michael Fitzgerald), Bill Elliott (Otis Foster)
Theme Song: "Love Is Crazy," by Jerry Fielding and Diane Hildebrand

Interracial dating and marriage were not exactly embraced by Hollywood during the first few decades of television thanks to miscegenation laws in the United States that forbade the practice in many states until as late as 1967. The topic of interfaith dating and marriage, despite no clear laws against it, also carried with it its own taboos and was rarely (if ever) the part of an ongoing television romance and story arc. That was until a situation comedy appeared in 1972 called *Bridget Loves Bernie*.

Depicting a marriage between a Catholic woman named Bridget and a Jewish man named Bernie, *Bridget Loves Bernie* introduced the topic of interfaith marriage, and with it came a storm of controversy that led to the show's cancellation after one season despite performing well in the Nielsen ratings, where it ranked at number 5. It is interesting to think that less than 50 years ago, people had such an issue with two people of different faiths joining in marriage.

The series was based loosely on the enormously popular Broadway play of 1922 called *Abie's Irish Rose* by Anne Nichols. It was the story of an Irish Catholic woman and a Jewish man who marry despite protests from their respective families. The play was one of Broadway's biggest hits of the era, running an unprecedented 2,327 performances. It is interesting to contemplate how *Bridget Loves Bernie* could shutter so quickly, yet an audience was there to keep *Abie's Irish Rose* running for years in New York City and then going on to receive two feature film adaptations. But then, theater audiences have historically been more progressive than television audiences.

On the television series, Bridget was from a well-to-do family, strong in their Catholic beliefs. Bernie was a cab driver and just as entrenched in Judaism. The couple met through a chance encounter at a bus stop where they quickly fell in love. Audra Lindley and David Doyle played Bridget's parents, the wealthy Walter and Amy Fitzgerald. Bernie's working-class parents were portrayed by Harold J. Stone and Bibi Osterwald as Sam and Sophie Steinberg, respectively. Bernie and Bridget lived in an apartment above the Steinberg's delicatessen. Plotlines of the series were typical of the sitcoms of the day, with the objections of various family members peppering the proceedings.

Bridget Loves Bernie, according to many detractors, made a mockery of both of the religions depicted within the context of the show. Rabbi Wolfe Kelman, executive vice president of the Rabbinical Assembly of America, thought the show was an "an insult to some of the most sacred values of both the Jewish and Catholic religions."[1] Orthodox rabbis met with CBS at regular intervals to make

Meredith Baxter and David Birney in *Bridget Loves Bernie*. CBS/Photofest © *CBS*

their disgust known. Some of the show's writers and producers had threats made against them, including a bomb threat on the show. Actress Meredith Baxter was confronted at home by members of the Jewish Defense League. It seems that the biggest problem people had with *Bridget Loves Bernie* had less to do with the interfaith marriage than with inaccurate depictions of religion within the show's story lines.

Although it is hard to know if *Bridget Loves Bernie* would have been successful outside of its plum time slot (sandwiched between *All in the Family* and *The Mary Tyler Moore Show*), it remains the highest-ranked sitcom to be canceled after one season. In one of the more cowardly displays of network leadership in the history of television, executives at CBS, who were becoming increasingly uneasy over a vocal minority and their negative reactions to the show's characters, their situation, and the way faith was depicted in the program, folded under pressure.

M*A*S*H

SUICIDE IS PAINLESS

Aired: September 17, 1972–February 28, 1983
Network: CBS
Created by: (Developed by) Larry Gelbart and Gene Reynolds, based on
   *M*A*S*H: A Novel about Three Army Doctors*, by Richard Hooker
Cast: Alan Alda (Hawkeye Pierce), Wayne Rogers (Trapper John McIntyre),
   Mike Farrell (B. J. Hunnicutt), McLean Stevenson (Henry Blake), Harry
   Morgan (Sherman T. Potter), Loretta Swit (Margaret "Hot Lips" Houlihan
   Penopscot), Larry Linville (Frank Burns), David Ogden Stiers (Charles Em-
   erson Winchester III), Gary Burghoff (Walter Eugene "Radar" O'Reilly),
   Jamie Farr (Maxwell Q. Klinger), William Christopher (Father John Patrick
   Francis Mulcahy)
Theme Song: "Suicide Is Painless," by Johnny Mandel

War and the sitcom have always been a peculiar combination, as there are so
many scenarios regarding war that just don't seem to lend themselves to jokes.
Yet television somehow navigated its way around the horrors of war and found
ways to make audiences chuckle regardless. Shows like *McHale's Navy*, *Hogan's
Heroes*, *Sgt. Bilko*, and *F Troop* juxtaposed soldier camaraderie and heroism
against situations of buffoonish leadership and caricature-like villains. In essence,
these sitcoms were not really about any kind of war situations that any Americans were likely to find themselves fighting.

Then, in 1970, Hollywood would produce one of the most unconventional
war films to date. *M*A*S*H*, which stood for Mobile Army Surgical Hospital,
was a black comedy directed by Robert Altman that took place during the
Korean War of 1950 to 1953. But the film made no effort to gloss over its
subtext, which was pointedly making commentary about the Vietnam War
(1955–1975), which was well under way and had resulted in myriad deaths

**Jamie Farr, Wayne Rogers, and Alan Alda in *M*A*S*H*. CBS/Photofest ©
CBS**

when the film premiered. *M*A*S*H* was both a box office and a critical hit, and in a surprising turn, the Oscar-winning film (Best Screenplay) was soon converted into a television situation comedy that proved to be one of the most groundbreaking and unconventional shows in history.

M*A*S*H the series was developed for television by comedy writer Larry Gelbart, who had written for many classic sketch comedy and variety programs of the 1950s and 1960s, including *Caesar's Hour*, *The Dinah Shore Chevy Show*, and *The Danny Kaye Show* (among many). Although his experience was in broad comedy, Gelbart would seek to create with *M*A*S*H* a situation comedy based on strong character development and story lines that blurred the lines between comedy and drama. *M*A*S*H* would be something that audiences hadn't quite ever encountered sitting at home and staring at the tube. No, *M*A*S*H* was going to make them think not just about the plot unfolding before them but also about the war that it paralleled, a war that was unfolding overseas and affecting their everyday lives with loss and fear. Just like the film, it would be a thoughtful representation of the survival and sacrifices made in the face of war.

Produced by 20th Century Fox for CBS Television, *M*A*S*H* followed the 4077th Mobile Army Surgical Hospital stationed in Uijeongbu, South Korea, and the medical staff who supported the unit. Among them in the show's beginning were the cocky surgeon Hawkeye Pierce; his amiable sidekick Trapper John McIntyre; head nurse, the opinionated Margaret "Hot Lips" Houlihan; the easygoing commanding officer Lieutenant Colonel Henry Blake; the inept Frank Burns, the nerdy but extremely efficient Walter "Radar" O'Reilly; the kindly Father Mulcahy; and the cross-dressing conscientious objector Maxwell Klinger. Some of these characters would depart over time for various reasons, and others would step in to fill their void, but this was the core cast of characters from the show's first season.

The brutality of war was captured perfectly on an episode of *M*A*S*H* titled "Point of View," which aired as episode 11 of season 7. A first-person camera tells the story through the eyes of an injured soldier whose throat wound has left him mute. Unable to talk, we simply see what he is seeing, watching as the members of the 4077th treat him, operate on him, and encourage him back to health. One of the most harrowing episodes in sitcom television, "Point of View" was one the series' most dramatic and least like a television comedy. But it wasn't just the wounded soldiers who struggled in the mobile hospital. In "Out of Sight, Out of Mind," Hawkeye Pierce is injured when a gas heater explodes and blinds him. The television audiences watched on the edge of their seats to see if the doctor's sight would return, even as he explored his other heightened senses and came to terms with his possible blindness.

Arguably, the series' most potent episode came when actor McLean Stevenson departed the series, seemingly frustrated with playing second banana. He asked to be released from his contract. With his departure, the writers decided to try something practically unheard of in the world of the situation comedy. In the final episode of season 3, titled "Abyssinia, Henry," it is announced that his character, Colonel Henry Blake, had earned enough points to return stateside. After his farewells, Blake boarded a plane to take him home. Everyone is under the impression that he has made it out, but in a startling twist during the episode's final moments, Radar bursts into the surgical tent and delivers the tragic news: Blake's plane has been shot down over the Sea of Japan, and there are no survivors. This was unprecedented in the annals of situation comedy. Never had a character in a half-hour program calling itself "comedy" been killed off. Larry Gelbart, in an interview where the death of Henry Blake was discussed, offered this context around the decision to kill off the character instead of having him fly off into the sunset:

> We resolved that instead of doing an episode in which yet another actor leaves yet another series, we would try to have Mac/Henry's departure make a point, one that was consistent with the series' attitude regarding the wastefulness of war; we would have that character die as a result of the conflict. After three years of showing faceless bit players and extras portraying dying or dead servicemen, here was

an opportunity to have a character die that our audience knew and loved, one whose death would mean something to them.[1]

Stevenson's departure from the program, along with the egress of Wayne Rogers, opened up the opportunity for some fresh blood and new avenues to explore at the 4077th. Instead of the affable Blake, the regiment was commanded by Colonel Sherman Potter, a tougher leader with a much sterner demeanor than the 4077th had been used to. He refashioned the loosey-goosey structure into what he hoped would be a tighter ship. Replacing Rogers (who had a far less significant good-bye than Stevenson) was Mike Farrell, playing B. J. Hunnicutt, a career physician with a wife and child at home. He would often receive letters from his spouse, epistles that reflected how difficult it was for those on the home front who had to endure (daily) the thought of their loved ones' lives in constant peril. The addition of these two gave *M*A*S*H* a breath of fresh air, but what these changes also achieved was to give the audience a real sense of how those who serve are shifted around, come and go, and live and die. There was a gravitas to this that made *M*A*S*H* feel authentic.

When series regular Larry Linville decided to part ways with *M*A*S*H* after season 5, his character of Frank Burns would be sorely missed for the comic relief he offered the program. Instead of just throwing another bumbling doctor into the mix to fill his void, writers gave us Charles Emerson Winchester III—a pompous, highly intelligent surgeon who would be a foil for Hawkeye and company.

Where *M*A*S*H* may have been at its most timely and controversial was that, despite being a show about war, it was a commentary against it. Again, when the series commenced, the Vietnam War had already taken many American lives, the violence and futility of America's efforts in Southeast Asia were at an all-time high, and though *M*A*S*H*'s story lines were not about Vietnam in the literal sense, figuratively they were. The idea of being a conscientious objector during the Vietnam War was an explosive issue. Many Americans believed that the United States had no business fighting in Vietnam and that the government shouldn't be so cavalier about the lives of the young men they were sending to fight it. On the other hand, there were those who felt that it was the patriotic duty of every young man to serve his country when called. To object to serving was anti-American, even treasonous. The character of Klinger was a conscientious objector who would do anything he could think of to be discharged and sent stateside. Klinger would don a variety of women's clothes in the hope that cross-dressing would be his ticket out. Although Klinger's schemes were intended mainly as comic relief, for a TV show to present a character who would go to such lengths not to serve offended many proponents of the Vietnam War. There was a generation that had served selflessly during World War II and the Korean War, and to even suggest in their presence that you didn't want to step up to the plate for your country could raise their ire.

M*A*S*H proved to be a popular television show, earning 14 prime-time Emmys, including Outstanding Comedy Series for its 1973–1974 season. Its final episode, titled "Goodbye, Farewell, and Amen," aired on February 28, 1983. The episode told of the final days of the Korean War at the 4077th, from the harrowing moments leading up to the cease-fire to the celebration and tearful good-byes that followed. Alan Alda wrote and directed the two-hour finale, which was eagerly anticipated not only by viewers but also advertisers who were coughing up $450,000 per commercial slot. This was more than the going rate for the Super Bowl in 1983. In all, 105.97 million Americans tuned in, a total audience of 121.6 million once international numbers were factored in. "Goodbye, Farewell, and Amen" shattered the record held by the "Who Shot J.R.?" episode of the nighttime drama *Dallas*. It still holds the record as the most-watched television series finale of all time and has been surpassed only by the February 2010 presentation of Super Bowl XLIV.

An interesting point to note about *M*A*S*H* is that the series was on television for 11 years, yet the Korean War lasted for just over three. Apparently, there were enough story possibilities and interested viewers to keep the skirmish going for much longer than history had already determined. *M*A*S*H* was so popular with the American viewing public that CBS even refused to let the franchise go when the original concluded. A spin-off called *AfterMASH* took the action back to the United States with Klinger, Colonel Potter, and Father Mulcahy all working in a hospital in Missouri. *AfterMASH* was not a success, surviving only 31 episodes before cancellation. But *M*A*S*H* would never be forgotten and continues to be a benchmark in television history, the place where comedy and drama collided into sitcoms that could tell serious stories.

Good Times

WATCHING THE ASPHALT GROW

Aired: February 8, 1974–August 1, 1979
Network: CBS
Created by: Eric Monte and Mike Evans, developed by Norman Lear
Cast: Esther Rolle (Florida Evans), John Amos (James Evans), Ja'net Dubois (Willona Woods), Jimmie Walker (James "J.J." Evans Jr.), Ralph Carter (Michael Evans), Bern Nadette Stanis (Thelma Evans Anderson), Johnny Brown (Nathan Bookman), Janet Jackson (Millicent "Penny" Gordon Woods)
Theme Song: "Good Times," composed by Dave Grusin, lyrics by Alan and Marilyn Bergman (performed by Jim Gilstrap and Blinky Williams)

Coming out of the 1960s, with the civil rights movement and the works of Martin Luther King Jr. fresh in our collective psyche, America was beginning to move in new directions. Some of them were positive. Change, however, wasn't coming fast enough, especially for black Americans, who were often relegated to slums, taking the brunt of unemployment, and facing the challenges of mere survival. Most of white America remained oblivious to this, while others turned a blind eye or remained willfully ignorant. How could anyone know what the lives and living conditions of many African Americans were when they were rarely depicted in film or on television, let alone given their due on the nightly news?

> Just lookin' out of the window.
> Watchin' the asphalt grow.
> Thinkin' how it all looks hand-me-down.
> Good Times, yeah, yeah Good Times.[1]

This snatch of lyrics written by Alan Bergman and Marilyn Bergman (music by Dave Grusin) closed each episode of *Good Times*. In a few carefully chosen words, the song captured the inner-city housing projects of Chicago and the poverty suffered by the multitudes, particularly minorities, that were packed into maze-like tenements in the 1970s. *Good Times*, created by Eric Monte and Mike Evans and developed and produced by Norman Lear, took a no-holds-barred look at the abject hardship experienced by blacks living in ghettos all over the country. Initially, the show, which ran from 1974 to 1979, made earnest attempts to tell serious stories (with humor), painting a stoic picture of those who clung to hope for a better life and, in its first few seasons, waking television audiences up to the plight of the struggling minority.

The genesis of *Good Times* started with another Norman Lear sitcom, *Maude* (itself a spin-off of the popular and socially charged *All in the Family*). Maude was an ultraliberal, four-times-married, outspoken, middle-aged woman who often felt at odds with her own white privilege. When hiring a maid, she was concerned with what people would think when she settled on Florida Evans, a black woman who takes the train up from the Bronx to Maude's suburban Tuckahoe home. Maude would make Florida's work harder by trying to do her household chores for her, insisting she use the front door to bring in groceries

Ralph Carter, Jimmie Walker, Esther Rolle, and Bern Nadette Stanis in
Good Times. CBS/Photofest © CBS

instead of the more conveniently located kitchen door in the rear. Rolle's dead-pan delivery and constant exasperation with Maude's antics made Florida an audience favorite. It was soon decided that the character should receive her own spin-off show, and Rolle's character was sandwiched into *Good Times*, a show that was already in development.

Moving the action from New York to Chicago and changing Florida's husband's name from Henry to James, *Good Times* introduced audiences to the Evanses' three children, who were often at the center of the show's story lines. James Jr. (referred to as "J.J.") was the eldest son. J.J. was an artist, a ne'er-do-well, often getting into trouble and trying to stay out of it. Daughter Thelma was a lovely girl who was dealt much of the household responsibility, particularly when Florida was taking jobs. The youngest child was Michael, sometimes re-ferred to as "The Militant Midget" for his strong political views and forays into activism. Florida also had a good friend, Willona Woods, who came and went, giving audiences a perspective on the single, middle-aged woman living in the projects.

Florida Evans was a pious woman, often turning to God with her prayers and her concerns. She was always reminding her family to be respectful of the Lord, chastising them if anything they said was blasphemous or even hinted at showing disrespect toward the Almighty. James Evans was a hardworking, curmudgeonly father who had high expectations for his kids. He often juggled two or three jobs, dealt with unemployment, and was always searching for bet-ter opportunities along the way. Together, James and Florida ran a structured household built on religion and their combined hopes that their children would someday have something better. They promoted education and a work ethic, instilling these values in their offspring. And yet, for all of their industry and their example of living with integrity, they were seldom rewarded by God or society for their efforts.

The challenges the Evans family encountered on *Good Times* were plenti-ful. Bigotry was often a major obstacle, keeping James from finding work and putting the kids into precarious situations at school and with the authorities. Unemployment was a constant worry. Jobs in the 1970s were already hard to come by, and being a minority in a system that favored whites only exacerbated the Evanses' plight. Inflation was often discussed on the show: money just didn't go as far as it used to, and salaries were not adjusting to keep up with the grow-ing costs of goods and services. James was consistently outspoken on all of these challenges, taking the government to task for creating the scenarios that led to the strife of the underclass.

Good Times was socially charged and socially conscious on many fronts. The Evanses faced eviction, as did many of their friends and neighbors. It is hard to pay rent when you cannot find work. "Keeping your head above water" was also a lyric of the show's opening theme, and the Evanses could barely manage that, living in a slum apartment with the barest essentials. In many episodes, the family would have only oatmeal for dinner, reminded by Florida that they should all be grateful for what the Lord had provided.

Gang warfare was always a looming specter in their lives, Florida keeping constant vigil that her children stay clear of the fray. If it wasn't gangs they were dealing with, muggers and con artists were also at the ready to take advantage of honest, hardworking people. *Good Times* painted a very real picture of the slums and the desperation felt by those therein. How do you get out and seek a better life when there is no money, no employment, and no opportunity? The program may have dealt with these issues with humor, but laughter only helped to make the horrible palatable. A palpable hopelessness permeated the show, giving television audiences a sense of what the underclass, inner-city minority suffered.

It is important to note that *Good Times* was a popular program, speaking to an audience far beyond an African American base that would seemingly tune in and relate. The show often stood secure in the ratings, ranking as high as number 7 during its second season. There was something about the show that spoke to everyone. In the 1970s, average people were struggling to make ends meet, burdened with inflation, and worried about rising crime. *Good Times* gave everyone the feeling of being in the same boat on these issues. In was half an hour each week to laugh at your problems while simultaneously digesting the state of the country.

Good Times also holds the significance of being one of the first sitcoms to feature an all-black cast. Until the time of its premiere, only *Amos 'n' Andy* (1951–1953) had endeavored to tell the story of black Americans. It would prove both overdue and timely to include a large but marginalized fraction of society in television storytelling. Their journeys had been left untold, and *Good Times* ventured to tell one of those myriad stories with respect and relatability. How significant it must have felt in 1974 for a person of color to turn on the television and finally see a show that reflected characters with whom they might identify.

Where the show strayed from its message came after the first two seasons. Although it didn't entirely neglect its original mission, it did veer toward the ridiculous. The character of J.J. became an audience favorite through his antics and his catchphrase "Dy-No-Mite!" Stories began to skew in his direction and center around his buffoonery. This did not sit well with Esther Rolle and John Amos, who felt that this was taking away from the serious story lines as well as perpetuating stereotypes that blacks were lazy and incompetent. They regularly voiced their concerns to the producers and writers. In a 1975 interview with *Ebony* magazine, Rolle stated,

He's 18 and he doesn't work. He can't read or write. He doesn't think. The show didn't start out to be that. . . . Little by little—with the help of the artist, I suppose, because they couldn't do that to me—they have made J.J. more stupid and enlarged the role. Negative images have been slipped in on us through the character of the oldest child.[2]

Amos also weighed in:

The writers would prefer to put a chicken hat on J.J. and have him prance around saying "DY-NO-MITE," and that way they could waste a few minutes and not have to write meaningful dialogue.[3]

Ultimately, it was Amos who was fired from the show, the character of James killed off at the end of season 3. Rolle soldiered on but chose to depart after season 4. After her exit, the show began to sag in the ratings. For the start of the show's sixth (and final) season, producers enticed Rolle to return, promising to revert to the show's initial format. J.J. was given a steady job, and story lines again took on meaning and substance. This was all for naught. *Good Times* never regained its momentum, and the groundbreaking show plummeted in viewership. In concluded its six-season run at number 83 in the Nielsen ratings.

Good Times was a benchmark in the evolution of television programming. It delivered to the world a portrait of honest, hardworking black Americans who lived with dignity, values, and a work ethic. This shattered stereotypes that had been perpetuated for centuries by those who chose to see otherwise. Through humor, it connected us all, helping us to see that, black or white, we are all just trying to keep our heads above water.

The Jeffersons

A PIECE OF THE PIE

Aired: January 18, 1975–July 2, 1985

Network: CBS

Created by: Don Nicholl, Michael Ross, and Bernie West, developed by Norman Lear

Cast: Isabel Sanford (Louise Jefferson), Sherman Hemsley (George Jefferson), Mike Evans (Lionel Jefferson #1), Damon Evans (Lionel Jefferson #2), Roxie Roker (Helen Willis), Franklin Cover (Thomas "Tom" Willis), Zara Cully (Olivia "Mother" Jefferson), Berlinda Tolbert (Jenny Willis Jefferson), Paul Benedict (Harry Bentley), Marla Gibbs (Florence Johnston), Jay Hammer (Allan Willis), Ned Wertimer (Ralph Hart),Danny Wells (Charlie the bartender), Ebonie Smith (Jessica Jefferson)

Theme Song: "Movin' on Up," by Ja'net Dubois and Jeff Barry (performed by Ja'net DuBois)

The 1970s brought America's synthesis of the turbulence of the 1960s. Entertainment reflected the change that was brought about through the civil rights movement, and African Americans offered the beginnings of a collective voice where network television was concerned. Until the 1970s, black characters had been typically relegated to the roles of servants (*Beulah* and *Make Room for Daddy*), featured players for stereotype-laden comedic relief (*My Little Margie* and *Trouble with Father*), and the occasional guest performance. Of course, there had been the series *Amos 'n' Andy* (1951–1953), the first to feature an all-black cast, but the show brimmed with undignified misrepresentations of the minority group and was a constant cause for concern among the black community for the stereotypes it perpetuated.

The 1975 sitcom *The Jeffersons* was a spin-off of the game-changing *All in the Family* (1971–1979). Blue-collar Archie Bunker and his wife Edith lived in Queens, New York. Archie was a bigot who didn't trust anyone who didn't look, act, or think like him, and he certainly never kept his mouth shut where political correctness was concerned. On the eighth episode of the series' first season, George and Louise Jefferson and their son Lionel moved in next door to the Bunkers. The Jeffersons were black, raising the ire of Archie and bringing out the worst of his ignorance and fears. Edith was much more open-minded, making friends with Louise, and Archie's progressive daughter Gloria and her ultraliberal husband Michael became fast friends with Lionel, but Archie struggled with the idea that a black family moved into the adjacent property. What was his neighborhood coming to?

The character of George Jefferson, who owned a dry-cleaning business and was often mentioned, was not seen on the show until 1973 due to Hemsley's prior commitment to the Broadway musical *Purlie*. Producer Norman Lear wanted him for the role and was willing to wait. Once Hemsley joined the cast as a recurring character, George and Archie enjoyed an explosive relationship, often fueled by Archie's racial stereotyping and George's short temper. Audiences loved the dynamic. This was the first time that a television sitcom was outwardly and consistently challenging and addressing the attitudes of white

Isabel Sanford, Sherman Hemsley, and Mike Evans in *The Jeffersons*. CBS/ Photofest © CBS

Americans and how they were adjusting to the new laws, freedoms, and opportunities that were finally being extended to minorities. For its time, this was cutting-edge television.

George Jefferson proved to be an effective and amusing foil for Archie Bunker. The character became so popular that it was inevitable that he would receive a spin-off show. The idea for it came from *All in the Family* producer Norman Lear, who set Don Nicholl, Michael Ross, and Bernie West to task to create the show. They imagined a scenario where George Jefferson's cleaning business took off with astronomical success. Now the hardworking entrepreneur had a large chain of dry-cleaning stores. The Jeffersons were wealthy, and they moved from their house next door to the Bunkers to a deluxe apartment on Manhattan's Upper East Side.

Until 1967, it was the law in many states that a person of color could not marry a white person and vice versa. Interracial marriage was frowned on, often by blacks and whites alike. Known as miscegenation, the practice was outlawed in many states, including Virginia, where the Racial Integrity Act of 1924 prohibited such unions. Mildred Loving (born Jeter), a woman of color, and Richard Loving, a white man, were sentenced to year in prison for violating the act by marrying each other. They took the matter to court. Argued on April 10, 1967, and decided June 12, 1967, *Loving v. Virginia* was a landmark Supreme Court case that struck down miscegenation laws, finding the 1883 case that set the precedent for the Racial Integrity Act, *Pace v. Alabama*, unconstitutional. Blacks and whites could finally marry, unfettered by any legal prohibition, but how would that translate to television? Would America embrace a television show that had an interracial marriage as part of its weekly makeup?

The Jeffersons was the first series to feature a recurring interracial couple (a white husband and a black wife) as part of its leading cast. George and Louise Jefferson had neighbors in their high-rise apartment building, Tom and Helen Willis, whose interracial marriage was a constant cause for concern on the program, particularly for George, who was opposed to miscegenation. George's frustration and closed-mindedness on the interracial marriage was exacerbated when his son Lionel fell in love with and married the Willises' biracial daughter Jenny. Although Jenny appeared to be black, George often referred to her as a "zebra" because of her mixed-race parentage. His feelings on the matter somewhat softened when Lionel and Jenny had children of their own.

Another way that *The Jeffersons* was revolutionary to television was in how it evolved audience perceptions of the black family. Up until *The Jeffersons*, African Americans were depicted as members of the working class, scraping to get by and barely making it. There was no living the high life. To quote the show's theme song, there were no "deluxe apartments in the sky." With George's dry-cleaning chain a success, *The Jeffersons* ushered the black America of television into the realm of possible wealth and prosperity, paving the way for shows like *Benson*, *The Cosby Show*, and *The Fresh Prince of Bel-Air*.

And yet, George Jefferson was no saint. Much like Archie Bunker, he was outspoken, closed-minded, quick to anger, and showed his own bigotry in uncomfortable situations. He often referred to his neighbor Tom Willis as a "honky," a derogatory term for a white person that certainly never equaled the contemptuous "nigger," an epithet that was used on *The Jeffersons* frequently to remind George and Louise where they had come from and to demonstrate the world that they were up against. George distrusted white people and often went on diatribes (many well founded) against the oppression of the opportunistic white man. But George was also a conniver, willing to work the system, sometimes accused of being an "Uncle Tom" in order to ingratiate himself with fellow business owners and the snobs in his building who looked down on him. He was wisely written as an imperfect man trying to succeed in a rigged establishment that didn't favor his participation, let alone his success.

Louise Jefferson, on the other hand, had trouble adjusting to her newfound wealth. She struggled with allowing herself to buy new clothes, have her hair done, and take special outings, having always had a propensity for frugality and industry. She didn't like putting on airs. George encouraged her, insisting that she had earned these comforts after a life of hard work, but the life she had led thus far wouldn't foster Louise's acceptance of deserving them. It was one of George's redeeming factors that he loved his wife so much that he wanted her to have these things and insisted that she would. Of course, some of that had to do with George's need to show off his money, but it was always clear that he loved Louise and would want the best for her. Exacerbating Louise's reluctance to enjoy her money was Mother Jefferson, the mother-in-law from hell, criticizing Louise regularly for entertaining even the slightest luxury. When George insisted that Louise get a maid (which they would eventually do in the form of the sassy "Florence"), Mother Jefferson ridiculed her, insisting that she never needed a maid. Louise had time on her hands and became restless in her new surroundings, and she eventually turned to charity work to fill her days.

Of special note: Isabel Sanford, who played Louise Jefferson for the series' record-breaking 11 seasons, was the first African American woman to win an Emmy Award for Best Actress in a Television Comedy. She was bestowed the accolade in 1981. Times were beginning to change, but it is telling about Hollywood that it took so long for the powers-that-be to create a situation/role where a woman of color could be recognized for her artistry.

The Jeffersons shattered many stereotypes in its 11-year run, even as it occasionally perpetuated others. It was a daring show, an achievement that is often overshadowed by the show's hilarity. It was great television comedy that entertained across racial lines. At the height of its success, the show ranked at number 3 in the Nielsen ratings. There were 253 episodes in all, and the show continues to have a healthy life in syndication. As the theme song for the show asserts, they "finally got a piece of the pie."

Welcome Back, Kotter

YOUR DREAMS WERE YOUR TICKET OUT

Aired: September 9, 1975–May 17, 1979
Network: ABC
Created by: Gabe Kaplan and Alan Sacks, developed by Peter Meyerson
Cast: Gabe Kaplan (Gabe Kotter), Marcia Strassman (Julie Kotter), John Sylves-
    ter White (Michael Woodman), Robert Hegyes (Juan Luis Pedro Felipo de
    Huevos Epstein), Lawrence Hilton-Jacobs (Freddie Percy "Boom Boom"
    Washington), Ron Palillo (Arnold Dingfelder Horshack), John Travolta
    (Vincent "Vinnie" Barbarino)
Theme Song: "Welcome Back," written and performed by John Sebastian

Ever since the movie *The Blackboard Jungle* premiered in 1955, the story of the
struggles to teach inner-city youth has proven a compelling avenue to explore in
the world of entertainment. The real-life combination of racial tension, poverty,
gang warfare, unemployment, and an endless horizon of concrete created the
seemingly insurmountable perfect storm to keep kids from succeeding. The kids
trapped in the ghettos of places like New York City, Los Angeles, Chicago, St.
Louis, Detroit, Philadelphia, Washington, D.C., and Atlanta all had their stories. The inner-city experience was a desperate one, a maze of challenges for the
youth requiring a guiding hand to help them find a way out.

By the 1970s, drugs and gun violence had also shaped ghetto living into a
frightful scene where the denizens felt in constant peril. Living in fear for their
lives, navigating a walk to school could be a daunting experience for even the
toughest and most resilient of kids. How were teachers going to reach these
youngsters who were juggling a multitude of stressors and provide them with an
education that would allow them to rise above their circumstances and live safe,
happy, productive lives?

In 1975, a television series came along that decided to address this challenge. Created by Gabe Kaplan and Alan Sacks, *Welcome Back, Kotter* was a sitcom set in Bensonhurst in Brooklyn, New York, and followed a dedicated teacher who hoped to make a difference at James Buchanan High School, where the students were surviving in that previously mentioned inner-city nightmare. In its early seasons (the show ran for only four), an earnest attempt was made to tell his story, as well as the stories of his students, with a heart and humor that never dodged the reality of that bleak vista.

Gabe Kaplan had been a stand-up comedian, starting as a teenager in the 1960s. His routine had started out as a string of one-liners, but as comedy began to evolve into storytelling with humor (think Bob Newhart, Bill Cosby, and Richard Pryor), Kaplan was inspired to tell stories about his time at a Brooklyn high school, honing in on a group of underachieving kids referred to as the "Sweathogs." In 1974, Kaplan recorded the comedy album *Holes and Mello-Rolls*, the impetus for *Welcome Back, Kotter*.

Gabe Kotter returns to the high school of his teenage years, where he has taken a job as a schoolteacher. It's a place (and a neighborhood) he had hoped to escape and never thought he'd return to, especially in the capacities of teacher and mentor. Kotter is hired to be a remedial instructor of the ethnically diverse group of misfits known as the "Sweathogs," which will prove to be his life's greatest challenge and reward. Gabe is married to Julie, an ever-patient spouse who supports his efforts with the Sweathogs even when they overflow into their home life. At work, Kotter was under the constant inspection of vice principal Michael Woodman, a crotchety and strict administrator who saw little potential in Kotter's charges, expecting the instructor to control them rather than educate them.

Mr. Kotter had his work cut out for him. The central quartet of the Sweathogs was an amiable but wayward lot: teenage boys without role models living in situations that were not conducive to optimum learning and navigating the temptations and challenges of their inner-city, ghetto environment. In Kotter's class was Vinnie Barbarino, a posturing Italian American who was a bit of a heartthrob, an attention seeker, and from a home with constantly arguing parents. Arnold Horshack was the geek of the group. Horshack was known for his frank observations, his inability to attract girls, and his peculiar laugh that sounded like a gasping wheeze. Of Polish descent, he was the most sensitive and potentially the smartest of the Sweathogs. Next up was Juan Epstein, a Puerto Rican Jew who was voted by his classmates as "most likely to take a life." Juan was the sixth of 10 children, and much humor was made of his crowded home life. Quick to temper and the Sweathog who gets into the most legal trouble, Juan was always trying to get away with something shady. Finally, there was Freddie "Boom Boom" Washington, a black student known for his basketball-

Robert Hegyes, Lawrence Hilton-Jacobs, Gabe Kaplan, John Travolta, and Ron Palillo in *Welcome Back, Kotter*. ABC/Photofest © ABC

playing skills, his hip personality, and his jive talk. He was the most mature member of the group, often invoking reasoning where the others seldom tread. Freddie was known for his signature salutation, "Hi, there!" spoken with a broad smile and the charm of a 1970s game show host.

Unfortunately, there was little focus on female Sweathogs on *Welcome Back, Kotter*. In the show's first season, there was the character Rosalie "Hotsy" Totsi (Debralee Scott), who came and went, but she disappeared after a few episodes. However, in a particularly startling and realistic twist for the show, she shows up again in season 3. "The Return of Hotsy Totsy" found the boys sneaking into a strip club where they find their old classmate working as an exotic dancer. She was now a divorced mother with no high school diploma, just trying to make a living to feed herself and her child. The episode demonstrated the societal double standard of how having a bad reputation can lead to something very different for girls than for boys. The Sweathogs are shocked to find their friend in this situation but are quick to judge the women working in the establishment.

The ultimate goal of a remedial teacher would be to get students up to speed with the outcome that they would rejoin the general student population. Unfortunately, not every kid functions well in the typical classroom setting. Arnold Horshack proves to be a capable student under Kotter's tutelage and quickly brings up his grades to the point where he will be reintroduced to regular classes. In "Arrivederci, Arnold" (season 1, episode 13), this transition occurs, leaving the Sweathogs upset over his departure and Arnold feeling isolated and depressed. In the end, it was decided that they should move Horshack back into Kotter's classroom, where he would feel more comfortable and continue to learn.

In the 1970s, it was still an acceptable practice in most schools for teachers to hit kids. Corporal punishment was a practice in both the home and the school and was an efficient means to an end that usually had immediate results but long-term consequences. Although society was beginning to move away from it, an episode of *Welcome Back, Kotter* titled "Caruso's Way" tackled the subject, offering a different approach for classroom discipline. The school's gym coach, Mr. Caruso, got tired of Vinnie's constant wisecracks and slapped the teen across the face. Kotter confronted the coach, questioning his methods but also fearful that Vinnie might retaliate against his colleague. A boy from the streets and the leader of his group, Vinnie was almost mandated by ghetto code to retaliate in order to save face. The season 2, episode 9, installment made a case for talking to kids and helping them work through their problems.

In one of the more hilarious episodes of *Welcome Back, Kotter*, the definition of art is debated. In "Epstein's Madonna" (season 3, episode 14), Juan Epstein created a nude mural as an art class assignment, and the Sweathogs and the faculty have a long debate over whether his work is really art or if it is better defined as smut. Even the forward-thinking Mr. Kotter has a hard time reconciling his feelings over the piece, which, he admits, makes him uncomfortable, particularly when he finds out that the face of the nude is inspired by his wife Julie. He does not, however, wish to squelch Epstein's enthusiasm and talent by passing judgment. One of his most difficult and challenging students is doing something positive, and Kotter's influence has helped propel him to a new place of hope and direction.

Things weren't always all laughs on *Welcome Back, Kotter*, though the series' legacy as a buffoonish sitcom would lead one to think otherwise. A poignant episode would come in the form of "What Goes Up" (season 3, episode 22), where Freddie Washington becomes addicted to painkillers prescribed for a knee injury suffered during a basketball game. The usually affable Freddie had a personality change and appeared groggy, and the boys eventually caught him in the bathroom taking pills. Kotter, of course, does his best to get Freddie help, which seemingly comes as Freddie has returned to his old self by the next episode. Still, it was one of the times that *Welcome Back, Kotter* was addressing very real and possible situations that kids could encounter in any high school, not just in the ghetto.

Two issues brought *Welcome Back, Kotter* to an untimely conclusion. First, Gabe Kaplan had a reputation for being temperamental on the set, throwing tirades and insisting that he get his way on rewrites and directing choices. By the time of the show's cancellation, costar Marcia Strassman wouldn't speak to him outside of their scenes. Kaplan began not appearing in episodes, as is apparent in his absence from much of season 4. The other problem was that John Travolta, the series' most popular star, was being courted by Hollywood to be a feature film star. Without the eye candy and laugh-inducing moments that Vinnie provided, audiences were less likely to tune in. So, though it may have had a lackluster run of only four seasons, *Welcome Back, Kotter* still managed to become an iconic sitcom of the 1970s (the show got its own lunch box, for crying out loud). More important, the show opened our collective eyes to what it was like to live in an inner-city environment, an urban plight that had been too long overlooked in television.

One Day at a Time

SOMEWHERE THERE'S MUSIC PLAYING

Aired: December 16, 1975–May 28, 1984
Network: CBS
Created by: Whitney Blake and Allan Manings, developed by Norman Lear
Cast: Bonnie Franklin (Ann Romano), Mackenzie Phillips (Julie Cooper Horvath), Valerie Bertinelli (Barbara Cooper Royer), Pat Harrington Jr. (Dwayne Schneider), Richard Masur (David Kane), Mary Louise Wilson (Ginny Wroblicki), Michael Lembeck (Max Horvath), Ron Rifkin (Nick Handris), Glenn Scarpelli (Alex Handris), Boyd Gaines (Mark Royer), Shelley Fabares (Francine Webster), Nanette Fabray (Katherine Romano), Howard Hesseman (Sam Royer)
Theme Song: "This Is It," by Jeff Barry and Nancy Barry (performed by Polly Cutter)

Since American marriage rates first started being accurately and consistently recorded in 1867, we see a steady increase in nuptials ending in divorce, escalating throughout the next century with occasional spikes occurring especially in the postwar years. Not surprisingly, this often followed spikes in marriage that were also the result of people reacting to the start of a war. The more marriages there were, the more divorces were ultimately going to follow. By the 1970s, divorce was at an all-time high (it would get worse into the 1980s before tapering off as more people chose not to marry at all). This led to an increasing change in family dynamics and, more significantly, a rise in the number of single mothers in the workplace.

It is also important to examine the rise of feminism in the 1960s and 1970s. The movement brought with it legislation and empowerment that gave women more choices outside what had traditionally limited them to "stay-at-home-mom" status. New laws, protections, and increased employment opportunities

Pat Harrington Jr., Valerie Bertinelli, Mackenzie Phillips, and Bonnie Frank-lin in *One Day at a Time*. CBS/Photofest © CBS

meant that they no longer felt compelled to stay in unhappy or abusive marriages where men were considered the primary (and often the only) breadwinners. Divorce had been taboo, painted as an admission of failure to "make things work," and the stigma of that alone made it challenging for women to overcome their circumstances. Gradually, it was becoming more socially acceptable for women to make the break and seek their own happiness, though equal pay and advancement opportunities would remain (and still remain) hurdles to overcome.

One Day at a Time, created by Whitey Black, arrived on the scene in 1975 and would bring to the forefront the struggles of the single divorcée, probing the world of broken families like no sitcom before it had. Produced by the groundbreaking television icon Norman Lear, *One Day at a Time* featured a recently divorced mother named Ann Romano who packs up her two daughters, Julie and Barbara Cooper, and moves them to Indianapolis to make a fresh start. Living in an apartment building supervised by the coarse but caring Schneider, Ann embarks on a new life and career while juggling the challenges of being both mother and father to her two teenage girls.

Although Ann Romano was not the first single divorced character to appear on television (Vivian Vance had played one as a supporting character on

The Lucy Show, and Diana Rigg portrayed one on the short-lived *Diana*, both preceding *One Day at a Time*), she was both the lead of a sitcom and represented a truer depiction of the realities faced by single mothers, raising children as divorcées. The popularity of *One Day at a Time* proved that there was a large television audience that related to the experience, not only adults but also kids who came from broken homes. *One Day at a Time* was capturing a growing demographic of viewers who could see their stories depicted in the Romano/Cooper household.

One Day at a Time found Ann Romano in very real situations that single mothers everywhere were experiencing and trying to overcome. Ann's ex-husband was mostly a deadbeat dad and seldom made his child support payments on time, creating a scenario where Ann struggled to make ends meet. She often fought to get this money, demonstrating to women in the same boat everywhere not only that they had a right to expect child support but also that they shouldn't accept anything less than every penny owed. Ann found challenges in the workplace as well, first in finding a job and then in navigating a world that was dominated by men. What *One Day at a Time* achieved was in presenting a relatable, sympathetic character who was written as neither perfect nor complacent. She was a character with rough edges, warts and all. It had to be a refreshing thing for women in television audiences to meet a character who reflected reality.

Ann was not the only character on *One Day at a Time* who escaped the caricatures painted of most women as submissive and delicate, baking pies, and knitting. In the characters of Julie and Barbara, a new type of teenage girl was being depicted on television. Both girls were curious about sex, Barbara even going so far as securing a *Playgirl* magazine to see what a naked male looked like. There was discussion of birth control, Barbara pretending that she was on the pill so that her classmates would think she was sexually active. It is interesting that, despite Barbara's preoccupation with sex, she remained a virgin until her wedding night (the show ran nine seasons, Barbara essentially growing up on the show). Julie found herself pressured with alcohol and drugs (something that would be paralleled in Phillips's private life, leading to her departure, return, and then second departure from the show due to substance abuse). When her character married and had a baby, she eventually left her husband and disappeared, leaving him to raise the child. Barbara and Julie were not your typical teens of television past, and *One Day at a Time* opened the doors for television programming that reflected real teen issues dealing with them head-on.

One other item that made Ann Romano a character unlike those who preceded her may seem trite but should not be taken lightly. Since Ann's last name on the show was Romano and her daughters' last name was Cooper, it was clear from the beginning that she had reverted to her maiden name after the divorce.

In the 1970s, this was a rare occurrence. Women typically moved on with their married name intact (it also cost additional money in a divorce to revert to your maiden name). This act by Ann served as a symbolic shedding of her marital ties, claiming both her independence and the person she was before the marriage crumbled. This was a big deal and had to reverberate with women who found themselves saddled with their ex-husbands' surnames.

One Day at a Time bore the imprint of a television series developed and produced by Norman Lear, who was never afraid to put the problems of women at the forefront of his shows (see *Maude* and *All in the Family*). Of the sitcoms he produced, *One Day at a Time* was the second longest running. The show consistently scored in the top 20 ratings and even managed to remain popular despite the network (CBS) moving it to 11 different time slots during its nine-season tenure. There was something special about *One Day at a Time* that really spoke to audiences. From the minute that its liberating and optimistic theme song "This Is It" by Jeff Barry and Nancy Barry, sung by Polly Cutter, commenced, audiences knew they were being ushered into a world where we could laugh at our problems and find humor in life's difficulties.

Laverne & Shirley

DOING IT OUR WAY

Aired: January 27, 1976–May 10, 1983
Network: ABC
Created by: Garry Marshall, Lowell Ganz, and Mark Rothman
Cast: Penny Marshall (Laverne Marie DeFazio), Cindy Williams (Shirley Wilhelmina Feeney), Michael McKean (Leonard "Lenny" Kosnowski), David Lander (Andrew "Squiggy" Squiggman), Phil Foster (Frank DeFazio), Eddie Mekka (Carmine Ragusa), Betty Garrett (Edna Babish DeFazio)
Theme Song: "Making Our Dreams Come True," lyrics by Norman Gimbel, composed by Norman Gimbel and Charles Fox (performed by Cyndi Grecco)

In 1974, a TV show premiered that was a nostalgic look at the more innocent times of the 1950s. It was a family sitcom that celebrated a world of burger joints with jukeboxes, sock hops, old-fashioned dating techniques, and teenagers having good, clean fun. The program centered on the innocent and amiable Richie Cunningham and his posse of goofy friends: Potsie, Ralph Malph, and the leather-wearing, motorcycle-riding, high school dropout and all-purpose cool guy Arthur "The Fonz" Fonzarelli. Richie enjoyed a happy home life with his loving mother Marion, his curmudgeonly but lovable father Howard, and his incorrigible sister Joanie. The show was, of course, the now iconic, long-running *Happy Days*, created by Garry Marshall. It was predictably about as wholesome as a sitcom in the 1970s could get, itself inspired by an episode of the anthology show *Love, American Style*. But after a modest reception in its first and second seasons, some retooling of the show (to put more emphasis on the character of Fonzie) elevated *Happy Days* to television's number 1 program during the 1976–1977 season.

This chapter is not about *Happy Days*, but it is necessary to introduce the important spin-off sitcom that it generated. During *Happy Days'* run, two characters were introduced who were acquaintances of Fonzie, older women who would occasionally go on dates with the teenage boys. These ladies were Laverne DaFazio and Shirley Feeney, a comedic duo that proved so popular with audiences that the producers of *Happy Days* saw potential in giving them their own show. Garry Marshall got to work with Lowell Ganz and Mark Rothman, and the trio created *Laverne & Shirley*.

For the show, it was necessary to flesh out the details behind the lives of the titular pair, making them best friends and roommates who share a basement apartment in Milwaukee, Wisconsin. The two young women held blue-collar jobs as bottle cappers at the fictitious Shotz Brewery. The girls shared a bedroom in what was a two-room dwelling, a central kitchen/living area with a window that looked up at the feet passing by on the street. Laverne and Shirley lived modestly but independently, seldom counting on anything but their own resourcefulness to make ends meet. Remembering that the show was set in the late 1950s, a time when young single women were discouraged from living independently and seldom did, *Laverne & Shirley* was demonstrating a world of independent women, a faction of society that most definitely existed but was rarely explored in entertainment.

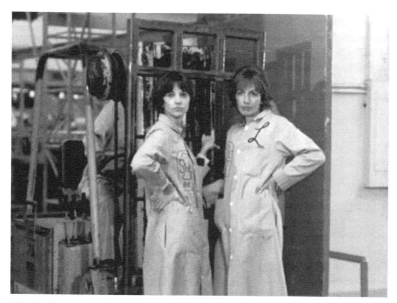

Cindy Williams and Penny Marshall in *Laverne & Shirley*. ABC/ Photofest © ABC

For the first half of the duo, Marshall's sister Penny was called on to play the tough-talking Laverne, complete with a monogrammed letter "L" on every stich of clothing she owned. For the other half of the show's namesake, actress Cindy Williams would play the upbeat, melodramatic Shirley, who was obsessively attached to her studded animal Boo Boo Kitty. In the same apartment building lived the girls' two obnoxious neighbors, Leonard "Lenny" Kosnowski and Andrew "Squiggy" Squiggman. Lenny and Squiggy were often on a libidinous search for companionship, occasionally making overtures toward Shirley and Laverne, but mostly they were just comic relief and good friends to the ladies. Other recurring characters included Shirley's on-again/off-again boyfriend Carmine "The Big Ragoo" Ragusa, Laverne's cranky but loving father Frank DeFazio, and their five-times-divorced landlady Edna Babbish, who eventually fell in love with married Frank.

It was easy to look at the plotlines of *Laverne & Shirley* and think that these two young women were merely fulfilling the expectations of women in the 1950s: the search for the perfect man to settle down with, get married to, and have children with. However, a deeper inspection of the series reveals that these were liberated women who made their own decisions and were quite content to take care of and think for themselves, being open to marriage only if and when they were comfortable with it. It was not uncommon to find them fighting for the rights of workers at the factory where they were employed. When the girls were overlooked for promotions, they resigned from the brewery and joined the U.S. Army, where they encountered tough-as-nails Sergeant Alvinia Plout (Vicki Lawrence), who held Laverne and Shirley to a high standard. Determined and undaunted, they rose to the occasion, showing that women could handle anything that men could.

Even the show's theme song evoked a spirited embrace of independence and drive. "Making Our Dreams Come True" by Norman Gimbel and Charles Fox and performed by Cyndi Grecco smacked of liberation and a pioneering spirit. The show commenced with Laverne and Shirley, arm in arm, confidently marching down the street and chanting "Schlemiel! Schlimazel! Hasenpfeffer Incorporated!," and then the theme song launched in an explosive burst of energy, "We're gonna do it! / Give us any chance, we'll take it / Give us any rule, we'll break it."[1] The song spoke to audiences, even gaining popularity on the radio and becoming a top 30 hit. But it was how the number set up the show's premise and defined its characters that really resonated. This was not the typical representation of women on television, and *Laverne & Shirley* was breaking down walls the way *The Mary Tyler Moore Show*, *That Girl*, and *Julia* had done prior. When that theme song started playing, everyone was called to the television and found themselves singing along, caught up in the show's spirit from the outset.

The opening montage that accompanied the show also painted the title characters as strong-willed, confident, and independent women. A collage of clips revealed Laverne and Shirley on the job at Shotz Brewery, from racing to work and punching in to daydreaming on the assembly line and then bringing us back to their apartment, where we also got a glimpse of their single lives shared with one another. Everything about that first 45 seconds that introduced each episode of *Laverne & Shirley* set the stage for a television show that was striving to tell a different story about women who could easily juggle a career, romance, friendship, and hope.

Laverne & Shirley was received with little controversy, audiences seemingly unfazed by a sitcom that featured two women living together and sharing a bedroom. A decade later, television would introduce another pair of women sharing a basement apartment in the form of *Kate & Allie*, a story about two divorced women sleeping in separate bedrooms but raising their kids together and sharing the expenses of living. That show, however, received an ongoing backlash over audience concerns that the title duo was perceived as a lesbian couple. It is interesting to speculate as to why, in 1976, this would not have been a problem, but in 1984, it caused a storm of outrage. In the decade between, the introduction of gay characters on television, the gay rights movement getting stronger, and the AIDS epidemic (and the misinformation that accompanied it) all cast a spotlight on issues that the masses had remained oblivious to prior. Had *Laverne & Shirley* been introduced in the 1980s, the show might have received a far different reaction.

But *Laverne and Shirley* was an unqualified hit. It ranked number 3 in the Nielsen ratings during its first season and number 2 in season 2, then took the top spot for two years running in its third and fourth seasons. In the fall of 1979, ABC executives decided to move *Laverne & Shirley* from its usual time slot of Tuesday night following *Happy Days* to Thursday nights, where it was forced to compete against *The Waltons* (CBS) and *Buck Rogers in the 25th Century* (NBC), both popular programs that had already established audiences. *Laverne & Shirley* suffered from the move, and ABC then tried Monday nights, where things didn't improve. By season 6, the show had slipped to number 20, and ABC finally realized its mistake and returned the show its original spot with the *Happy Days* lead-in. It was too late, and *Laverne & Shirley* never regained its spot in the top 10. Still, it remained in the top 30 and managed to last eight seasons.

Laverne & Shirley's decline in the ratings cannot entirely be attributed to schedule changes. At the start of season 6, the characters gave up their Milwaukee apartment and moved to Burbank, California, where they found jobs in a department store. The transition was ludicrous, with everyone they knew in Milwaukee seemingly following them to their new destination. Lenny and Squiggy, Laverne's father, Edna, and even Carmine all picked up their lives and moved to the West Coast. Plotlines skewed toward the screwball (even by the show's already farcical standards), and the show just didn't retain that edgy, "free spirits on a mission" feeling that had made it so groundbreaking in the beginning. *Laverne & Shirley* was starting to wind down.

As the show began preparations for season 8, Cindy Williams became pregnant and approached the producers with a list of demands that involved contingencies for the birth of her child, which Paramount refused to accommodate. This was an unchivalrous move from a studio that was funding a TV show that seemingly was promoting a world where women were making strides.

Williams departed the show and filed a multimillion-dollar lawsuit against Garry Marshall and Paramount that would eventually be settled out of court. Her character was written off the show, a somewhat unceremonious departure where she fell in love and married over two episodes, finds out that her character is with child, and leaves Laverne a note telling her she has left to be with her husband, who is an overseas army medic. By the end of season 7, there was no more Shirley Feeney.

Surprisingly, the absence of one-half of *Laverne & Shirley* did little to hurt the show's ratings, which held at number 25 in its final season. Penny Marshall soldiered on and continued to deliver her usual sidesplitting performances. Producers wanted to continue the show for another season, but Marshall had her own demands, including moving the show from Los Angeles to New York City, a move that would not be cost effective. Instead, *Laverne & Shirley* was brought to a conclusion with no real resolution. Instead, the final episode served as what was construed as a backdoor pilot spin-off for Carmine Ragusa, who would move to New York City to star in a Broadway production of the musical *Hair*. That actual spin-off never materialized, and Laverne appeared for only a few minutes in the final episode of *Laverne & Shirley*.

On the surface, *Laverne & Shirley* may not seem all that groundbreaking of a sitcom. The characters were often played with broad strokes, and physical humor often won out over intellectual humor and character development. Regardless of that perception, the sitcom conveyed a strong bond between two independent women and retroactively rectified the lack of liberated, feminist, female characters who were absent from television programming in the actual 1950s by showing audiences that they had always been there. The 1970s yielded a changing landscape for women, and *Laverne & Shirley* was an inspirational if lighthearted comedy that indicated that potential and change were in the air.

Three's Company

WHERE THE KISSES ARE HERS, AND HERS, AND HIS

Aired: March 15, 1977–September 18, 1984

Network: ABC

Created by: Don Nicholl, Michael Ross, and Bernie West, based on the ITV series *Man about the House*, by Johnnie Mortimer and Brian Cooke

Cast: John Ritter (Jack Tripper), Joyce DeWitt (Janet Wood), Suzanne Somers (Chrissy Snow), Norman Fell (Stanley Roper), Audra Lindley (Helen Roper), Don Knotts (Ralph Furley), Richard Kline (Larry Dallas), Ann Wedgeworth (Lana Shields), Priscilla Barnes (Terri Alden), Jenilee Harrison (Cindy Snow)

Theme Song: "Come and Knock on Our Door," composed by Joe Raposo (performed by Ray Charles and Julia Rinker)

Television is almost always a decade behind the times when it comes to dealing with social change, so it should be no surprise that it didn't really start addressing the sexual revolution, which exploded in the 1960s, until the 1970s. Until then, the mention of sex on television was taboo, glossed over, and insinuated. With an embarrassed look, a character might refer to "making whoopie" with the result of collective canned gasps to suggest that it shouldn't be taken any further. Television of the 1970s, however, brought with it, if not an ease, then at least an understanding that human beings did indeed have sex. It also had the audacity to suggest that sex was not just for procreational purposes but also recreational. *All in the Family*, *Maude*, and *M*A*S*H* were the sitcoms that most blatantly opened the doors for the discussion, but it wasn't until 1977 that a show came along where almost every episode was steeped in innuendo and libidinous salaciousness that pushed the boundaries of television.

In Great Britain, there was a popular sitcom called *Man about the House*, which ran on ITV from 1973 to 1976. That program had been created by Brian

Cooke and Johnnie Mortimer and told the story of two single women sharing a flat with a single man. For the 1970s, whether in Europe or in the United States, it was frowned on for single people of the opposite sex to cohabitate. In fact, landlords often wouldn't rent to a couple unless they were married. To create a television show that said otherwise was a daring leap for its day, but *Man about the House* took things one step further. In order to convince the landlord to allow their male friend Robin to live with them, the two women, Chrissy and Jo, tell him that Robin is gay. Of course, he is not, but keeping up the ruse was an ongoing ingredient of the show's farcical nature.

If this sounds a bit familiar, then you are obviously thinking about the long-running American sitcom *Three's Company*, which was inspired by *Man about the House*. Developed by Don Nicholl, Michael Ross, and Bernie West, *Three's Company* presented practically the same scenario. Janet Wood and Chrissy Snow are roommates in an apartment complex in Santa Monica, California. Their third roommate, Eleanor, is leaving, and they throw a going-away party. The next day, they find a stranger passed out in their bathtub. That man is Jack Tripper, a college student studying to be a chef. When it is revealed that Jack lives at the YMCA, Chrissy and Janet are quick to suggest that Jack take over Eleanor's spot in the house. There is one problem, however. Mr. Stanley Roper (Norman Fell), their landlord who lives directly below with his sexually driven

Joyce DeWitt, Suzanne Somers, John Ritter, and Don Knotts in *Three's Company*. ABC/Photofest © ABC

wife, Helen, is conservative about unmarried males and females living together. In order to convince him to approve the arrangement, Janet tells Mr. Roper that Jack is gay. Despite his detestation of homosexuals, Mr. Roper agrees. Eventually, Mrs. Roper is let in on the secret and helps the "kids" keep their secret from Stanley.

Three's Company did not treat the issues of homosexuality on television with much understanding or compassion, instead making it a recurring joke that furthered stereotypes. Whenever Mr. Roper would interact with Jack, it usually involved him making a prissy face and holding his thumb to his forefinger and shaking his hand in the "Tinkerbell" motion that was a popular gesture used to indicate a gay man. When Jack was cornered by Mr. Roper on issues of unpaid rent, he would put on an effeminate persona and bat his eyes to scare him off. Just the recurring suggestion that being gay made one less of a man (enough so that the taboo of cohabitating with women was apparently, in this case, acceptable) did more to perpetuate stereotypes about being gay than helping to put them at rest.

What *Three's Company* did achieve was to make the case that people of the opposite sex could cohabitate based on necessity and friendship in platonic relationships. Although Jack would often flirt with Janet and Chrissy, it was an understood rule of the household that none of them could be anything more than friends. All three were supportive of each other and loving. A bonus for the two women was to have a man in the house who helped them feel safer. The harsh reality that women on their own could become targets of sexual assault was always an underlying worry on *Three's Company*, and having Jack in the apartment was considered added security that would help ward off unsavory characters and help them feel more safe. This argument and logic was applied when both Janet's and Chrissy's parents found out that their daughters were living with a single man (Chrissy's father was a minister, with the additional religious strictures forbidding such an arrangement).

Another point regarding Jack challenged gender roles of the time period. Neither Chrissy nor Janet was a capable cook (they could barely boil water, and this became a recurring joke of the show), so there was an allure to having Jack, who was studying to be a professional chef, around the house to prepare gourmet meals. It is unfortunate to have to recall that cooking was once deemed "women's work," a stereotype of the patriarchal society where men mowed the lawn and brought home the bacon and women cleaned house and popped out babies. *Three's Company* dared to suggest (rightfully) that no person should be confined by their gender and the societal mores that discouraged stepping outside of your prescribed expectations.

Three's Company went through myriad cast changes throughout its eight seasons. The first came at the end of season 3. It involved the spin-off series *The*

Ropers, which took the popular couple of Stanley and Helen out of the equation and whisked them away to a new living situation. Understandably, *Three's Company* needed to retain the tenant–landlord dynamic that was at the center of its plotlines, not to mention the central conceit of Jack's alleged homosexuality to create farcical situations. Enter Ralph Furley in the form of character actor Don Knotts, who was well known for his goofy awkwardness from years on *The Andy Griffith Show*. Mr. Furley fancied himself a ladies man, dressed in outrageous getups that were his idea of a swinging bachelor. In reality, he was a hilarious mess under the impression that he could teach Jack to be straight.

A bigger change would come early in season 5 when contract negotiations regarding Suzanne Somers went sour. Somers, who was an audience favorite as the dim-witted Chrissy, was demanding higher pay that would match the top-paid leading men on television. Producers would not budge, so halfway through that fifth season, Somers was ushered to a separate soundstage, essentially banished from interaction with her cast mates as an intimidation tactic, where she filmed phone calls to Jack and Janet with the explanation that Chrissy was home visiting with her parents. By the end of the season, it was clear that an agreement could not be reached, and Somers departed the show in one of the ugliest exits resulting from an actor–producer standoff. Somers was replaced in episode 7 by Jenilee Harrison, who played Cindy Snow, Chrissy's accident-prone cousin. From the start, it became obvious that Cindy was merely seen as a stopgap to get the sitcom through the end of the season. When season 6 commenced, Cindy was packing up to go to college at UCLA and appeared for a handful of episodes afterward, eventually fading into obscurity. The new roommate would be the smart, witty, and sexy Terri Alden, played by Priscilla Barnes, a nurse who was not afraid to challenge Jack's machismo. Barnes would remain with the show until its conclusion, adding another sexy, unattainable lady in Jack's circle.

Three's Company was not, however, all that sensitive to how it depicted women. Jack and his best friend, Larry, often treated women like objects to be attained and conquered, drooling over any buxom beauty who wandered into the Regal Beagle, the local pub that was their favorite hangout. For one season, the writers did turn the tables on Jack by the addition of the character of the sultry Lana (Ann Wedgeworth), who lusted after Jack, putting him in compromising positions and always trying to get him to come over to "change a lightbulb" or some other ruse to land him in bed. Lana was not a three-dimensional character by any stretch but really just a one-recurring-joke caricature that outstayed her welcome for one season, after which she disappeared into the ether.

After eight seasons, *Three's Company* had exhausted its premise, and it was time for everyone to move on, save Jack Tripper, who would receive a short-lived spin-off called *Three's a Crowd*. John Ritter had won an Emmy Award late in the show's run (1984) and, as an audience favorite for his physical antics, was the likely choice for the spin-off. The end of *Three's Company* saw Jack falling in love with a woman named Vicky Bradford (Mary Cadorette), and *Three's a Crowd* found the two moving into their own apartment, only to be given little privacy by her father and new landlord James Bradford (Robert Mandan). For Janet, she would find love and get married, and Terri would move to Hawaii, where she found a new nursing position. Neither of the ladies would appear on *Three's a Crowd*, but there was very little opportunity since the spin-off was canceled after one season.

In the end, *Three's Company* was first and foremost a farce with recurrent sexual overtones. Although very little sex actually happened on the show (in fact, it almost never did), it was hinted at frequently. This in itself made the show revolutionary because sex was often a taboo subject of television, something that might be alluded to but was rarely the thrust of situation comedy. *Three's Company* was just ribald enough to seem saucy and salacious, opening the doors for future TV shows that would prove to be far more laden with lust and blatant sexual situations (see *Soap*), but was itself mostly an innocuous brew of physical humor and comedy of errors.

Soap

THE STORY OF TWO SISTERS

Aired: September 13, 1977–April 20, 1981
Network: ABC
Created by: Susan Harris
Cast: Katherine Helmond (Jessica Gatling Tate), Robert Mandan (Chester Tate), Jimmy Baio (Billy Tate), Diana Canova (Corinne Tate Flotsky), Sal Viscuso (Father Timothy Flotsky), Jennifer Salt (Eunice Tate-Leitner), Donnelly Rhodes (Dutch Leitner), Arthur Peterson Jr. (The Major), Cathryn Damon (Mary Gatling Dallas Campbell), Richard Mulligan (Burt Campbell), Jay Johnson (Chuck and Bob Campbell), Ted Wass (Danny Dallas), Billy Crystal (Jodie Dallas), Robert Urich (Peter Campbell), Robert Guillaume (Benson DuBois), Roscoe Lee Browne (Saunders), Dinah Manoff (Elaine Lefkowitz), Inga Swenson (Ingrid Svenson), Rod Roddy (Narrator)
Theme Song: "Theme to *Soap*," composed by George Aliceson Tipton

The American soap opera used to be a staple of radio and television, the continuing tales of romance and drama targeted at housewives who were at home during the day and in need of entertainment. Soap operas typically followed a particular clan, taking a close look at their personal lives. Because the stories aired daily (weekdays), scripts were churned out quickly, and story lines could be outrageous, exhausting any and all points of intrigue and ending each episode with some sort of cliffhanger to keep the listener or viewer tuning in the next day. It was inevitable that such a format would ultimately be spoofed as the melodrama and the wide array of colorful characters could border on the ridiculous. In 1977, a TV sitcom would do just that, and *Soap* entered on the scene.

The idea for *Soap* came from the mind of Susan Harris (who would go on to create the TV series *The Golden Girls*), and the audacious and scandalous show would take television to places it had never ventured.

Billy Crystal and Jay Johnson In *Soap.* **ABC/Photofest © ABC**

Unlike the genre that it spoofed, *Soap* was a weekly sitcom, each episode half an hour in length, but it maintained the serial format with the action picking up the following week where it had left off the week before. *Soap* told the story of two sisters, Jessica Tate and Mary Campbell, as well as delving into the lives of their extensive family. Jessica was a kindhearted but often oblivious character who danced to the beat of her own drummer. She lived in a stately mansion with her philandering husband Chester, who was constantly scheming and running around behind Jessica's back. Their three children, the adult Eunice and Corinne, and their pubescent teenage brother Billy also resided at the Connecticut estate. The caustic, social-climbing Eunice initially was in a relationship with a married congressman but eventually went on to have a long-term relationship with Dutch Leitner, a convicted murderer. The kinder but flighty Corinne had her own problems, falling in love with and marrying Father Tim Flotsky, defrocking him, and having his child (which was possessed by the devil). Billy enjoyed the usual teenage boy problems, like getting caught up in a cult and having an affair with one of his high school teachers. Also in the house was Jessica and Mary's father, known as "The Major," a shell-shocked World War II vet who dresses in uniform and believes that the war is still under way. Finally, there is the butler, Benson DuBois, the clever servant whose acerbic nature and no-nonsense approach to managing a household kept him at odds with the chaos that often engulfed the Tates' lives. Benson was also African American and regularly suffered the bigoted indignities thrown his way by certain members of the Tate and Campbell broods.

Mary Campbell, on the other hand, did not enjoy the luxury that Jessica does. Put-upon and a worrywart, Mary was married to second husband Burt Campbell, a middle-class building contractor who accidentally killed Mary's first husband. Burt was both high-strung and prone to getting into bizarre situations, such as being abducted by aliens. From her first marriage, Mary had two sons. Jodie Dallas was an openly gay man and occasional cross-dresser who found himself suicidal, contemplating gender reassignment surgery, and often confused about how to reconcile his sexuality with his hopes and dreams. Danny Dallas was a dim-witted but kindhearted guy who was involved with the mob and who was given the task of killing his stepfather in retribution for his real father's murder. Danny was also forced to marry the mob boss's daughter, Elaine Lefkowitz, a pushy, overbearing girl with whom he eventually fell in love. Burt had a son from his first marriage, Chuck Campbell, a ventriloquist with a doll named "Bob," who Chuck sees as a living human being and insists that the family treat him as a member.

Soap also featured one other regular character, "The Announcer," who would recap the lunacy of the previous week's episode at the beginning of each new episode. He would also conclude each episode by posing a series of questions about that week's episode that the television audience is hoping to have resolved in the next installment. The Announcer was a tour guide of sorts, navigating the viewer through the complicated twists and turns of the show's multiple story lines and myriad characters.

From the outset, *Soap* proved to be a controversial show for its network, ABC (which had passed on *All in the Family* a decade earlier, fearful of how audiences would respond to its content). In March 1977, ABC screened the first two episodes of *Soap* for the executives of its affiliate stations, and the feedback was not positive. Most of them were disgusted by the show's sexual content, its emphasis on infidelity, and its inclusion of a gay man among the show's recurring characters. A handful of detractors thought the show was not fit for television. If their concerns cast an immediate pall over the proceedings, it was nothing compared to a June 1977 *Newsweek* article by Harry F. Waters previewing the fall TV lineup. Waters tore the show to shreds, alluding to its content as blasphemous and outright characterizing the show as a "sex farce."[1] Although this cancerous word of mouth might have been detrimental toward creating an audience for an adventurous new show, it also sparked an intrigue surrounding *Soap* that almost guaranteed that the curious (good and bad) would tune in to see for themselves.

The *Newsweek* piece stirred up a movement by religious groups that were ardently opposed to a show like *Soap* airing on network television, especially during prime time. Among the groups that mobilized were the National Council of Churches, the United Methodist Church, the National Council of Catholic Bishops, the United Church of Christ, the Christian Life Commission of the Southern Baptist Convention, and the Board of Rabbis of Southern California, calling on their followers to boycott the show and the sponsors to withdraw from buying commercial time. Letter-writing campaigns of more than 32,000 letters inundated the network itself, demanding that *Soap* be pulled from the fall lineup—all of this before most of the viewing public (including Waters) had actually seen an episode.

Religious communities were not the only detractors. The International Union of Gay Athletes and the National Gay Task Force were concerned about how the character of Jodie Dallas and his pro football–playing partner would be characterized. Despite the fact that *Soap* would feature the first recurring homosexual character in a sitcom—or perhaps because of it—these organizations wanted Jodie to be depicted in a light that was not detrimental to their cause. Considering that the show was premiering in the 1970s, the gay rights movement was still relatively young, and stereotypes perpetuated by homophobia were a real concern. As progressive as the idea of a recurring gay character was and would seemingly open some eyes in audiences, the reality was that *Soap* often drifted toward perpetuating misconceptions about homosexuals and would often paint Jodie in an unflattering light.

Producers had a reason to worry. The network had reasons to panic. A show's success lies in its ability to draw both audiences and the sponsors who are hoping to advertise their products. If viewers weren't tuning in, then the cost of a typical time slot at the time ($75,000) was not going to yield the return that was strived for. ABC dropped the price of advertising during *Soap*'s time slot to $40,000 per commercial spot, a motivator to keep their advertisers on board. Ultimately, 20 ABC affiliates out of 195 chose to boycott the show and refused to air it on their stations. Nevertheless, the show premiered on September 13, 1977, and ran for four seasons. For such a debated and contested sitcom, *Soap* fared relatively well in the ratings. Neither a blockbuster nor the ratings nightmare that was predicted, *Soap* ranked number 13 in the ratings for its first year, falling to number 19 and number 25 for the next two seasons, and ultimately dropping out of the top 30 before its cancellation at the end of season 4.

Soap's eventual decline had less to do with audiences finding offense or losing interest and more to do with internal issues at ABC. The show's creator, Susan Harris, had laid out an entire plan for the story arc of *Soap*, a "show Bible" of sorts that explained where each character started and where each would finish. ABC's Broadcast Standards and Practices Department reviewed Harris's plan and had a litany of concerns over the show's content. "The Soap Memo," a document citing a long list of revisions, eliminations, and rules that were expected to be adhered to, sought to tame the show as it was imagined by its creator. On June 27, 1977, this memo was leaked to the *Los Angeles Times* before the show premiered, adding fuel to the already growing fire. Throughout its four years on television, the Broadcast Standards and Practices Department continued to monitor the sitcom, and its insistence and influence would often render plot turns and characterizations both incoherent and ridiculous.

Once *Soap* was launched, with a disclaimer preceding each episode of the first season warning for adult content (subsequent seasons dropped the warning), the response to the show was surprisingly positive. The premiere won its time slot (this was aided by a strong lead-in from a lineup that included *Happy Days*, *Laverne & Shirley*, and *Three's Company*). Although the show never won an Emmy Award for Best Comedy, it was nominated for three of its four seasons. Richard Mulligan, Cathryn Damon, and Robert Guillaume all won in acting categories, and Guillaume was given a spin-off series called *Benson*, which found the butler taking a job working in the governor's mansion and eventually rising to the role of lieutenant governor. *Benson* was a political satire that outperformed its parent series, running for seven seasons. Guillaume won an Emmy for Best Actor in a Comedy Series for his work on *Benson*.

The two most important items to acknowledge about *Soap*'s influence are how it pushed the envelope with regard to content on television and how it adventurously endeavored to put a gay character in the limelight. It created a national dialogue in both regards, opening the doors to explore more fully realized characters that reflected a wider range of who we were as Americans. If we happened to laugh hysterically along the way, all the better because humor has always been a successful way to look at our differences and find our commonality.

Diff'rent Strokes

A SPECIAL KIND OF STORY

Aired: November 3, 1978–March 7, 1986

Networks: NBC (1978 –1985) and ABC (1985–1986)

Created by: Jeff Harris and Bernie Kukoff

Cast: Conrad Bain (Philip Drummond),Gary Coleman (Arnold Jackson), Todd Bridges (Willis Jackson), Dana Plato (Kimberly Drummond), Charlotte Rae (Edna Garrett), Nedra Volz (Adelaide Brubaker), Mary Jo Catlett (Pearl Gallagher), Dixie Carter (Maggie McKinney Drummond #1), Mary Ann Mobley (Maggie McKinney Drummond #2), Danny Cooksey (Sam McKinney)

Theme Song: "Diff'rent Strokes," by Alan Thicke, Al Burton, and Gloria Loring (performed by Alan Thicke)

Adoption has occurred in television sitcoms occasionally, but the popular NBC sitcom *Diff'rent Strokes* shed a compelling light on the subject, often looking at the challenges children have adjusting to a new family and living situation. *Diff'rent Strokes* was created by Jeff Harris and Bernie Kukoff and premiered on November 3, 1978, on NBC, where it remained for seven seasons before transferring to ABC for its eighth and final season.

The story concerned the wealthy, Caucasian Philip Drummond (Conrad Bain), who adopts the two African American sons of his black housekeeper when she passes away. The two boys, the scamp Arnold (Gary Coleman) and his cool older brother Willis (Todd Bridges), are whisked away from their home in a bad area of Harlem to the Drummond household, a Manhattan penthouse apartment. Also in the home is Kimberly (Dana Plato), Phillip's likable teenage daughter by his deceased wife, and Edna Garrett (Charlotte Rae), the practical and motherly housekeeper who offers good advice. Edna's character would eventually be spun off to her own sitcom, *The Facts of Life*, and the Drummonds'

Gary Coleman and Todd Bridges in *Diff'rent Strokes*. NBC/Photofest © NBC

would employ other domestics, including the crusty Adelaide Brubaker (Nedra Volz) and the flighty Pearl Gallagher (Mary Jo Catlett). The role of the house-keeper, however, always remained a surrogate mother and kindly mentor of the Drummond children.

In its early seasons, *Diff'rent Strokes* was not reluctant to address the boys' adjustment to losing their mother, leaving their home, and trying to settle in with their new family without being disloyal to their mother's memory or forgetting their former life. Philip was always patient with the boys, never requiring them to take his surname and encouraging them to keep their connections in Harlem. The boys continued to go by "Jackson" for the entirety of the show, which was an important part of keeping a piece of their mother with them. Kimberly was a welcoming sister to her new brothers and rarely appeared to be jealous of sharing her father's attention. It was an arrangement that worked well for all.

It is of consequence to note that the Drummond household was about as unconventional a family dynamic as one was likely to see on network television in the late 1970s. For many, adoption was something that they were initially being exposed to. Adoption, in society and on television, was typically treated as a secret that should be kept until a child was grown up and could process the information. As progressive as the Drummond/Jackson scenario appeared to be, the idea of a white, single male adopting two African American boys was the perfect recipe to incite the ire of bigots. Indeed, NBC received some negative feedback over this multiracial family from white supremacy groups that felt that the show had stepped over a line. Fortunately, NBC had a hit show on its hands and was unlikely to shut *Diff'rent Strokes* down as long as the advertising revenue continued to roll in.

In the 1980s, it was typical of popular sitcoms to have what was referred to as "very special episodes," seriously plotted stories that touched on current issues and/or subjects of a sensitive nature. *Diff'rent Strokes* produced what is remembered as one of the most iconic of these. In 1983, a two-part episode titled "The Bicycle Man" found Arnold and his best friend Dudley (Shevar Ross) targeted by a bicycle shop owner (Gordon Jump) who attempts to seduce the boys and molest them. The episode ran with a parental advisory warning, suggesting that adults take the time to talk to their kids about the episode after viewing. Many a conversation was had in homes warning against stranger danger and preda-tors who will give you gifts in exchange for your young body. It was a haunting episode of sitcom television, bearing a gravitas that shaped the minds of many children on making safe choices. This "episode" would lead to several others, ranging in topics from bulimia to epilepsy and from alcoholism to the dangers of hitchhiking.

Another place where *Diff'rent Strokes* had an impact on the youth of America was in the war on drugs. First Lady Nancy Reagan, wife of popular

1980s President Ronald Reagan, had launched an antidrug program called "Just Say No." In the season 5 episode "The Reporter," the First Lady made a guest appearance on the show, warning against the use of and abuse of controlled and illegal substances. "Just Say No" caught on, gaining its own iconic status as a 1980s cliché. Whether it managed to be taken seriously is another question, but the *Diff'rent Strokes* episode got the word out and helped to facilitate a national discussion.

As the series wore on, things changed in the house. Actress Dana Plato became pregnant and was written out of the series for a while. The scandal of having an unmarried, single woman with child was still too much for NBC to handle in those days, so she was sent off and would return only as a guest star toward the show's end. Philip would also marry an aerobics instructor named Maggie with a child named Sam, who made the perfect little brother for the now aging Arnold.

Although a popular sitcom well into the 1980s (the show was iconic in many ways but is particularly remembered for Arnold's signature catchphrase, "What you talkin' about Willis?"), *Diff'rent Strokes* was not exactly a critical darling. Many reviewers found the show trite, a sugary sitcom that always had a happy ending. In many ways, what they said was true. It didn't matter, however, because audiences continued to tune in to *Diff'rent Strokes*. The show's popularity made it the perfect tool for reaching mass audiences, which is probably why it was so often utilized as a means for getting out information and for addressing topical issues. People often underestimate the show's influence because of its typical sitcom corn. But *Diff'rent Strokes* could pack a subtle wallop when given a chance, living up to the lyrics of its theme song that declared, "The world don't move to the beat of just one drum / What might be right for you, may not be right for some" and that "it takes diff'rent strokes to move the world."[1]

Diff'rent Strokes was a little bit of everything, something for just about everyone, that special kind of story that could speak to many people on a variety of levels.

The Facts of Life

YOU TAKE THE GOOD, YOU TAKE THE BAD

Aired: August 24, 1979–May 7, 1988
Network: NBC
Created by: Dick Clair and Jenna McMahon
Cast: Charlotte Rae (Edna Garrett), Lisa Whelchel (Blair Warner), Mindy Cohn
(Natalie Green), Kim Fields (Dorothy "Tootie" Ramsey), Nancy McKeon
(Jo Polniaczek), John Lawlor (Steven Bradley), Jenny O'Hara (Emily Ma-
honey), Felice Schachter (Nancy Olsen), Julie Anne Haddock (Cindy Web-
ster), Julie Piekarski (Sue Ann Weaver), Molly Ringwald (Molly Parker),
Pamela Segall (Kelly Affinado), Mackenzie Astin (Andy Moffett), George
Clooney (George Burnett), Cloris Leachman (Beverly Ann Stickle), Sherrie
Krenn (Pippa McKenna)
Theme Song: "The Facts of Life," by Al Burton, Alan Thicke, and Gloria Loring
(performed by Gloria Loring)

Up until the 1970s, the life and concerns of the American teenager had been relegated mostly to malt shops, drive-in movies, and high school sock hops. Going
steady was the only goal of almost every teen. Not much screen time was given
to painting the problems of teens, and teenage girls were given particularly short
shrift in this arena. *One Day at a Time*, which premiered in 1975, had broken
the mold somewhat, taking a more authentic approach to the subject and giving
the show's two teenagers, Barbara and Julie, story lines that addressed sex, drugs,
and the myriad pangs of growing up. But *One Day at a Time* wasn't just a show
about teenage girls. Another show arrived on the scene four seasons later that
made telling the story of the female teenager its priority.

The Facts of Life was a spin-off of the popular sitcom *Diff'rent Strokes*, about
a wealthy man named Philip Drummond who adopts his black housekeeper's
two sons after she dies. In the Drummond household is the sage and caring

housekeeper Mrs. Garrett, who looks after the two boys, Arnold and Willis, as well as Philip's biological daughter, Kimberly, who attends the Eastland School for Girls, a boarding school in Peekskill, New York. When Eastland finds itself in need of a housemother for one of its dormitories, Mrs. Garrett agrees to help out in the interim. Once she arrives at the campus, it becomes clear that the girls need her, and she decides to stay around in a permanent capacity. This scenario was created with the idea that, if *The Facts of Life* didn't succeed as its own entity, Charlotte Rae could seamlessly return to *Diff'rent Strokes*. They need not have worried. *The Facts of Life* ran for nine seasons, though Rae would stay with the show for only seven.

In its first season, *The Facts of Life* was a very different show than what it would eventually evolve into. Mrs. Garrett's job as housemother saw her offering motherly advice to the spoiled rich girl Blair, the incorrigible Tootie, the funny Natalie, the tomboyish Cindy, the brainy Sue Ann, the pretty but insecure Nancy, and the frank Molly. Among the other adults involved with the girls were Principal Steven Bradley and teacher Emily Mahoney. With so many characters to juggle, it was challenging for the show's writers to home in on their individual personalities, defeating the show's implied purpose of giving a realistic understanding of the problems and challenges of teenage girls.

Still, *The Facts of Life* did attempt some groundbreaking moments in its first season. In the show's pilot episode, titled "Rough Housing," the popular Blair makes the insinuation that Cindy, who is always hugging the other girls and who likes sports and roughhousing, might be a lesbian. She drops many offhanded remarks about the girl, bullying Cindy to the point that she doesn't want to attend the school's Harvest Ball. Of course, Mrs. Garrett steps in and galvanizes Cindy's self-worth. More important, she approaches Blair and makes some carefully chosen, manipulative insinuations of her own about Blair's reputation, suggesting that she has "been around." Blair bristles at the assumption, telling Mrs. Garrett that she shouldn't believe everything that she hears or listen to rumors that might ruin someone's reputation. In return, Mrs. Garrett points out how Blair has essentially done the same thing to Cindy. Of course, in true half-hour sitcom fashion, the lesson is learned, Blair apologizes to Cindy, and the two become friends. What makes this episode stand out is twofold. First, in 1979 the idea of lesbianism was rarely addressed on television and certainly not as boldly as *The Facts of Life* was tackling the subject. Second, the writers never discussed being gay as "right" or "wrong" but rather suggested that girls being intimate with each other, platonically or otherwise, was okay. For a pilot episode, this was a bold kickoff to a show that would occasionally move past its laugh track–buoyed humor and probe life's realities.

Nancy McKeon, Lisa Whelchel, Kim Fields, Mindy Cohn, George Clooney, and Mackenzie Astin in *The Facts of Life*. NBC/Photofest © NBC

Season 1 featured other episodes that delved into important topics. In one, titled "Dieting," Sue Ann, who was a healthy-looking girl, decides to go on a crash diet when (of course) Blair suggests that a particular boy won't like her because of her weight. In "The Facts of Love," Mrs. Garrett teaches a sex education class and insists on covering topics that are pertinent to teenage girls, much to the dismay of Mr. Bradley, who prefers a more conservative approach to the topic. Season 1 would also take on the topics of divorce, adoption, and smoking marijuana and how a teenager might respond. It was a lot to pack into the program's truncated first season of 13 episodes.

After season 1, *The Facts of Life* was retooled, addressing the show's challenge of too many characters. Mrs. Garrett was given a promotion to school dietician and lived in a small room above the cafeteria. Only Blair Warner, Tootie Ramsey, and Natalie Green continued as regulars, while the other girls would occasionally have recurring appearances, mostly in what amounted to glorified walk-ons. Also out were Mr. Bradley, who would be replaced by Mr. Parker (Roger Perry) and Ms. Mahoney (who actually disappeared after episode 4 of season 1 and wasn't replaced at all). New to the cast was Blair's roommate, Jo Polniaczek, a scholarship kid from the Bronx who had just been accepted at Eastland. Jo drove a motorcycle and was tough, smart, outspoken, and poor, everything that Blair was not. If Blair had been appalled by Cindy's tomboyish nature, it was nothing in comparison to her detestation of Jo. The pairing of the two diametrically opposed forces of Blair and Jo led to one of the show's most successful and interesting dynamics. Blair immediately wanted to change rooms, but Mrs. Garrett worked her advisory magic and convinced her to give the new girl a chance.

In the opening of season 2, Jo dares Blair to help her steal a school van and go with her to a local bar. Through peer pressure, Blair reluctantly agrees. The much younger Tootie and Natalie tag along, insisting they aren't going to miss out on the fun (they also make it a condition of their not squealing on Jo and Blair). At the bar, the two older girls are picked up by an undercover cop while the two younger ones accidentally wreck the school van. They face expulsion, but Mrs. Garrett comes to the rescue and makes arrangements for the girls to remain in her care, working off the damages to the van by assisting her in the cafeteria. A storage room across the hall from Mrs. Garrett's quarters is converted into a dorm room for all four girls, and there they remained for three seasons. It is in this period of time that the show was its most effective.

Season 2 introduced a new, recurring character, one that was a big step for television. In the episode titled "Cousin Geri," Blair's cousin visits Eastland. She is a stand-up comedian who has cerebral palsy. When Geri (Geri Jewell) arrives at Eastland as a surprise, Blair begins to act strangely and doesn't appear happy to have her relative, whom everyone else seems to love, around. The girls assume that Blair is embarrassed by Geri's handicap. As the story progresses, we learn that Blair is jealous of her because what she has overcome is extraordinary. When Geri is around, she gets lots of attention from family and friends, something Blair is used to being the center of. The episode is noteworthy because, foremost, it was presenting a character with physical challenges and a speech impediment having a relatively normal life: a career, success, and desires. Open dialogue was had between Geri and the girls where certain stereotypes were put to rest. This was the first character with a visible disability to have a recurring role on a television program. Cousin Geri would return over the show's seasons for a total of 12 appearances.

When it was time for Blair and Jo to graduate from Eastland, it became clear that the show had to evolve beyond the boundaries of the cozy dormitory of its high school setting. In the opening of season 5, Mrs. Garrett leaves her post at the school to open a bistro called Edna's Edibles just a few blocks away from Eastland. Both Jo and Blair attended local Langley College, and Natalie and Tootie continued at Eastland. In a bit of a forced attempt to keep the relationships under one roof, all four girls move into the spare room of the home adjacent to Mrs. Garrett's new premises, living with their favorite mentor and motherly figure while helping out in the shop. The girls were becoming women and growing up, and this offered *The Facts of Life* the opportunity to explore more mature content. Even though the transition felt relatively inorganic, the show continued to be a success for NBC, and audiences tuned in.

Edna's Edibles didn't last for long. After two seasons of serving the town of Peekskill quiches and other specialty baked goods, a fire wiped out the establishment. Since Mrs. Garrett was insured (which also covered her tenants), the money was used to build a new shop called Over Our Heads, where Edna and the four girls used the money to go into a partnership. The store featured novelty items, record albums, and other odds and ends. This brought aboard the character of George, a handyman who would do the remodel, played by a young George Clooney. This new scenario was created to give Mrs. Garrett fewer appearances per Charlotte Rae's request for a lighter load. Realizing that the story was becoming more about the young women, Rae eventually departed the show, and Cloris Leachman, playing Edna's sister Beverly Ann Stickle, stepped in to be the new matriarch of the household. Also joining the show was Andy Moffat, a troubled foster child whom Beverly Ann ultimately adopts.

An episode of particular significance came in season 9, the show's final season. Realizing that this was a sitcom about four young women who were well into their 20s at this point, the writers decided it was time to address one of them losing her virginity. Initially, they had hoped to cater that story line to Blair, but Lisa Whelchel, who held strong religious beliefs that rejected premarital sex, wanted nothing to do with the episode. Mindy Cohn, however, thought that her character of Natalie, who had been in a long-term relationship with her boyfriend Snake (Robert Romanus), would be the right character to (as Cohn put it) "have her cherry popped." She pitched the idea to writers, and the episode "The First Time" was the result.

At the show's conclusion, Eastland School finds itself in financial straits and is in danger of closing. Blair decides to use her trust fund to keep the school open. It is decided that it is time to begin allowing boys to enroll. The final two episodes gave the indication that perhaps a spin-off was in the works, with Blair overseeing the education of a batch of new kids (among them Seth Green, Mayim Bialik, and Juliette Lewis). A new show or continuation never happened, and the four young women who had become the show's center were given pat endings: Blair is at Eastland, Tootie leaves for London to attend acting school, Natalie goes to New York City to pursue her writing career, and Jo, who married in the show's final season, joins her husband.

The Facts of Life is one of the most iconic shows to come out of the 1980s. Its theme song alone (by Al Burton, Gloria Loring, and Alan Thicke) is legendary with its catchy melody and its tongue-twisting lyrics. The tune perfectly summed up what the show was trying to capture: the world of the teenage girl and the challenges she faces, from simple growing pains to life's trials and tribulations of surviving as a woman in a male-centric society. *The Facts of Life* has been honored, parodied, and spoofed in pop culture for decades since its final episode. A reunion television movie in 2001 demonstrated its lasting impact. That same year, TV Land bestowed the show with its Pop Icon Award. It would be misguided to dismiss the effects that a sitcom that on the surface appeared to be simply a show aimed at teens about a quartet of teenage girls had on reshaping television's depiction of young women.

Kate & Allie

JUST WHEN YOU THINK YOU'RE
ALL BY YOURSELF, YOU'RE NOT

Aired: March 19, 1984–May 22, 1989
Network: CBS
Created by: Sherry Coben
Cast: Susan Saint James (Kate McArdle), Jane Curtin (Allie Lowell), Ari Meyers (Emma McArdle), Frederick Koehler (Charles "Chip" Lowell), Allison Smith (Jennie Lowell)
Theme Song: "Along Comes a Friend," by Ralph Schuckett, composed by John Loeffler and Ralph Schuckett (performed by John Loeffler)

With divorce in the United States climbing and peaking in the 1980s, a number of single mothers found themselves trying to raise their kids on salaries with gender disparity. Women simply were not making the same money as men. As is mentioned in the chapter on *One Day at a Time*, single mothers were depending on child support to make ends meet and not always getting it or getting it late. There were also the challenges of single-parent households. Who would watch the kids while Mom was working? How do you juggle the responsibilities of two parents when you are all by yourself? Obviously, women acclimated the best they could, and many made a success of single parenting. However, one TV show dared to suggest an alternative plan that would lessen the burdens of single parenting and in doing so would invite harsh criticism and audience pushback for its audacity.

Kate & Allie, which ran on CBS from 1984 to 1989, was created by Sherry Coben and featured two divorced mothers (and best friends since childhood) cohabitating and raising their children together in a Greenwich Village basement apartment. Kate McArdle was a free-spirited travel agent who had already been divorced from her husband for some time. She was raising her daughter Emma on her own when her old friend Allie Lowell found herself divorced from

110

a cheating husband and needing a place to live and to raise her two kids, Jennie and Chip. This is how the two families came together and began living as one. Initially, Kate went to work each day while Allie stayed at home and handled the domestic side of the arrangement and doing some catering on the side. As time went on, Allie went back to school and pursued a degree, which she completed. Eventually, Allie found romance with sportscaster Bob Barsky (Sam Freed) and married him. In the show's final season, Kate moves in with Allie and Bob in their new upscale apartment and together start a catering business.

This basic explanation of *Kate & Allie*'s premise sounds relatively innocuous, but the network was concerned about an aspect of the show that might become an issue with more conservative viewers. Would the two women be misconstrued as lesbians? This was long before shows like *Ellen*, *Will & Grace*, and *The New Normal* dared to challenge these social mores, so the idea of a gay couple on television could translate into poor ratings. However, Kate and Allie were not a lesbian couple, but the producers, who felt the pressure from network executives, made a point in most episodes to show the two characters entering

Jane Curtin and Susan Saint James in *Kate and Allie*. CBS/Photofest © CBS

separate bedrooms at night. Although *Kate & Allie* was inherently about women finding their identities apart from men, it was also interpolated into many plots that they were open to, and actively dating, men. There would be no mistaking them as lesbians. They were heterosexual, and it was going to be abundantly apparent, even if it did occasionally undermine the show's theme, that these two women were regrouping after their respective divorces and searching for their own identities outside of the prescribed norms that women should simply couple with men as their ultimate goal. Such was the climate of 1980s television and society as a whole.

Ironically, in season 2 the two women are faced with a rent increase when their landlady (Gloria Cronwell) finds out that two families are sharing a one-family dwelling. The titular pair pretend to be a lesbian couple to make the case that they are truly one family. The plan goes awry, however, when the landlady introduces Kate and Allie to her lesbian partner (Chevi Colton). The duo liked this older couple, leading to Kate and Allie, out of respect for their newfound friends, confessing to the ruse. In the end, the argument is made and accepted that the definition of "family" is those with whom you share your life. The lesbian couple admit that they, too, have felt discrimination and had their definition of family challenged. They drop the idea of the proposed rent increase. Although this episode clearly utilized the comedy-of-errors trope of pretending to be gay (à la *Three's Company*) to dodge a difficult situation, it was poignant nonetheless, and it fueled more fire regarding Kate's and Allie's supposed sexuality. Some audience members were not pleased, and the network received letters from disgruntled viewers who balked at even the suggestion of a lesbian couple on prime time. The higher-ups had been put on notice.

Interestingly enough, viewers had not felt the least bit concerned almost a decade earlier when *Laverne & Shirley* premiered on ABC in 1976. That scenario had two single female factory workers sharing a basement apartment (and a bedroom) and two upstairs neighbors, single men, also sharing an apartment (and a bedroom). In many ways, *Laverne & Shirley* was considered family entertainment, following its lead-in parent show, *Happy Days*, but there was not much that was different from the basic premise of *Kate & Allie* other than that the two women were not raising children. This didn't raise the suspicion or ire of television audiences, so what was societally different for *Kate & Allie* 10 years later?

In the 1970s, gay characters seldom appeared on television sitcoms or dramas. Early episodes of *The Mary Tyler Moore Show* and *All in the Family* had addressed the topic in one-off episodes, but a recurring gay character would not appear until 1977, when *Soap* introduced Jodie Dallas. *Soap* received backlash from both the right (who thought a gay character on television was immoral) and the left (who didn't feel that the character of Jodie Dallas was projecting a positive image for gays). What *Soap* had done was open the door for discussion and criticism around the topic. Producers had to lower the price of commercial advertising during *Soap*'s time slot, fueled particularly by letter-writing campaigns by viewers to sponsors asking them not to advertise. Did the fear of what happened with *Soap* influence decision making regarding *Kate & Allie* and put the network executives on high alert against the supposition that they could be lesbians? Had *Soap* conditioned audiences to question anything that even looked like homosexuality on television and to try to stamp it out before it could be influential? Certainly, *Kate & Allie*, though nothing close to being a gay-centered sitcom, was being treated as one, and network executives were aggressively trying to keep that perception at bay.

All of these worries and misconceptions aside, the concerns around Kate and Allie's alleged lesbianism started an important dialogue that was timely in the 1980s. What is family? In a decade when AIDS had reared its ugly head, gay couples in particular were experiencing a prejudice that attempted to diminish their definition of family. But this extended to anyone who was living in a relationship that was not defined as "traditional marriage." Partners of the dying were given no rights. In many cases, they were not allowed to see their loved ones on their deathbeds. Blood family members could excise a partner from funeral proceedings. *Kate & Allie* established that family can mean many things and, through its example, offered heartwarming alternatives for audiences to rethink its feelings on the matter.

Kate & Allie was far more than just the previously mentioned game changer where family definitions were concerned. It was a television show that gave a voice to both the independent woman and the woman seeking independence. Although both ladies shared story lines and had a chance to shine in their own right, it was the character of Allie around whom the show galvanized its message that women had options outside of what tradition and a male-dominated society had so unkindly limited their mothers to. Allie had been married to Dr. Charles Lowell (Paul Hecht) and had prided herself on being the perfect housewife and mother, a Donna Reed for the 1980s. With Charles's infidelities and their marriage severed, Allie was thrust into the world of single parenting and a job market that didn't offer many well-paying options for her skill set. Even more challenging was Allie's self-esteem. Her confidence had been destroyed by her failed marriage and her reticence exacerbated by leaving the security of her Connecticut home and starting life anew in the overwhelming playground of New York City. These situations created a tabula rasa for Allie, a chance for her to explore her individual identity and become the autonomous person she would eventually embrace. Through going back to school, building her own business, making the tough choices of parenting, and, most important, acknowledging the transition of gender roles, Allie Lowell was demonstrating what many women were already feeling: they no longer felt confined to the rules and strictures that were put on their mothers. Much of her phoenixlike reemergence was aided by Kate, who had already dealt with many of the demons that Allie was facing. It was women sharing with women, taking each other by the hand and lifting them up. This was *Kate & Allie* at its best and most effective.

Kate & Allie was a modest success, reaching number 8 in the ratings during its first season, middling in the teens for the next three seasons, and then plummeting for its final two seasons. It won two Emmy Awards for Jane Curtin, and Susan Saint James was nominated three times. Writer/director/producer Bill Persky was also honored with an Emmy for Outstanding Direction of a Comedy Series. The show's decline is often attributed to the completion of Allie's story arc. When she remarries, the dynamic of the show changed, and the two women no longer needed each other in the way that made the series work. But for a time, *Kate & Allie* told a story that was fresh, affirming, and relevant, serving many purposes, from entertainment to empowerment.

The Cosby Show
REDEFINING BLACKNESS

Aired: September 20, 1984–April 30, 1992
Network: NBC
Created by: Edwin "Ed" Weinberger, Michael Lesson, and Bill Cosby
Cast: Bill Cosby (Dr. Heathcliff "Cliff" Huxtable), Phylicia Rashad (Clair Hanks Huxtable), Lisa Bonet (Denise Huxtable Kendall), Malcolm-Jamal Warner (Theodore "Theo" Huxtable), Tempestt Bledsoe (Vanessa Huxtable), Keshia Knight Pulliam (Rudith "Rudy" Lillian Huxtable), Sabrina Le Beauf (Sandra Huxtable-Tibideaux), Geoffrey Owens (Elvin Tibideaux), Joseph C. Phillips (Lieutenant Martin Kendall), Raven-Symoné (Olivia Kendall), Erika Alexander (Pamela "Pam" Tucker)
Theme Song: "Kiss Me," by Stu Gardner and Bill Cosby (performed by Stu Gardner and Arthur Lisi, instrumental, seasons 1 to 3; Bobby McFerrin, season 4; Oregon Symphony, season 5; Craig Handy, seasons 6 and 7; and Lester Bowie, season 8)

Television has demonstrated a dubious history in how it has represented the African American experience in the United States over the first few decades since its popularity began. When it bothered to include blacks as sitcom families, they have been either laden with stereotypes à la *Amos & Andy* or painted in extremes, as in the poverty-stricken Evans household of *Good Times* or the wealthy George and Louise Jefferson of *The Jeffersons*. Where was the successful middle-class family with typical teenage kids who happened to be African American? In 1984, that representation would change with the arrival of *The Cosby Show*.

Comedian Bill Cosby was already an established star of the comedy circuit and a television personality known for his lead roles on shows such as *I Spy* (1965–1968) and *The Bill Cosby Show* (1969–1971) as well as the Saturday morning cartoon *Fat Albert and the Cosby Kids* (1972–1985) built out of his most famous stand-up character. In 1983, Cosby's stand-up act *Bill Cosby: Himself* was taped and aired on cable television to great success. Portions of the routine focused on Cosby's home life and the challenges of raising five "brain-damaged" kids (as he mused) with his successful, opinionated wife. Audiences connected with the piece, finding a commonality with Cosby's family-based humor. *Bill Cosby: Himself* would be the impetus for the creation of *The Cosby Show*, which, during its first season, drew on many of the scenarios Cosby shared in the act.

The Cosby Show followed the lives of the Huxtable family, with Heathcliff Huxtable and Clair Huxtable at the helm as father and mother. "Cliff" was an obstetrician who conducted business in his office in the basement of their Park Slope, Brooklyn, residence. Cliff could easily keep tabs on the house and then run downstairs and see a patient, a stay-at-home dad with a full-time job. Clair was a successful lawyer but always had her finger on the pulse of the household. She was the modern mother who worked full-time and wore the boots in the home, always calling out Cliff and the kids on their shenanigans.

Phylicia Rashad and Bill Cosby in *The Cosby Show*. NBC/Photofest © NBC

The Huxtables had five children: the adult Sondra, who had successfully completed college and was embarking on a marriage with the chauvinistic but awkward Elvin. Next was the flaky but hip Denise, who was concerned with the latest trends and music. She was followed by Theo, a kindly but stupid boy who often made dumb decisions in the name of popularity. Vanessa came next, an opportunist who would throw a sibling under the bus to make sure she got what she wanted. Finally, there was the sassy little Rudy, who incorrigibly offered frank observations and wisecracks and who was a feminist in the making. What was nice about the Huxtable kids was that they offered a nice cross section of interests and abilities while simultaneously being imperfect and typical of most American kids.

The Huxtables, as a TV family, were an upper-middle-class unit, living comfortably but not without careful planning. They certainly weren't the Jeffersons, nor were they the Evanses. This was the most realistic portrayal of a middle-class, black family on television to date. One has to consider the impact that this representation had on generations of African American viewers who had seldom experienced a TV show that just let their minority population exist as an average, typical family. In fact, this would be a revelation for *all* TV audiences. Without stigma and without pretense, *The Cosby Show* gave us that. We were all watching a TV show that gave us a view of black America that we hadn't seen before in the world of sitcoms.

One place where *The Cosby Show* shed much-needed light was on the learning disorder dyslexia. Dyslexia, according to the Mayo Clinic, "is a learning disorder that involves difficulty reading due to problems identifying speech sounds and learning how they relate to letters and words (decoding). Also called reading disability, dyslexia affects areas of the brain that process language." It was relatively unheard of by the average American. In the 1989 episode "Theo's Gift," *The Cosby Show* helped television audiences understand dyslexia and how it affects those challenged by the disorder. Theo Huxtable had always had a difficult time with school, often to the concern of his parents, who thought the boy wasn't applying himself. Although Theo had a lazy streak, we soon learned that kids with dyslexia will often feel defeated by what they perceive as an inability to learn. Their fear of failure could lead to their giving up, not trying, or becoming discouraged when they do try, only to have it not translate to good grades on their report card. Theo, while attending college at New York University, learned that he had dyslexia and was given new hope by a specialist who showed him how to approach learning in a different way. Soon, Theo was excelling at school and, through his journey, was teaching viewers that dyslexia existed and could be managed and bringing national attention to learning disabilities as a whole.

The character of Clair Huxtable was a sitcom mother quite unlike any who had been experienced before on television. Although she was seemingly the perfect mom of the 1980s (who wouldn't have loved to have Mrs. Huxtable as their parent?), balancing a career and home life with aplomb and dexterity, she was not the typical sitcom mom by any stretch. Clair was an articulate, progressive woman who exhibited an outspoken feminism that was seldom restrained. In fact, for her daughters, her son, and particularly her son-in-law, she would monologue about the misconceptions society had on the role of women as subservient to men. One icy stare from Clair let the other characters (and audiences) know that the status quo in how women were regarded, which had been deemed acceptable up to that point, held little water in the Huxtable household. Women were equal to men and, in Clair's estimation, perhaps just a bit superior.

Then there was the character of Cliff Huxtable himself. Cliff was not the typical sitcom father. He exhibited a zest for life and a playfulness with his children that few television fathers had ever revealed to that point. He was a warm, participant parent, not the dad who went to work and left the rearing of the kids to the mother. In fact, Cliff was at home more than Clair was. It was a marriage of equals, with Cliff stepping up to the plate when Clair's career took her away from the home and she reciprocating when the situation called for it. One of the hallmarks of the show's humor derived from the creative punishments and repercussions that the couple devised when disciplining and teaching their children. This was not a home where spankings happened. Clair and Cliff were far too clever for that.

The *New York Times* offered a perspective on *The Cosby Show*'s legacy, describing it as television's "biggest hit in the 1980s" and citing that it "almost single-handedly revived the sitcom genre." It also suggested that

> *The Cosby Show* is often credited for breaking new ground in the media visibility of African-Americans, laying track for later shows with predominantly black casts: *The Fresh Prince of Bel-Air* (1990–96), *Family Matters* (1989–98), and the progressively minded campus-comedy spinoff *A Different World* (1987–93). Though some might say the show merely picked up where *The Jeffersons* (1975–85) and *Good Times* (1974–79) left off, *The Cosby Show* remains the most-watched show featuring a predominantly black cast in the history of American TV. For five of the eight years it ran, it was the most-watched show in America—period—beloved by audiences of all colors and walks of life.[1]

Mark Whitaker, author of the book *Cosby: His Life and Times*, had this to say about the program:

The Cosby Show has been described by some as a show which redefined Blackness, presenting a nuclear construct that, until its 1984 debut, was not even considered a possibility.[2]

In a September 2014 article by Jake Flanagin, "Why *The Cosby Show* Still Matters," that perception was challenged:

> According to an editorial for News One, "Black America knew better." For a number of African-American viewers and critics, *The Cosby Show* did not "redefine Blackness" in so much that it showcased another aspect of black American life: "a Black narrative that focused on education instead of poverty. A Black narrative that focused on art instead of gang violence. A Black narrative that focused on love instead of pathology." This is true. Though *The Jeffersons* focused on an upper-class African-American family, their wealth and quality of life was intentionally novel—the windfall with which they "moved on up to the Upper East Side" being the literal basis for the show.[3]

The Cosby Show sought to lend a dignified narrative to the story of black America. Cosby himself was insistent that the show's plotlines focused on African Americans succeeding, achieving, and making responsible decisions that demonstrated their inherent value and productivity in the face of a white-dominated society. Indeed, *The Cosby Show*'s spin-off series *A Different World* (1987–1993) brought Denise Huxtable to the mostly minority-attended, fictional Hillman College in Virginia. The series was an opportunity to show one of the Huxtable kids making good, enjoying the fruits of what hard work and proactive living could yield. It was setting an example for every African American girl and boy, giving them a chance to witness better options than what television had deemed was a bleaker lot in life.

Holding the position of the number 1 television show in America for five years running, *The Cosby Show* was a cultural phenomenon. It wasn't just black audiences who were tuning in to spend time with the Huxtables; viewers from every demographic, race, religion, and income level were as well. Even in its final season, the lowest-ranked of all seasons, the show had fallen only to number 18. For its other seven seasons, it had remained in the top five. *The Cosby Show* also won a handful of Emmy Awards, including Outstanding Comedy Series in 1985. Overall, it generated $2.5 billion in television revenue between advertising and its ongoing success in syndication.

In recent years, the legacy of *The Cosby Show* has been tainted by the actions of its star, who was accused and then convicted of drugging and sexually assaulting women, with several victims coming forward, offering compelling enough testimony to land him in prison. At the time of this writing, Cosby is serving a three- to 10-year sentence. It is a shame that his inexcusable actions have put a stain on a classic TV series that opened so many doors, gave so many people a weekly dose of laughter, and reframed how America would view the African American family. Cosby's actions aside, *The Cosby Show* remains an important sitcom in the history of television, breaking down many barriers in its eight years on the air.

Who's the Boss?

THERE'S A PATH YOU TAKE
AND A PATH NOT TAKEN

Aired: September 20, 1984–April 25, 1992
Network: ABC
Created by: Martin Cohan and Blake Hunter
Cast: Tony Danza (Tony Micelli), Judith Light (Angela Robinson Bower), Alyssa Milano (Samantha "Sam" Micelli), Danny Pintauro (Jonathan Bower), Katherine Helmond (Mona Robinson)
Theme Song: "Brand New Life," composed by Larry Carlton and Robert Kraft, lyrics by Martin Cohan and Blake Hunter (performed by Larry Weiss, 1984–1986; Steve Wariner, 1986–1989; and Jonathan Wolff, 1989–1992)

Gender roles in our society were once defined by what the patriarch-guided establishment said they should be. Women were often left out of the workplace unless they were single and entered professions such as teaching and nursing. Otherwise, it was the assumption that a woman's job was to get married, keep house, and raise children. Men had their prescribed duties as well: go to work, mow the lawn, take out the trash, and keep order in their households. The reality was that not every family and individual worked this way, but from watching television in the 1950s and 1960s, no one would guess that an alternative dynamic had evolved. When men went away to fight in World War II in the early 1940s, women stepped up and proved themselves adept at running businesses, working in factories, and handling much of the work left behind by their soldier husbands. They did this while managing households and raising children. Many women who had not experienced otherwise found that being out of the home was invigorating and fulfilling in ways that they typically were not in a position to explore. Some would not be eager to return to their prewar lives.

When the men returned from the war, it was generally expected that women would return to their household duties, but that was not always what was wanted or required. In the ensuing decades, it became clear that some women wanted to remain in the workplace and/or needed to join it, and though employment opportunities and equal pay with men would be a mountainous struggle to over-come (an ongoing one to this day), there was a growing contingent who would change the labor landscape. With the burgeoning women's rights movement gaining ground in the 1960s and into the 1970s, these women found a voice. They were not just baby machines—they had much to offer society with their perspectives and their industry. As their voices grew louder and more plentiful, the more visible their influence became. Divorce rates were also rising exponen-tially, and by the late 1970s and early 1980s, many women were raising children on their own with the necessity of holding full-time jobs to keep their children fed and clothed.

There was also the single woman to consider. Not every female was inter-ested in marrying and having children as soon as she left high school or college. Some didn't want either of those things. Many endeavored to pursue careers and did so successfully, legitimizing their individuality and capability outside the parameters that had been set for their mothers and grandmothers. There was something more to life than that. Some TV shows in the late 1960s and early 1970s began to recognize this, such as *That Girl*, *Julia*, and particularly *The Mary Tyler Moore Show*, breaking those June Cleaver and Donna Reed stereotypes that rigidly cast women in one very narrow beam of light: that of the perfect homemaker.

Men staying at home to raise the kids and keep the house was also becoming more common despite the stigma that it somehow challenged their masculinity. So engrained was society in the belief that gender defined what you could and could not do that the majority behaved as though this situation was one that should be avoided. The success of women was viewed as a castration of sorts, a defeat of man and what he was supposed to be. As ridiculous as this sounds, gen-eration after generation had been taught to think this way. In marriages where women suddenly became the breadwinners, the shift often required men to stay home and handle the domestic responsibilities. By the 1980s, this was becoming more and more common, enough so that the movie industry took notice. Films like *Kramer vs. Kramer* (1979) and *Mr. Mom* (1983) found compelling premises in placing men in the situations of these evolving gender roles. As the 1980s wore on, television would finally find a way to catch up with the changing times, and a TV show would enter the collective psyche of America that reversed as-signations of these prescribed duties, giving television audiences the perspective that how we view families and the roles each member takes need not be so rigidly defined. Fluidity was the mark of how *Who's the Boss?* captured America's heart

Tony Danza, Judith Light, Alyssa Milano, and Danny Pintauro in *Who's the Boss? ABC/Photofest © ABC*

with humor while simultaneously giving us a new way of understanding that we are *all* more than a checklist of what we should and should not do.

Who's the Boss? told the story of an unlikely duo, Angela Bowers, an advertising executive in Connecticut, and Tony Micelli, an ex–Major League Baseball player whom Angela hired as a housekeeper. A divorcée, Angela was busy with her career and needed someone in the house to cook, clean, and help look after her little boy, Jonathan. Tony, a widower, had been injured playing ball and had to retire. He needed work that took him away from the limited opportunities of his old life. He brought with him his little girl, Samantha, hoping to find a safer community in which to raise her outside their Brooklyn neighborhood. Another regular on the show was Mona Robinson, Angela's confident and sassy mother who lived in an apartment above the garage. Mona liked the company of men and, despite her age, was regularly seen dating, partying, and living a life of fun in her bachelorette pad. She was the antithesis of Angela and often gave her daughter a hard time for being reserved and uptight.

Having a strange man living in her house was difficult for Angela, and Tony had certain difficulties adjusting to his new role as a domestic. In season 1, episode 2 called "Briefless Encounter," we learn that Tony is doing an excellent job cooking and cleaning in the Bower household. The only place he seems to be failing is in the upkeep of Angela's bedroom and bathroom, a place he is uncomfortable invading. Angela, on the other hand, wants her spaces cleaned and insists that Tony do so. He reluctantly agrees. When he discovers that she has a big, beautiful, private bathtub, he decides to take a soak as part of his time cleaning. What he doesn't realize is that Angela is home and already in it. As he enters the bathroom, she is climbing out of the tub, and he sees everything. Of course, this creates a tension between them, Angela being both modest and reluctant to have a male housekeeper. What is important to note is that despite Tony's macho, overt heterosexuality, he never once wants to be disrespectful of Angela or enter her spaces of privacy. *Who's the Boss?* could easily have gone in that clichéd direction of the dominant male stereotype and made the show into a sex farce à la *Three's Company*. The temptation must have certainly been there to capitalize on that ribald scenario. Instead, the writers chose to explore alternatives where a man could be inherently decent, a gentleman.

Who's the Boss? did not just reserve its stereotype shattering for the adults on the show. The kids were also depicted in a way that broke the molds of typical family sitcoms. Samantha was a tomboy: she was tough, assertive, and an athlete, but she also wanted to be feminine, respected for all aspects of who she was. Jonathan liked his snakes and insects but dressed in sweater vests and regularly revealed a sensitive side. Although television had introduced audiences to kids who broke stereotypes, *Who's the Boss?* was insistent in maintaining that kids are just as diverse, possessing complex personalities that span a spectrum of masculine and feminine traits.

The show also helped to redefine television families and what made up those units. Could two separate families come together, each with a very different background, and survive? Sure, Tony was an employee, but he was raising his child in the home of his employer alongside her son. At first, Tony and Angela could be at odds, but as the show progressed, they developed a deep friendship that eventually blossomed into romance. The two had to learn to give and take (never an easy feat) and also take into consideration the other one's child. In the episode "Samantha's Growing Up" (season 1, episode 11), Tony has to bring his daughter to purchase her first bra. Overcome with emotion over his little girl becoming a woman and simultaneously uncomfortable with taking her to buy feminine undergarments, he turns to Angela, who steps up to the plate and handles it with a motherly tenderness and affection that hints at the important influence she will have on the girl over time. Even though they were not stepparents in the traditional sense, these are the roles that they would essentially assume. There were times that it was hard for Samantha to adjust to Angela's mothering efforts, fearful that she might be replacing her deceased mother in the process. Jonathan was more comfortable with Tony, seeking a male role model in his life. Angela's soon-to-be ex-husband traveled a lot and had very little interaction with the boy other than to occasionally sweep in and spend time with him. In fact, Jonathan was an impressionable boy who looked to Tony as a role model. In the season 1 episode titled "Just Like Tony," the child begins to get into trouble, stealing a hubcap off a police car and mixing with an unsavory crowd. It turns out that Tony has been telling him stories about his own childhood and experiences in the Bronx. Jonathan wants to emulate his ideal, which is, of course, their new housekeeper. Tony quickly grows to understand the influence he has on the little boy and begins pointing him in the right direction while choosing his words more carefully. Still, Jonathan could rebel against Tony just as Samantha would have her moments of teenage stubbornness with Angela. Each adult had to carefully navigate their respective seas carefully.

Who's the Boss? was also one of the first sitcoms to address age discrimination in the workplace. In season 2, episode 11, titled "The Graduate," Mona, who had recently graduated from college, was asked to help bring down a company that had a reputation for refusing to hire older employees. Angela, who is unware that Mona is a part of a sting operation, uses her influence to get her mother the job. Although the plan backfires, the episode shed light on a topic that had been mostly ignored: how difficult it was (and still is) to find employment once you have passed a certain age.

As a few seasons passed, Angela began to gain confidence in herself and learned to be far more assertive than she had been initially. She is a hardworking career woman at the advertising agency, but she loses an important client and is fired at the beginning of season 3. Desperate to find a new job, she doesn't know what to do. Tony and Mona point out that she has all the necessary resources to open her own ad agency: time, talent, money, and family support. She does this, and, though it is a struggle at first, she makes the Bower Agency an unqualified success. It is a testament to the acting skills of Judith Light that she always managed to keep Angela both strong and independent and fragile and vulnerable. This eclectic mix of attributes was never more effective than in this three-episode arc.

Who's the Boss? may not have been as explosively revolutionary as some sitcoms, but in its own gentle, unimposing way, it helped redefine much of how television writing approached the male–female dynamic and broke down gender stereotypes that had been painted as staunchly unyielding. Men could be sensitive and macho. Women could be strong and vulnerable. It suggested that a world where everyone is able to explore the gamut of their potential, their emotions, and their interests is an okay world to live in. As the Martin Cohan and Blake Hunter (lyrics) and Larry Carlton and Robert Kraft (music) theme song "Brand New Life" suggests, "There's a path we take and a path not taken, the choice is up to you my friend."

Who's the Boss? took an alternative path with an out-of-the-box scenario, asserting that, in avoiding the conventional and known and exploring new territory, the result could be a successful sitcom full of more fully realized characters who exhibit both masculine and feminine traits.

The Golden Girls

TRAVEL DOWN THE ROAD AND BACK AGAIN

Aired: September 14, 1985–May 9, 1992
Network: NBC
Created by: Susan Harris
Cast: Beatrice Arthur (Dorothy Zbornak), Betty White (Rose Nylund), Rue Mc-
   Clanahan (Blanche Devereaux), Estelle Getty (Sophia Petrillo)
Theme Song: "Thank You for Being a Friend," by Andrew Gold (performed by
   Cynthia Fee)

Until 1985, television had represented grandmothers mostly as bespectacled
blue hairs in housecoats and matronly dresses, limping around on canes, baking
pies, or dropping by to visit their families for a guest appearance. Sometimes
revered for their sagacity and usually cartoonish in their inability to grasp the
mores and lingo of the contemporary generation, women of a "certain age" were
too often depicted in entertainment as caricatures, having expired and played
their part and expected to take a backseat to those younger and allegedly more
vital. This marginalization may have come as a result of television demographics that skewed toward the young (the 18-to-49 age-group), with the over-50
crowd given short shrift where starring roles and age-defining story lines were
concerned. In an entertainment medium where ratings are the determining factor of how and why shows are made, why in the world would Hollywood want
to produce a show that catered to an older audience and that featured a cast that
was over 50?

Based on a premise known as *Miami Nice* (the title a spin on the iconic
NBC cop drama *Miami Vice*), the idea for a show about four elderly women living together had been bandied about for some time. The idea came from Susan
Harris, who had created the earlier groundbreaking sitcom *Soap*. Then NBC
chief Brandon Tartikoff liked the idea, as did the vice president of company

programs, Warren Littlefield, but they found that most of the people surrounding them in the company did not think the show would succeed. Still, they knew that they had a hit, something that hadn't been done before, and that there was a large pool of beloved older actresses who were no longer getting work because Hollywood saw them as past their prime. It was a chance that NBC was willing to take. Something about the idea just felt "right."

The Golden Girls (as it would be rechristened) would look like this: three women—two widows and a divorcée—all over the age of 50, would share a home in Miami, Florida. The divorcée's mother (a widow herself) would make the trio a quartet when her nursing home burned down in the opening episode. They would become a family, evolving, loving, arguing, and surviving together. Dorothy Zbornak (played by Emmy Award–winning *Maude* actress Beatrice Arthur) was divorced from her unfaithful husband, making ends meet as a substitute schoolteacher. Acerbic and tenacious but masking a heart of gold and poor self-confidence, Dorothy represented the backbone of the group. Rose Nylund (brought to life by Emmy Award–winning actress Betty White of *The Mary Tyler Moore Show*) was the guileless housewife from Minnesota who had lost her husband. Rose was the show's heart: dippy and sincere as she recounted

Bea Arthur, Rue McClanahan, Betty White, and Estelle Getty in *The Golden Girls*. NBC/Photofest © NBC

ridiculous stories of her life in the town of St. Olaf but always the most affectionate and forgiving of the tribe. She would have a job as a grief counselor. Blanche Devereaux (played by *Maude* and *Mamma's Family* actress Rue McClanahan) would be the owner of the house. A fiery vixen who had grown up in the South, Blanche, also a widow, represented sexuality and vitality. Working in a museum where she was surrounded by beauty and a favorite of all the men, she would have the hardest time with the hurdles of aging. Sophia Petrillo (played by stage actress Estelle Getty) was Dorothy's mother. A sassy, no-holds-barred immigrant from Sicily, Sophia escaped the nursing home fire at Shady Pines to move into the house, becoming the "wisdom that comes with age" character. A spunky octogenarian, Sophia filled her days holding jobs at fast-food restaurants and volunteering at the hospital. Due to her stroke, her brain's filter for appropriateness sometimes malfunctioned, and Sophia spoke exactly what she was thinking. The girls also had a live-in gay cook named Coco (played by Charles Levin), who was excised after the pilot episode not because he was gay but because it was decided to put more focus on Sophia, who was winning most of the laughs.

Premiering on September 14, 1985, *The Golden Girls* was an instant hit, often winning its time slot. The show became a staple of NBC's Saturday night lineup. It ran for seven seasons, garnered 68 Emmy nominations, and produced three spin-off series: *Empty Nest, Nurses,* and *The Golden Palace.* All four leading ladies won Emmys for their performances, and the show won twice in the Outstanding Comedy Series category. These achievements are important to underline because this was a show that many believed wouldn't appeal to a wide audience. For this kind of ratings success, more than just retirees and the early-bird-special crowd were tuning in. It turns out that people were not turned off by a show about mature women and, in fact, were delighted by how they were being portrayed. Getting older no longer had quite the same stigma. It offered a lifetime of hope. Grandmothers on the tube shed their aprons and took their hair out of buns. *The Golden Girls* broke this stereotype not only on television but also in society itself.

The Golden Girls didn't just break the barriers of ageism in Hollywood by making a success of a show about four women over 50; it also tackled many of the issues and fears that Americans were or would be experiencing with aging. Blanche, initially thinking she was pregnant from one of her many hookups, finds out from a doctor that she is going through menopause. Her self-confidence is based on her sexuality, and she wrestles with the stigma brought about by "the change" and how this could affect her desirability as a woman. Dorothy and Rose, who are living from paycheck to paycheck, constantly deal with ageism in the workplace. Sophia is forced to watch many of her friends fade as Alzheimer's disease, dementia, and illness take them from her world. She herself, having already suffered a stroke, goes on to have her own battles with life-threatening pneumonia and memory loss. Rose has a heart attack, and the girls must adjust to the idea that they might lose one of their quartet, facing the specter of death that is staring down all of us. *The Golden Girls* captured these moments of our humanity in an unyielding way.

Even though *The Golden Girls* was a situation comedy constructed mainly for laughs, it managed to explore many important issues, sometimes courageously doing so when no other program was addressing them. When the show decided to tackle the topic of AIDS, the writers interestingly (and effectively) chose to make the person facing the scare not the libidinous Blanche (the obvious choice) but rather the naive and prudish Rose, who may have received the virus through a blood transfusion. First, a TV show was addressing AIDS, which in the mid-1980s was a taboo subject despite its growing relevancy and the pall of fear it cast over the country (and the world). Second, the person who was possibly infected was an aging woman who lived a relatively tame life where sex was concerned, thus breaking a long-standing stereotype that young gay men were the only people at risk of contracting HIV. Third, it was taking us along for the ride, forcing us to deal with both our fear of and (then) our lack of information on AIDS.

Another illness that was given attention on the show was chronic fatigue syndrome, a then mostly unheard-of sickness that continues to be hard to diagnose. Dorothy, who was usually energetic and the pillar of strength on the show, starts to have symptoms of a cold as well as a malaise that simply will not go away. Doctor after doctor tells her that it is psychosomatic or that she is imagining it, leaving her in a state of despair. She knows that this feeling of total exhaustion is not in her mind. Not only did this story line introduce a very real disease to the TV-watching public, but it was also challenging how we let our health care professionals treat us. It suggested perseverance in finding the answers to our medical concerns and not letting condescension from patriarchal doctors intimidate us into silence. The aging should persevere for better answers.

The Golden Girls has an enormous gay following, which many have marveled at. It should not be surprising since the show is about community and redefining the meaning of family, both topics that are near and dear to the gay community. *The Golden Girls* never shied away from gay/lesbian issues; in a few episodes, the subject was handled head-on. Dorothy's good friend Jean comes to visit the girls. Jean is a lesbian and finds herself attracted to Rose. Rose doesn't know how to deal with it; she doesn't understand those feelings. Unable to hurt another person, Rose works through her fears and finds she can be Jean's friend even if the attraction is not mutual. It was simply laid out for viewers to observe and learn. There is no need to be afraid of a person of the same sex who is attracted to you. There is no need to shun a friend who feels that way about you. Another episode features Clayton, Blanche's brother, who reveals to his sister that he is gay. Blanche wrestled with her phobias on the subject, calling it "unnatural" and insisting that he just hasn't met the right woman. A subsequent episode features Clayton showing up with the man he wants to marry, which resurfaces all his sister's misgivings. Blanche eventually concludes that her fears are about how she will be perceived having a gay brother and reluctantly (but lovingly) gives her blessing. Only the bravest of shows were addressing gay and lesbian story lines in the 1980s, and *The Golden Girls* did it with honesty and respect.

Perhaps the most astonishing thing about *The Golden Girls* has been the longevity of its appeal. This is not a program that had its moment in the spotlight and then faded away. During its initial run, it entered into syndication and played successfully in reruns. Networks such as Lifetime and the Hallmark Channel made *The Golden Girls* a part of their regular repertory, often playing multiple episodes a day and marathons on the weekend. Hulu recently added it to its options on their streaming site, and the show has been enormously successful, playing to a whole new generation of fans. The show has never really gone away. Something worked when a few believers looked at a missed demographic and designed a show that spoke for a forgotten generation. Old and outspoken became cool. Life didn't end at 50, and it turns out that it never had. *The Golden Girls* reminded us that you are only as old as you feel and that you should never let society's estimation of your worth be the barriers by which you live. This is arguably—but most assuredly—why the show continues to resonate.

Valerie / Valerie's Family / The Hogan Family

THE MORE YOU LEARN, THE LESS YOU KNOW

Aired: March 1, 1986–May 7, 1990 (NBC), and September 15, 1990–July 20, 1991 (CBS)

Networks: NBC and CBS

Created by: Charlie Hauck

Cast: Valerie Harper (Valerie Hogan), Sandy Duncan (Sandy Hogan), Jason Bateman (David Hogan), Danny Ponce (Willie Hogan), Jeremy Licht (Mark Hogan), Josh Taylor (Michael Hogan), Edie McClurg (Mrs. Patty Poole)

Theme Song: "Together through the Years," composed by Charles Fox, lyrics by Stephen Geyer (performed by Roberta Flack)

For much of television's early history, the subject of sex was particularly taboo. The censors kept even the slightest suggestion of intercourse at bay. The collective morality of the country seemed to like it that way, preferring to keep even husbands and wives mostly in separate beds until the late 1960s. In the 1970s, a few shows suggested "making whoopie," a ridiculous euphemism for having sex that always seemed to incite gasps on game shows like *The Newlywed Game* and *The Dating Game*. Even on sitcoms such as *Soap*, *Three's Company*, and *WKRP in Cincinnati*, shows that were ribald, suggestive, and cutting edge on the topic, the focus was more on allusions to sex than the actual act, comedies of errors, mistaken assumptions, and characters who were always out to have sex but rarely ever achieved their goal.

Around this time, the AIDS epidemic began in the United States, and by the mid-1980s it was clear that the disease was spreading through bodily fluids, blood and semen being the chief vessels for the retrovirus. Although it became imperative that people protect themselves by using condoms during sex, reducing the chance of spreading the HIV virus, that information was not being

Josh Taylor, Jason Bateman, Jeremy Licht, Luis Daniel Ponce, and Valerie Harper in *Valerie*. NBC/Photofest © NBC

delivered to the masses. The Reagan administration had turned a blind eye to the growing AIDS crisis and was certainly making no efforts to arm people with lifesaving information. School health teachers were reluctant to broach the subject of safe sex for fear of being reprimanded (or worse, fired) when conservative and religious families, many of whom already objected to instruction of sexual education in the classroom, would oppose any suggestion that this was an alternative to abstinence. The necessary message about condoms was not reaching the people who needed to hear it the most: teenagers who were just beginning to experiment with sex and who were becoming a growing risk group where HIV was concerned. *Valerie / Valerie's Family / The Hogan Family* was a sitcom that arrived on the scene in 1986 that addressed the topics of condoms and AIDS but with particularly unyielding results, especially for a sitcom that was considered light family fare.

Valerie / Valerie's Family / The Hogan Family was a typical family sitcom, created by Charlie Hauck, about a working mom named Valerie Hogan, raising her three teenage sons: the popular David, the brainy and sensitive Mark, and the incorrigible Willie. Their father, Michael, being an airline pilot, came and went, usually leaving Valerie to fly solo with her three sons and their journey through adolescence. The reason for the program's three different titles grew out of a contract dispute between the show's star, Valerie Harper, and the producers, Miller-Boyett Productions, Lorimar-Telepictures, and the producing network, NBC. Harper (and her producer/husband Tony Cacciotti) wanted greater control of the show and its direction, salary increases, and a larger cut of the syndication profits. When she was turned down, Harper parted from the show, her character killed off and replaced by Sandy, the sister of the family patriarch, Michael. Although this is irrelevant to the themes discussed here, an explanation is necessary for why the program went by three different names at different times during its run. Episodes of consequence are coordinated appropriately with the show's title at the time it first aired.

Written by Chip Keyes and Doug Keyes and directed by Howard Storm, the first episode of consequence (with regard to social evolution) aired on February 8, 1987. Titled "Bad Timing," this episode of *Valerie* revolved entirely around the use of prophylactics. The episode, accompanied by the usual preshow warnings addressing the sensitive content of the show, not only tackled the subject directly but also captured the collective discomfort and apprehensions that most Americans were experiencing when it came to having a dialogue about safe sex. Some network affiliates refused to air the program, while others chose to run it at a later hour than the show's usual time slot. Although the show courageously journeyed into uncharted territory, its efforts to create a meaningful dialogue were thwarted.

The episode featured the Hogans hosting some old family friends, the Morgans, who are in town so that their daughter Lori can attend a college interview. It is soon revealed that Lori and David were childhood sweethearts and that their affections for each other have remained intact. Lori approaches David in the night, climbing into bed with him. The two consider having sex, with David asking her what kind of birth control she is on. When she admits that she isn't on anything, the discussion turns toward using a condom, which David regrets he does not have. Wishing to behave responsibly, they postpone their plan until the next day, and David goes to the pharmacy to purchase condoms and to buy his mother, Valerie, some cough drops. The bags get mixed up, and Valerie is alerted to her son's plans. Although she awkwardly stumbles through the conversation, she commends her son on his being responsible and for making the adult choice to use contraception. She reassures him that the feelings he is having are normal and that she understands the pressures of someone his age to have sex. Valerie also asks David to remember all of the things that his father and she have taught him about sex—that it shouldn't be done lightly and should be done with someone who is special. The next day, David and Lori are left alone in the house and prepare to make love. Under time constraints to complete the act before the adults return, David confesses that he is a virgin and that he doesn't want his first time to be rushed or without meaning. The episode concludes with their deciding to wait until Lori's next visit.

"Bad Timing" was unabashedly earnest and direct in its discussion of both sex and contraception, retaining the humor of a sitcom while simultaneously conveying the gravity of the situation. Although the first time we had heard it on television was in an episode of *Cagney & Lacey* a year earlier, the use of the word "condom" no longer seemed quite so taboo when it was used in a sitcom. It was certainly the first time that an episode of prime-time television revolved almost entirely around the use of a condom as the "situation" for situation comedy. Deeper discussions of safe sex would creep into other programs—comedy and drama alike—all thanks to the door opened by *Valerie*.

Another important episode tackling a difficult but important subject aired on December 1, 1990. At this point, the show was called *The Hogan Family*, and the episode was titled "The Best of Friends, the Worst of Times." During the show's evolution, the series added a recurring character named Rich, played by Tom Hodges. Rich was a macho buddy who palled around with the eldest son, David. At the end of season 5, Rich parted from the show. In season 6, while David is working on a documentary in the hospital, he comes upon Rich in one of the hospital beds. As the friends reunite, we find out that Rich has AIDS and is expected to die. David is devastated and looks to his Aunt Sandy for information and comfort. She reveals that an old college friend of hers died from the disease. Throughout the episode, we are given a great deal of information about HIV and AIDS, clearly an attempt to inform audiences who, in the early 1990s, were still afraid of HIV-positive individuals. The "The Best of Friends, the Worst of Times" endeavored to dispel the myth that AIDS was a disease that affected only homosexuals and drug addicts. The episode concludes with David and Sandy speaking at the local high school, explaining how to prevent becoming infected. David concludes the presentation by sharing that Rich has died from the disease.

Actor Tom Hodges, who played Rich, cowrote the episode, the decision to conclude his character's tenure with the show in such a startling way an effective and noble one. *The Hogan Family* wasn't the first sitcom to discuss HIV and AIDS, but it was the first sitcom to kill off a recurring character from the dreaded disease. In the early 1990s, most people were still terrified of AIDS and generally ill informed. "The Best of Friends, the Worst of Times" helped to provide a platform for discussion on the topic, using the character of Rich's tragedy as a means to make the monumental losses that AIDS was accumulating a palpable one for those who had no experience with it firsthand.

Head of the Class

LET THE LEARNING BEGIN

Aired: September 17, 1986–June 25, 1991

Network: ABC

Created by: Michael Elias and Rich Eustis

Cast: Howard Hesseman (Charles P. "Charlie" Moore), Billy Connolly (Billy MacGregor), William G. Schilling (Harold Samuel), Jeannetta Arnette (Bernadette Meara), Leslie Bega (Maria Borges), Dan Frischman (Arvid Engen), Robin Givens (Darlene Merriman), Khrystyne Haje (Simone Foster), Jory Husain (Jawaharlal Choudhury), Tony O'Dell (Alan Pinkard), Brian Robbins (Eric Mardian), Kimberly Russell (Sarah Nevins), Dan Schneider (Dennis Blunden), Tannis Vallely (Janice Lazarotto), Michael DeLorenzo (Alex Torres), Lara Piper (Vicky Amory), Rain Pryor (Theola June "T.J." Jones), Jonathan Ke Quan (Jasper Kwong), De'voreaux White (Aristotle McKenzie)

Theme Song: "Theme to *Head of the Class*," composed by Ed Alton

In the 1980s, it was a trend to set sitcoms in the classroom and reveal the questions and concerns of teenagers as they journeyed through one of life's most trying and confusing obstacles: puberty. *The Facts of Life* gave us a compelling understanding of the female jaunt through adolescence, and *Good Morning, Miss Bliss* (and its ultimate transformation into *Saved by the Bell*) gave us a sanitized, more wholesome look at the teenager's world. What was lacking in these sitcoms was a sense of diversity. They skewed toward perspectives of the average (often generalized) Caucasian experience with an occasional minority in the cast to perhaps open the door for episodes of topical social relevance.

In 1986 came *Head of the Class*, a sitcom created by Michael Elias and Rich Eustis that found a wider variety of stories to tell. The show followed aspiring actor and teacher Charlie Moore (Howard Hesseman of *WKRP in Cincinnati* fame), an instructor of a classroom full of gifted, Individualized Honors Program (IHP), high school students at Manhattan's Millard Fillmore High School. First brought in as a substitute teacher, Mr. Moore had some unconventional teaching methods that clicked with his 10 brainy students. He was asked to continue his work by the blustering principal, Dr. Harold Samuels, who was in constant disagreement with Moore's methods, and the more levelheaded vice principal, Bernadette Meara.

What set *Head of the Class* apart from other high school set sitcoms was the diversity found in Mr. Moore's classroom. Not since *Welcome Back, Kotter* had such a cross section of ethnicities, races, and creeds populated a TV sitcom. In the case of *Head of the Class*, however, focus was split equally between boys and girls. Among the intelligent menagerie were Arvid Engen (Dan Frischman), the nerdiest of the bunch in the stereotypical way (math genius, eyeglasses, and pocket protectors). Arvid's best friend was the overweight, sarcastic chemist, physicist, and computer whiz Dennis Blunden (Dan Schneider, who would go on to create series for Nickelodeon such as *Drake & Josh*, *iCarly*, and *Zoey 101*). Alan Pinkard was the classroom preppy. Self-absorbed and often condescending, sporting pretty-boy looks, Alan's specialty was political science (he leaned conservative and championed the administration of then President Ronald Reagan). Speech and debate were covered by the equally spoiled and arrogant Darlene

Dan Schneider, Leslie Bega, Khrystyne Haje, Jory Hussain, Tony O'Dell, and Tannis Vallely in *Head of the Class*. ABC/Photofest © ABC

Merriman, an African American girl from an affluent family. Sarah Nevins was the most diversely talented of the bunch, without specialty, but also the least eccentric in the IHP class. Maria Borges was a young Latina girl who seemed less interested in quality of learning and more focused on getting straight A's, a goal that led to her putting a lot of pressure on herself. A foreign exchange student from India came in the person of Jawaharlal Choudhury, an affable young man with a penchant for natural science. Janice Lazarotto, the youngest member of the class and advanced beyond her years, sometimes felt out of place with the older kids. Simone Foster was the artistic one in the class, with interests in drama and poetry. Simone would eventually have a relationship with classmate Eric Mardian, a creative writer with a terrible (and sometimes aggressive) attitude that made him hard to like.

The students of Mr. Moore's class offered viewers a classroom that most likely gave them someone they could relate to. With such a range of diversity and personality types, it was hard to feel like you were left out of the equation. Sure, the show often dealt in generalizations and stereotypes (this was the 1980s after all), but it felt more inclusive than any other high school–set sitcom to date. It also sought to extinguish the stigma of being smart—that being gifted did not make a kid an outcast but instead presented him or her as having something special to offer. Although the kids in Mr. Moore's class found themselves regularly at odds with one another, they became a family and would look out for each other, especially if an outsider came after one of their own. Bullies beware, the IHP students had each other's backs.

Of course, changes in the cast happened when students departed for college or moved away, making room for new students in the classroom. Maria went to a performing arts high school. Janice was accepted at Harvard and went on to the university. Jawaharlal's family moved to California. New students included Alex Torres a parochial school transfer; Aristotle McKenzie; quantum physicist Vicky Emory; T.J. Jones; and another exchange student, Jasper Kwong. The biggest change, however, was not in the student body but rather in the departure of their teacher, Mr. Moore, at the end of season 4.

When season 5 commenced, the students in the IHP classroom are shocked to learn that Mr. Moore will not be returning, his acting career having finally taken off. He would be replaced by Scottish teacher Billy MacGregor (Billy Connolly), a less laid-back teacher whom the kids initially didn't care for but ultimately embraced. The reason for Hesseman's departure was that he had grown frustrated with the show and its direction:

> We're not doing the show that I was led to believe I'd do, and it's difficult for me to get off that. I don't want to air dirty laundry in public, but I do feel that the educational arena is one that offers a

variety of story ideas as a means of investigating our lives—what we mean to one another and what's important.[1]

He felt that the show was resorting to one-liner jokes and not humor that derived from the situation, which he felt was rife for dealing with more topical, character-driven humor.

Head of the Class lasted for only that one additional season on Hesseman's exit. Connolly's character was given a spin-off show called *Billy*, where he moved to Berkeley, California, and married a single mother with children so that he could get his green card and avoid deportation. Billy lasted for half a season and was canceled after 13 episodes.

Designing Women

GEORGIA ON MY MIND

Aired: September 29, 1986–May 24, 1993
Network: CBS
Created by: Linda Bloodworth-Thomason
Cast: Dixie Carter (Julia Sugarbaker), Annie Potts (Mary Jo Shivley), Jean Smart (Charlene Frazier-Stillfield), Delta Burke (Suzanne Sugarbaker), Meshach Taylor (Anthony Bouvier), Julia Duffy (Allison Sugarbaker), Jan Hooks (Carlene Frazier-Dobber), Judith Ivey (Bonnie Jean "B.J." Poteet), Alice Ghostley (Bernice Clifton)
Theme Song: "Georgia on My Mind," by Hoagy Carmichael and Stuart Gorrell (performed by Doc Severinsen, instrumental, seasons 1 to 5, and Ray Charles, season 6)

A TV show that rivals *All in the Family* for its audacity and willingness to take on difficult topics in a comedic way is *Designing Women*. Running on CBS from 1986 to 1993, the program is practically a checklist of the contemporary issues that were on many people's minds. *Designing Women* was created by Linda Bloodworth-Thomason, and together with her husband Harry Thomason they produced the program. Bloodworth-Thomason, who was a close personal friend of Bill and Hillary Clinton, was not afraid to infuse the program with her liberal bent, often using the program to address the social issues that were important to her. This is, perhaps, why *Designing Women* could be such a divisive program, viewers either embracing its message or rejecting it. Never a top 10 show in the ratings, it held strong at the height of its popularity in the top 20 to 30. Regardless of where one stands on the program's political agenda, one has to admit that it was addressing potent and polarizing issues in a way few television sitcoms dared. Moreover, it did so in abundance. *Designing Women* delved deeply into a litany of subjects, including feminism, body image, politics, homosexuality,

AIDS, sexual assault, racism, health care, single parenting, immigration, aging, spousal abuse, the Gulf War—you name it.

Designing Women was set in Atlanta, Georgia, at the interior design firm known as Sugarbakers. The business occupied the home of Julia Sugarbaker, the founding partner in the firm. Julia was a regal, elegant woman, dripping of etiquette and propriety until her ire was raised. Then Julia morphed into an outspoken soldier for issues that were important to her. Erudite and eloquent, she would launch into monologue tirades that decimated the object of her scorn, leading to her coworkers affectionately nicknaming her "The Terminator." Joining Julia at Sugarbakers was her sister Suzanne, an often married former beauty queen who spoke her mind to the chagrin of Julia, who found Suzanne's opinions uninformed and politically incorrect (think a much sweeter, prettier Archie Bunker). Suzanne often found herself at odds with her more progressive coworkers and regularly served as a foil to the show's penchant toward liberal-tilting story lines. She was, however, vivacious and charming, possessing a heart of gold and capable of evolving through her experiences. Mary Jo Shively was a recently divorced mother of two who was initially mousey and indecisive. As the show progressed, Mary Jo came out of her shell, trying new things and sampling the variety of life afforded by her independence from a cheating, manipulative husband. By the show's conclusion seven seasons later, she had become a confident, self-realized woman. Completing the initial *Designing Women* quartet was Charlene Frazier, the firm's business manager. Charlene had grown up in the rural South, in a large religious family. Often trusting to a fault, Charlene could be naive but preferred to see the best in everyone. She and Mary Jo were close friends. During her tenure on the show, Charlene met and married Air Force colonel Bill Stillfield (Douglas Barr), and she eventually gave birth to a daughter, Olivia.

Sugarbakers also employed a delivery man named Anthony Bouvier, an ex-convict who ultimately had his conviction overturned. In time, Anthony went to college to study law and bought into Sugarbakers, becoming a partner and overcoming many of the obstacles that society's perceptions of his race and background had put in his path. Anthony had a close relationship with Julia, whom he looked to as a godmother, and with Suzanne, who, despite her early reservations about hiring an ex-con, grew to see Anthony as her best friend. Also along for many of the *Designing Women* adventures was Bernice Clifton, a family friend living in a retirement community. Suffering an "arterial flow problem to the brain," Bernice brought crazy antics to the program (often some of the show's more hilarious), but she also provided an opportunity to explore how the aging were treated in America. Bernice fiercely loved the inhabitants of Sugarbakers, though she often caused them a great deal of embarrassment with her unfiltered stream of thought and peculiar notions. All of these characters came

Dixie Carter, Jean Smart, Delta Burke, and Annie Potts in *Designing Women. CBS/Photofest © CBS*

together to create the perfect storm for addressing the myriad social concerns that the show sought to shed light on.

A poignant episode featured Charlene's doctor finding a lump in her breast but dismissing it and telling her to let him do the worrying. Julia insists that Charlene get a second opinion, with the result that the growth is cancerous. "Old Spouses Never Die" was a two-part episode that culminated in Julia doing her research and approaching Charlene's initial doctor, icily reprimanding him for the women whose cancer had spread under his care. Quoting his statement about doing the worrying, she points out that "you're not the one who has to do the dying." The episode underlined the importance of women getting regular mammograms and not being complacent about their health, especially when patriarchal male doctors are involved.

As has been mentioned several times in this book, the 1980s was a time when AIDS was casting a pall over the United States, frightening everyone with both its death toll and misinformation. "Killing All the Right People" found the Sugarbaker ladies facing the disease when one of their friends and colleagues, Kendall Dobbs (Tony Goldwyn), reveals that he is dying from it. One of their customers overhears a discussion with Kendall and attacks both Kendall and the ladies, exclaiming, "This disease has one thing going for it: it's killing all the right people." An incensed Julia dresses her down for her insensitive, ignorant remarks and then closes out the woman's account, practically defenestrating her in one of her best tirades. Meanwhile, Mary Jo attends her school's PTA meeting, where the discussion turns to the distribution of condemns to teenagers. Mary Jo, deeply moved and conflicted by Kendall's scenario, speaks up on behalf of keeping kids safe. Nicknamed "The Condom Queen," she is tasked with leading the debate in favor of contraception. In the end, she makes the argument that "more important than what any civic leaders, PTA, or Board of Education think about teenagers having sex, or any immoral act that my daughter or your son might engage in . . . the bottom line is I don't think they should have to die for it." "Killing All the Right People" was undoubtedly inspired by Thomason's experience with her mother, who contracted AIDS through a blood transfusion. In her mother's final days, while wandering the hospital, Thomason overheard someone say that AIDS was "killing all the right people." Art reflects and imitates life, with Bloodworth-Thomason receiving an Emmy nomination for writing the episode, which closed with the ladies attending Kendall's funeral.

Soap opera star Kim Zimmer made a guest appearance on *Designing Women* in an episode called "The Rowdy Girls." Playing the role of Mavis, an old friend of Charlene's, she is helping the ladies choreograph an act they are putting together for a fund-raiser. Mavis's husband, however, though warm and welcoming to the ladies when they are around, beats Mavis and verbally abuses her when they are not. Charlene accidentally walks in on one of the incidents and pleads with Mavis to take her kids and leave. Mavis has nothing—no job, no money, no home, and no security without her husband—so she is terrified to walk out on her abuser. Charlene promises to help her through it and finally convinces her to take the steps. The ladies also pitch in and write checks to help give Mavis a fresh start. "The Rowdy Girls" helped to combat the stigma suffered by those trapped in abusive relationships, demonstrating that there was no shame in leaving.

In a hilarious episode titled "Big Haas and Little Falsie," Mary Jo finds herself coming into unexpected money and decides that she wants to spend it on a breast augmentation. Trying out false pairs of different sizes, she feels that she is being treated differently, that the bigger the set, the more power they seem to wield. Her personality changes, making her aggressive and preoccupied with how people respond to the bigger cup size she is flaunting. Most of this is in her mind, her insecurities exacerbated by the societal celebration of buxom body types. In the end, she decides that she is happy with what she has and reverts to the Mary Jo everyone loves. What makes this a standout episode is that it puts under a magnifying glass how many people suffer from negative body images and how they compare themselves to others in estimating their own self-worth.

Arguably the show's most affecting episode was titled "They Shoot Fat Women, Don't They?" Delta Burke had gained a significant amount of weight over her five seasons with the show, and it became apparent that this needed to be addressed with her character. The episode involved Suzanne going to her high school reunion only to be ridiculed by former classmates for the pounds she had put on, then throngs delighting in the idea that a former beauty queen was no longer the ideal. This story line was juxtaposed against a secondary plot where Anthony was fund-raising for starving Ethiopian children, signing up Julia and Mary Jo for a fast wherein they could barely stand to go without food for 24 hours. "They Shoot Fat Women, Don't They?" took a hard look at the First World problem of having more than enough food to eat while simultaneously drawing attention to the cruelty of fat shaming and how many Americans resort to food as an emotional crutch.

It is, however, through the character of Julia Sugarbaker and Dixie Carter's indelible performance that the show spoke with the most political ferocity. In an episode called "The Candidate" written by Bloodworth-Thomason, Julia finds herself running for city commissioner against an opponent with repugnant views on women, the poor, and so on. Julia lets loose with a diatribe that sums up both her character and *Designing Women*'s undaunted approach to tackling pertinent issues:

> I do not think everyone in America is ignorant! Far from it!! But we are today, probably, the most uneducated, under read, and illiterate nation in the Western Hemisphere. Which makes it all the more puzzling to me why the biggest question on your small mind is whether or not little Johnny is gonna recite the Pledge of Allegiance every morning! I'll tell you something else, Mr. Brickett. I have had it up to here with you and your phony issues and your Yankee Doodle yakking! If you like reciting the Pledge of Allegiance every day then I think you should do it! In the car! In the shower! Wherever the mood strikes you! But don't try to tell me when or where I have to say or do or salute anything, because I am an American too, and that is what being an American is all about! And another thing . . . I am sick and tired of being made to feel that if I am not a member of a little family with 2.4 children who goes to Jerry Falwell's church and puts their hands over their hearts every morning that I am unreligious, unpatriotic, and un-American! Because I've got news for you, Mr. Brickett . . . all liberals are not kooks, any more than all conservatives are fascists! And the last time I checked, God was neither a Democrat nor a Republican! And just for your information, yes I am a liberal, but I am also a Christian. And I get down on my knees and pray every day—on my own turf—on my own time. One of the things that I pray for, Mr. Brickett, is that people with power will get good sense, and that people with good sense will get power . . . and that the rest of us will be blessed with the patience and the strength to survive the people like you in the meantime!!

After *Designing Women*'s fifth season, the program went through many changes. Both Delta Burke and Jean Smart chose to exit the program and were replaced with characters that were ineffective attempts to fill their void. Julia Duffy (more or less) replaced Burke, playing the character of Alison Sugarbaker, a snooty family cousin who bought Suzanne's share in the business and had designs on taking over. Jan Hooks, playing Charlene's dimwitted sister Carlene Dobber, took over as the office manager. After one season, Duffy departed and for the final season was replaced by a kindly wealthy woman named B.J. Poteet (played by Judith Ivey), who joined the firm. The show never regained the sense of camaraderie that was felt among the original four, and *Designing Women* was canceled after season 7 and 163 episodes. Despite its revered writing, unforgettable performances, and important legacy in television, *Designing Women* won only one Emmy Award (for Outstanding Achievement in Hairstyling), in 1988. Interestingly enough, the show did receive a spin-off called *Women of the House* (1995), starring Delta Burke reprising her role as Suzanne Sugarbaker, her character going to Washington, D.C., to take over a congressional seat left vacant by her deceased husband. The show lasted half a season (13 episodes).

Full House

WHATEVER HAPPENED TO PREDICTABILITY?

Aired: September 22, 1987–May 23, 1995
Network: ABC
Created by: Jeff Franklin
Cast: John Stamos (Jesse Katsopolis), Bob Saget (Danny Tanner), Dave Coulier (Joey Gladstone), Candace Cameron (D.J. Tanner), Jodie Sweetin (Stephanie Tanner), Mary-Kate and Ashley Olsen (Michelle Tanner), Lori Loughlin (Rebecca Donaldson Katsopolis), Andrea Barber (Kimmy Gibbler), Scott Weinger (Steve Hale), Blake and Dylan Tuomy-Wilhoit (Nicky and Alex Katsopolis)
Theme Song: "Everywhere You Look," by Jesse Frederick, Bennett Salvay, and Jeff Franklin (performed by Jesse Frederick)

Fathers raising children without mothers was nothing new on television when the sitcom *Full House* arrived on the scene in 1987. *Nanny and the Professor*, *The Courtship of Eddie's Father*, and *Diff'rent Strokes* had all featured widower dads getting by, albeit with domestics in their houses to handle the housekeeping, cooking, and tender side of raising the kids. But *Full House* took a big step in rewriting that script.

From 1987 to 1995, *Full House* took audiences into the home of Danny Tanner, a recently widowed father of three little girls living in San Francisco. A local television personality for the morning program *Wake Up, San Francisco*, Danny was having a hard time juggling both his work and his home life while also healing over the death of his wife Pam. Coming to the rescue were his brother-in-law, the Elvis-worshipping, motorcycle-riding, all-purpose cool dude Jessie Katsopolis, and Danny's goofy, practical joking best friend Joey Gladstone, who was a stand-up comedian and voice-over artist. The duo moved into Danny's house and helped him raise his three little ladies, with sticky sweet moments of family comedy that had a preachy aftertaste.

The kids were a darling brood, incorrigible but each cute as a button. Donna Jean, or "D.J." as she was typically addressed, was a bit of a know-it-all but always caring for her family. She spent most of her time with her obnoxious best friend Kimmy Gibbler, who lived next door. Next there was Stephanie, a frank and funny kid whose favorite catchphrase was "How rude!" Then there was the baby Michelle, a cute little cherub who had great facial expressions and one-liner deliveries to put the Pampers baby to shame. After a time, Uncle Jessie got married to Becky, Danny's coworker, and she moved into the growingly crowded home, where she became a surrogate mother to the Tanner girls as their "Aunt Becky." But, for a few seasons, it was just the men in the Tanner household, and much of the show's humor derived from their baptism by fire of adjusting to raising three girls.

So what was so revolutionary about *Full House*? The character of Danny Tanner was a television father that not only redesigned the model of a sitcom dad but also broke that model altogether. Danny was tender, he was affectionate with his kids, and he was always hugging everyone, including the adult men in the house. Danny was an immaculate housekeeper, a neat freak who loved to dust, polish, organize, and vacuum. He was a good listener, seldom angry, and could recognize his own shortcomings and limits. Not many sitcom dads had been painted in this light.

What *Full House* also did very well was show children (and adults) how boys can grow up to be good men. Despite his machismo, Uncle Jessie could put aside his rugged exterior to cradle a crying child or change a diaper. Uncle Joey could confess his failures and fears to his housemates. The male characters on the show were not afraid to be vulnerable in front of each other. How many television series, before or after *Full House*, have shown men exhibiting such sensitivity? *Full House* did not perpetuate the myth that men have to be tough, stoic, and commanding to run a household, but rather are capable of incorporating both masculine and feminine traits to be a parent who better serves and loves their children.

In 2016, the *Full House* story continued with the series returning on the streaming site Netflix under the title *Fuller House*. An adult D.J. (her last name is now "Fuller") has been recently widowed and left to raise her three boys on her own. Her dad has her family move into their old San Francisco house, then announcing that he is leaving for Los Angeles to be on a new morning program. To help D.J. out, her single sister Stephanie and her best friend Kimmy Gibbler (now a divorced mother with a teenage daughter) move in to help her. Sound familiar? *Fuller House* basically repeated the scenario of *Full House*, switching

Dave Coulier, Jodie Sweetin, John Stamos, Mary-Kate/Ashley Olsen, Bob Saget, Candace Cameron, and Andrea Barber in *Full House*. *ABC/Photofest © ABC*

out the raising of girls for the raising of boys. The cast also included Michael Campion, Elias Harger, and the duo of Dashiell and Fox Messitt to play D.J.'s sons Jackson, Max, and Tommy, respectively, as well as Soni Nicole Bringas as Kimmy's daughter Ramona, Juan Pablo Di Pace as Kimmy's ex-husband Fernando, John Brotherton as D.J.'s coworker and love interest Matt Harmon (the two ran an animal clinic together), and Kimmy's brother and Stephanie's love interest Jimmy Gibbler (Adam Hagenbuch). The cast of the original *Full House*, save the Olsen twins, made regular appearances on *Fuller House*.

The reboot was hardly as revolutionary as *Full House* had been, especially since it was modeled so closely after the original concept. The new incarnation, however, was extremely popular and, as of this writing, was just renewed for a fifth (and allegedly final) season. It is a testament to the popularity of the original, both in its first run on ABC as part of its TGIF lineup and then in syndication, that viewers flocked back to spend more time in the Tanner household.

Roseanne

IF WHAT DOESN'T KILL US IS MAKING US STRONGER

Aired: October 18, 1988–May 20, 1997, and March 27, 2018–May 22, 2018

Network: ABC

Created by: Matt Williams

Cast: Roseanne Barr (Roseanne Conner), John Goodman (Dan Conner), Laurie Metcalf (Jackie Harris), Sara Gilbert (Darlene Conner-Healy), Michael Fishman (Daniel Jacob "D.J." Conner), Alicia "Lecy" Goranson (Rebecca "Becky" Conner-Healy, seasons 1 to 5 and 8), Sarah Chalke (Rebecca "Becky" Conner-Healy, seasons 6, 7, and 9), Natalie West (Crystal Anderson Conner), Estelle Parsons (Beverly Harris), Johnny Galecki (David Healy), Glenn Quinn (Mark Healy), Emma Kenney (Harris Conner-Healy), Ames McNamara (Mark Conner-Healy), Jayden Rey (Mary Conner)

Theme Song: "Theme to *Roseanne*," composed by Dan Foliart and Howard Pearl, with John Juke Logan

Television comedy has typically tried to capture a rosy side of America, staying clear of issues that might put a damper on the purpose of comedy, which was always about creating escapist entertainment. Early television families were painted as perfect, the parents beyond reproach for anything more than offering a heavy-handed lesson for the wayward scamps and date-crazy teenagers who might stay out 10 minutes past curfew. Serious matters simply were not discussed, as writers hadn't quite figured out how to use comedy as commentary on life's bigger challenges.

In the 1970s, television took a sharp turn in its depiction of sitcom families. Shows like *All in the Family* and particularly *Good Times* began telling real stories of working-class families and their day-to-day struggles. Problems were not always neatly wrapped up at the end of each episode, and often the characters and their lives were left in a state of ambiguity regarding their eventual outcomes. A family such as the Evanses of *Good Times* didn't always settle in for a nice supper of meat and potatoes but often had to content themselves (and barely fill their bellies) on a pot of oatmeal. Archie Bunker worried about his job and wasn't sure from week to week if he could take care of his bills and keep a roof over his family's head. Television comedy had embraced the concerns of the blue-collar American clan and begun to lend credence to the burdens of survival that many Americans were experiencing due to inflation, unemployment, and the financial black holes that were almost impossible to climb out of as a result of their stations in life.

A groundbreaking TV show that started in 1988 and ran until 1997, only to return in 2017 to cause a whole new whirlwind of controversy for different reasons, was the hit sitcom *Roseanne*. The series was built around the talents of stand-up comedian Roseanne Barr, a loud and abrasive personality who prided herself on her brazen humor and no-holds-barred delivery. The sitcom followed the Conners, a family in Lanford, Illinois, who had a hard time making ends meet. Often living in constant worry of the electricity being turned off and not being able to make their mortgage payments, *Roseanne* was one of the few TV shows to directly deal with the struggles of the working class and capture their

Laurie Metcalf, Michael Fishman, Roseanne Barr, Alicia Goranson, John Goodman, and Sara Gilbert in *Roseanne*. ABC/Photofest © ABC

fears, their realities, and their inherent fortitude. Along the way, the series regularly delved into topical issues of an ever-changing America and how the family would adjust and evolve to deal with them.

The matriarch of the home was Roseanne Conner, a homemaker and mother who also held several low-paying (and sometimes degrading) jobs in order to supplement the family income. She held positions in fast-food restaurants, in a factory, in a hair salon, selling magazine subscriptions, and waitressing. Her thorny and outspoken manner made her a lovable curmudgeon, but her personality often found her at odds with employers, customers, and certain members of her family. Roseanne was a survivor of abuse in a dysfunctional family, often turning to food to eat her feelings as she dealt with the ghosts of her childhood. Her sister Jackie was a neurotic mess, coming to Roseanne in search of answers to her myriad problems, even as she lent her unwavering support in return. Jackie cycled through several jobs as well, including factory work, becoming a cop and a truck driver, and ultimately going into business with her sister, running a diner called The Lunch Box, where their signature dish was loose meat sandwiches. Roseanne's husband Dan was a hardworking man who labored in construction, taking jobs doing drywall (something he detested) to keep his family fed. Dan had weight issues as well, and though he was a teddy bear at heart, he could be quick to temper and was typically set in his ways. He could get depressed, discouraged, and sometimes fly off the handle, yet he and Roseanne enjoyed each other, had a healthy sex life, and were always each other's rock.

The Conners also had three children who were atypical of the sitcom brood as painted by television up until that point. The eldest was Becky, a smart and clever girl who Roseanne often relied on to run the household while she and Dan were working. Becky appeared to be college bound, but she dropped all of her future plans (at least for the time being) to elope with her tough-guy boyfriend Mark in an effort to give her parents one less mouth to feed. She could also be self-centered, concerned about getting what she wanted at any cost, so her motives were rarely as altruistic as her reasons for elopement might suggest. Mark is offered a job in Minnesota, so rather than see her boyfriend move away and their relationship end, Becky uses the family's financial woes as an excuse for running away and keeping the man-boy she loves. The middle child is Darlene, a sarcastic kid who is an athlete and a promising writer. Moody, morose, and usually caustic toward family members, Darlene dreams of escaping the town of Lanford and becoming an author of comic books. When she meets Mark's brother David, a sensitive artist, she teams up with him to create their comics and graphic novels. Afraid of exploring her emotions, Darlene ultimately falls for David, the two sharing a dysfunctional relationship where she is domineering and he is a pushover. The third child was D.J., an oblivious scamp with strange hobbies, such as collecting doll parts under his bed, and a generally bad attitude where his older siblings were concerned. D.J. was the least clearly drawn character of the show, serving as a means of annoyance for his two sisters and the occasional comedic shenanigans that catered to the show's subplots. As the series progressed, D.J. developed an interest in filmmaking and would begin dating, but he never shed his strange-kid persona. These three kids made up the balance of Roseanne and Dan's family, and there was nothing conventional about them with regard to how television kids had been depicted. They were mouthy. They didn't learn lessons easily. They made bad choices. They resented things about their parents. There was an authenticity about them that we had yet to encounter on television. But more on that later.

Where *Roseanne* was most riveting and, ultimately, most effective was the way it tossed reverence aside and delved into the imperfect, human side of humanity. America had simply been too uptight and conservative about how it represented a cross section of America as it really was. *Roseanne* was not afraid to introduce characters that challenged late 1980s/early 1990s television audiences. It featured a parade of recurring characters that looked nothing like what America was used to and utilized these characters to address a wide range of topics that were, at the time, relatively new and shocking to find in a sitcom. Among them was Roseanne's gay boss Leon Carp (Martin Mull), with whom she enjoyed an adversarial relationship, though she was very supportive of his sexuality, even volunteering to plan his wedding to his partner Scott (Fred Willard). This was long before gay marriage would be legalized in all 50 states in 2015. Roseanne and Jackie were friends with a woman named Nancy (Sandra Bernhard), who initially was enamored with and then married to the dimwitted Arnie (played by Barr's then husband Tom Arnold), but after their divorce decided to declare herself interested in women and enter into a lesbian relationship with Marla (Morgan Fairchild). Although these characters were depicted with a great deal of humor, they were also given a great deal of heart. By making them recurring characters, *Roseanne* cast them as a part of the television world, not just as guests of one-off episodes dealing with a timely topic that would fade away.

There were many episodes of *Roseanne* that became iconic, specifically for how they handled the truth of who we are as people. This was a refreshing change for television, which had tried to paint characters mostly as incapable of having weaknesses, faults, and idiosyncrasies that could be resolved within the confines of a half hour. Although it is hardly groundbreaking in terms of the change it brought to television, one episode in particular illustrates how *Roseanne* embraced our faults, foibles, and differences with unyielding honesty and hilarious comedy. The first episode of season 2, titled "Inherit the Wind," took on a topic we had never seen explored in situation comedy: flatulence. Becky, who is always concerned about other people's perceptions of her, is making a speech in front of the student council (including a boy she is interested in dating). In the middle of her big moment, she accidentally breaks wind and becomes the laughingstock of the whole school. When had television done this? When had it taken something so basic as the human function of farting (a taboo subject on television at the time) and addressed it head-on? A teenager's humiliation can be devastating, but "cutting the cheese" is also funny. The series married the two in a way that paved new avenues for the show to probe delicate subjects.

In season 4, episode 1, another story revolving around Becky was treading uneasy territory. With teenagers growing more sexually active as each decade progressed, the eldest Conner girl was becoming sexually active with her boyfriend Mark. Becky approached her mother and asked to be put on birth control pills. Roseanne is torn. She wanted to maintain an open dialogue with her daughter about safe sex but also believed that Becky was too young to be having intercourse. "A Bitter Pill to Swallow" was addressing concerns that many parents were having over their kids' sexual activities. By example, *Roseanne* offered a template for parents to follow on how to have this discussion or, at the very least, offered an alternative scenario to blowing up at the teen and saying no. Roseanne agreed to get Becky the pills, even as her husband Dan unwittingly hires Mark to work as a mechanic in his bike shop, creating a tense situation when he finds out that Mark and Becky are having sex.

An episode that rubbed some people the wrong way (no pun intended) came in season 6, episode 7, called "Homeward Bound." D.J., who has launched into puberty, has begun masturbating and is horrified when the family figures out that this is the reason why he has been locking himself in the bathroom for long periods of time. In one of the more awkward parent–child scenes made for television, Dan tries to talk to his son about his newfound hobby. He tries to relate to the kid, reassuring him that masturbation is okay and that almost everyone does it. D.J. turns the tables on his father, asking him, "Do you do it?" Dan, embarrassed as most fathers would be, tells him that even though it is natural and a part of growing up, nobody talks about it. What a compelling message to put out there on a hit television show, letting the multitudes know that self-pleasure is not something to be embarrassed by and that we can have an open dialogue about it. Hasn't every teenager wrestled with the closet guilt of this situation? Hasn't every parent been mortified that he or she would have to address this at some point or another?

In "Don't Ask, Don't Tell" (season 6, episode 18), soon after Roseanne found out that Nancy is interested in women, she agreed to go on a girls' outing to a gay bar to prove that she is cool with her friend being a lesbian. She, Jackie, Nancy, and Nancy's girlfriend Sharon (Mariel Hemingway) visited the pub "Lips," and everything appeared to be going well until Sharon planted a kiss on Roseanne. Obviously, this threw her, and she began questioning just how "okay" she was with homosexuality. The episode itself caused more controversy at the network (ABC) than was initially expected. Producer Tom Arnold (Barr's husband at the time) was told that fear of sponsor backlash would keep them from airing the episode and that a million dollars in revenue was at stake. Roseanne herself, always an advocate of LGBTQ representation on television, threatened to take the show and move to another network. The Gay and Lesbian Alliance Against Defamation came to her side, asking ABC to reconsider and show the kiss. *Roseanne* was one of ABC's top-performing shows in the ratings and, reluctantly, agreed to air "Don't Ask, Don't Tell." Barr spoke out about the standoff in the weeks leading up to the episode, questioning how a network that continually represented women being beaten, raped, shot, and mutilated could have a problem with two women sharing a kiss.

But *Roseanne* was not a show that was focused purely on sexual discovery and sexual orientation; it simply revolutionized how television could and would comment on these prickly topics. There were other pressing social issues that the show would explore, sometimes with harrowing results and to great effect. In season 5, episode 13, "Crime and Punishment," and its follow-up, "War and Peace," Jackie is having a relationship with a man named Fisher (Matthew Roth), and everything seems to be going well for her. Darlene walks in on Jackie when she is changing her clothes and sees that she has been beaten black and blue. When Darlene reveals this to Roseanne, she confronts Jackie, who admits that Fisher has been hitting her but blames herself and the pressures that he is under from being unemployed for the abuse. Roseanne wants her to go to the hospital to be checked out, but Jackie is afraid that everyone in town will find out. Roseanne convinces her to go to a hospital out of town while Dan, ever protective of his sister-in-law, beats Fisher up and is arrested. Insisting that Jackie leave him immediately, Roseanne accompanies her to Fisher's apartment so she can get her things. There, they encounter Fisher, and despite Roseanne's instincts to take control of the situation, Jackie summons the strength to end the relationship. Domestic violence had been handled on television before, but the stark brutality and Jackie's palpable fear and conflict in these two installments spoke volumes to the reality of the situation. Women (or anyone is an abusive relationship) needed options, resources, and support, and here was a television sitcom character, someone audiences knew intimately, keeping this dark secret and having the subsequent epiphany that she had to find a way out. According to domesticviolencestatistics.org, a woman is assaulted or beaten every nine seconds in the United States, a staggering figure. In many ways, this story line cast a ray of hope for the viewers in that situation.

What *Roseanne* also did very well was paint the dysfunctional family dynamic with authenticity. This family fought. The Conners and Harrises could hold a grudge and carry resentment toward each other. In one emotionally charged episode called "Wait till Your Father Gets Home" (season 5, episode 16), Roseanne must deal with the death of her philandering and abusive father. As her mother Beverly (Estelle Parsons) goes on a tirade toward the father's mistress (in a moment of comic genius), Roseanne stands over her father's casket and reads a letter, unloading all of the pent-up hurt and resentment she has been carrying for years. Also, the program was no less forgiving toward Roseanne and Jackie's mother Bev, a high-pitched shrew who criticized everyone, used her money in controlling ways, and gouged at the self-esteem of her two girls. There was never any question that Bev loved Jackie and Roseanne, but she very seldom encouraged them or had anything positive to say about them. This spoke perfectly to any viewer who had been in a similar boat. You can love your family without necessarily liking them. Dan loved all three of his children immensely and, despite his occasional crustiness, showed them affection regularly. However, this didn't stop him from shutting out Becky for a period after her elopement. He hurt, and he didn't know how to process it.

Although Roseanne could be controversial and topical, it was most certainly and foremost a funny program. It took the angle that we are stuck with our family, so why not make the best of the situation and laugh at how we behave as a unit? Arguably, the show's most delightful installments were the annual Thanksgiving episodes, which often found the entire family (including the cool but crazy Nana Mary played by Oscar-winner Shelly Winters) gathering for a yearly argument that would have audiences in stitches. A close second were the Halloween episodes, complete with the Conners, who felt that they were the masters of clever costumes (they were), showing off their yearly creations at the lodge Halloween party. For many, the Conners were simply relatable, and their story mirrored much of what working-class America was about. If, perhaps, the show sometimes took on too many issues or felt a little over the top for some, the earnestness and heart with which the show gave a voice to working-class families made it an unqualified, unmissable hit. Indeed, the show ranked number 1 in the Nielsen ratings after its second season, dethroning the beloved *Cosby Show*, which had held that position for five seasons running. During its first six seasons, *Roseanne* landed in the top five. Whether or not some people were turned off by the show, it's audacity did little to decrease audiences.

As the show wore on, it began to unravel. The final season brought with it the ridiculous premise that the Conners had won the lottery and suddenly their worries and woes were gone. Dan suffered a heart attack and then cheated on Roseanne. Jackie was courted by royalty. Roseanne went on a whirlwind travel excursion. The dynamics, the relationships, and the situations that the audiences loved about *Roseanne* were no longer there. Perhaps the controversy had all been used up. In the final episode, we find out that the whole series had been a book written by Roseanne and that some of the realities we had come to accept about characters had been fictionalized. For example, Dan had died after the heart attack, and making him a cheater was Roseanne's coping mechanism, preferring to think that he was away instead of gone for good. So little of what happened in that final season or the explanations that were offered in that final episode were true to the show's first eight seasons. *Roseanne*, unfortunately, ended on a low note.

Until . . .

On March 27, 2018, *Roseanne* returned for a tenth season, more than two decades after it had ended. The program had remained alive in the hearts of those who had grown up watching it, and ABC saw fit to give it a reboot with the entire original cast returning. The writers basically decided to pretend that season 9 had never happened (something most viewers were glad to embrace). This meant that Dan was still alive and still doing drywall. Roseanne was now a doting grandmother. Jackie had become a life coach but had Bev living with her. Becky, whose husband had died, was working in a Mexican restaurant and trying to have a baby. Darlene and David were divorced, with Darlene and her two kids, the snarky Harris and the gender-fluid Mark, all living with Grandma and Grandpa. D.J. was married to a deployed soldier named Geena (Maya Lynne Robinson), and together they had a daughter named Mary. Despite having many unanswered questions and plot points that didn't quite match up with character story arcs of the original, the reboot's premiere was a ratings lovefest. It set records, having been seen by 18.45 million viewers, and continued to perform well.

Frustratingly, however, Roseanne Barr had changed over the two-decade hiatus, and her tone and influence on the program reflected that. Roseanne (Barr and Conner) was a Trump supporter. She was suspicious of her Muslim neighbors. She wrestled with the gender fluidity of her grandchild. Where was the Roseanne Conner we knew and loved? How could she have become so conservative in her old age? In all fairness to Barr, this did create an interesting dynamic for the show, offering two sides on a multitude of issues that were dividing the nation. It just didn't feel true to a character that had bolstered confidence and pushed progressive points in the late 1980s and early 1990s. Ultimately, Roseanne Barr would make an egregious mistake that would result in the show's cancellation. A vocal conservative on social media, Barr took to her Twitter account and made some racially insensitive comments about Valarie Jarrett, an African American woman who had been a senior adviser to President Obama, suggesting that Jarrett was the result of the Muslim Brotherhood and Planet of the Apes having a baby. There was an understandable uproar, and ABC bore the brunt of it. Unable to reconcile the actress's words with the character she played, they decided to cancel the *Roseanne* reboot after one season.

Until . . .

Audiences loved the reboot, and the writers, performers, designers, and technicians wanted to keep their jobs. There were whisperings that the show might return sans Barr. Barr herself, who owned the show, gave her blessing for all involved to move ahead without her. In the fall of 2018, the show (redubbed *The Conners*) returned. Barr's absence was attributed to her character's accidental overdose from painkillers. All other plot points essentially stayed the same. *The Conners*, however, did not enjoy the same ratings as season 10 of *Roseanne*, but it did well enough. It remains to be seen where the story of the Conner clan will lead next and for how long audiences will continue to embrace them. Without Barr's signature personality and wit, the show is missing what always made it unique. That nine-year run was a freight train of humor, heart, and comedy delving into the difficulties of life.

Murphy Brown

R-E-S-P-E-C-T

Aired: November 14, 1988–May 18, 1998, and September 27, 2018–present
Network: CBS
Created by: Diane English
Cast: Candice Bergen (Murphy Brown), Faith Ford (Corky Sherwood Forrest Silverberg), Charles Kimbrough (Jim Dial), Robert Pastorelli (Eldin Bernecky), Joe Regalbuto (Frank Fontana), Grant Shaud (Miles Silverberg), Pat Corley (Phil), Lily Tomlin (Kay Carter-Shepley), Jake McDorman (Avery Brown), Nik Dodani (Pat Patel), Adan Rocha (Miguel), Tyne Daly (Phyllis)
Theme Song: "Theme to *Murphy Brown*," by Steve Dorff

From the mid-1960s on, television has provided us with a bevy of female characters that are strong, successful, independent minded, and career driven: *That Girl*, *Julia*, *The Mary Tyler Moore Show*, Ann Romano of *One Day at a Time*, and the ladies of *Designing Women*. Each time this happens, it is greeted with a feeling of novelty, one that television has taken a giant step forward in representing "unconventional" females for the first time when in reality these women have always been a part of society. Why is it that these characters spent decades fighting to be part of the television norm only to be treated as an anomaly rather than the rule?

In 1988, another one of these compelling and fascinating characters joined the television landscape. Created by Diane English, *Murphy Brown* was a series that featured a titular character that broke with television convention on a variety of fronts, some of which brought new and polarizing perspectives on the sitcom woman and what she stood for. Murphy was a relentlessly driven reporter who seemed to function just fine with or without male companionship, she was used to getting her way at work, and could hound a source or an interviewee with dogged determination. She was a recovering alcoholic, and she also made the active choice to raise her child as a single parent. The combination of these things made Murphy Brown something fresh (and sometimes subversive) in the eyes of viewers. The show was not without its critics and detractors.

Murphy Brown was an investigative journalist for the popular nighttime newsmagazine program *FYI* (think *60 Minutes*) based in Washington, D.C. The locale provided plenty of opportunities for Murphy and her cohorts to encounter the politicians of the day and to make commentary on current policies. Murphy was a vocal liberal and feminist but also had hilarious quirks, such as her inability to go an episode without firing a secretary and an overt distaste for the musicals of Andrew Lloyd Webber (*Cats*, *The Phantom of the Opera*, and *Starlight Express*). She was also an ardent fan of singer Aretha Franklin, particularly her song "Respect."

At work, Murphy navigated (with little diplomacy) a crew of crazy co-workers. The wunderkind Miles Silverberg was a twitchy, nervous "kid" and the executive producer of *FYI* whom Murphy resented taking directives from, particularly because he was concerned with what the higher-ups would think. Jim Dial was the anchor of *FYI*, a rigid veteran newsman who tended toward an old-school approach to the news. Corky Sherwood was a perky, fluff-piece

Robert Pastorelli, Candice Bergen, Faith Ford, Charles Kimbrough, Pat Corley, and Joe Regalbuto in *Murphy Brown*. CBS/Photofest © CBS

reporter (Murphy's polar opposite) who was hired to replace Murphy while she was at the Betty Ford Clinic. The Murphy–Corky dynamic started as a frosty rivalry that eventually melted into friendship. Frank Fontana was Murphy's best friend and a feature reporter for *FYI* who typically opted for high adventure and daredevil assignments. Frank looked after Murphy and was often the only person in the office who could reason with her.

Outside of the office, the *FYI* gang would convene at the local restaurant/ pub "Phil's," run by its crusty but likable namesake. Phil's had been the hangout for politicians for decades, and the owner would often regale Murphy and friends with stories about his encounters. At home, Murphy was in constant state of renovation. Eldin Bernecky was a painter and handyman in charge of Murphy's never ending projects. It is suggested that Murphy liked having him around and kept the home improvements going, Eldin becoming a constant confidant whom she relied on.

In the show's 1991–1992 season, the series found Murphy Brown pregnant by her former husband Jake Lowenstein (Robin Thomas). Although Jake was willing to give up his current situation as an underground, leftist radical and help her raise the child, Murphy opted to be a single parent and rear the child on her own. This choice incited real-life protests against *Murphy Brown* and the character, with the likes of conservative pundits and personalities, as well as family groups, speaking out against the decision. Most notably, Vice President Dan Quayle, during his 1992 reelection campaign, spoke out against Murphy's choice of single motherhood, lamenting that it was "mocking the importance of fathers by bearing a child alone." Women and liberals were outraged because Murphy Brown was representative of a contingent of America who had demonstrated that they could raise children without a man and have them grow into well-adjusted adults.

The writers for *Murphy Brown* were not likely to remain silent over Quayle's judgment and condemnation. Remember, the show was already liberal leaning and quite adept at challenging real-life politicians within its fictional world. In the series' 1992 season premiere, *FYI* produced a special on family diversity in America, celebrating all the different configurations that reflected the wide range of possibilities in America. By manipulating footage of Quayle, they made it look and sound as though his diatribe was aimed directly at Murphy Brown as a person, not just a character on a sitcom. To add to his comeuppance, the series made fun of one of Quayle's public mishaps earlier that year. On June 15, 1992, at a spelling bee in Trenton, New Jersey, Quayle had corrected an elementary school student's spelling of "potato" to "potatoe." Quayle was often ridiculed in the media for incorrectly stating facts and making amusing gaffes. The episode of Murphy Brown that rebutted Quayle's argument was titled "You Say Potatoe, I Say Potato" and culminated with Murphy sending a truck full of spuds to be dumped outside the gate of Quayle's home. When Candice Bergen won an Emmy that season, she thanked the vice president in her acceptance speech.

Murphy Brown was a series that was not afraid to tackle anything. One particular story arc challenged the big-time tobacco industry. *FYI* attempts to do an exposé on the health risks of smoking only to have upper management try to put a lid on the piece. Jim Dial resigned in protest, then the other characters followed suit. For a time, they went to work for a struggling, fledgling network, taking over the news department. In the end, however, Miles, in a rare instance of backbone, stood up to the executives, reminded them of their obligation to report the news without bias, and championed the credentials and integrity of his *FYI* team. The network caved, the tobacco piece ran, and the team was reinstalled in their rightful place at the *FYI* news desk.

Murphy Brown enjoyed 10 seasons during its initial run. As controversial as the program often was, it was a critical darling and awards magnet. It won 18 Emmy Awards, including Outstanding Comedy Series in 1990 and 1992. Bergen won five Emmys for Best Leading Actress in a Comedy Series. The show was also celebrated with wins for its writing and directing. The show held tight in the ratings for many years, usually remaining in the Top 20.

In 2017, *Murphy Brown* was given a reboot, with most of the original cast returning for the fun. Murphy was host of her own show called *Murphy in the Morning*. With the advent of Donald Trump in the White House and the Republicans holding power in all three branches of government, it seemed like the optimal time for television's vocal liberal to rejoin television and provide commentary on the goings-on in Washington. As a clever plot twist, Murphy's (now grown) son Avery (Jake McDorman) is a staunch conservative who hosts his own program on a rival network, creating a tense relationship between mother and son.

The return of *Murphy Brown* struggled in large part because of its placement by CBS against the ratings juggernaut of football. However, the show also suffered from audiences being without her for two decades. Unlike the reboots of *Will & Grace*, *Roseanne*, and *Full House*, which have enjoyed a healthy life in syndication, *Murphy Brown* hadn't had that longevity. Due to royalty issues surrounding the popular music used on the show, it was not cost effective for networks to buy into *Murphy Brown* for syndication. Legwork would have had to be done to renegotiate terms on every individual song that was, in many cases, an intrinsic part of each episode. A similar fate had befallen *WKRP in Cincinnati* when the series went into syndication and also wanted to benefit from home video release. This was handled by editing out most of the music. *Murphy Brown*, however, was tethered to its sound track. Arguably, this lack of exposure to *Murphy Brown* may have inhibited audiences from tuning in for the reboot.

Ellen

YOU ONLY WANT US
WHEN WE'RE AT OUR BEST

Aired: March 29, 1994–July 22, 1998
Network: ABC
Created by: Neal Marlens, Carol Black, and David S. Rosenthal
Cast: Ellen DeGeneres (Ellen Morgan), Joely Fisher (Paige Clarke), Holly Fulger (Holly Jamison), Arye Gross (Adam Green), David Anthony Higgins (Joe Farrell), Clea Lewis (Audrey Penney), Jeremy Piven (Spence Kovak), Maggie Wheeler (Anita Warrell)
Theme Song: "So-Called Friends" (performed by Texas)

LGBTQ characters on television seem to be everywhere. In today's inclusive climate, they are far more frequent than they had been up until the 1990s. Sure, there would be a show that would throw a gay character in here or a lesbian character in there, more as the novelty of a very special episode touching on the AIDS crisis. There had also been Jodie Dallas, the recurring gay character on *Soap*, and as groundbreaking as that was, that had been mostly an exploration of gay stereotypes. Then the population of gay characters began to increase thanks to groundbreaking shows like *Roseanne*, which made them a big part of its parade of recurring supporting characters, and *Will & Grace*, which was making them a regular part of the leading-role landscape. It was, however, one lesbian performer and her alter ego on a popular sitcom that would do more for the representation and inclusion of LGBTQ characters on television than any other person or program.

Comedian Ellen DeGeneres was a lesbian succeeding in Hollywood as a seemingly straight performer (at least that was the assumption most people made). DeGeneres wasn't being intentionally duplicitous but simply navigating a business that favored a heterosexual persona to achieve success (sadly, that continues to be the case despite some strides toward diversity in the arena of sexual identity). Although being unconventional for the day, and her style and look evoking a certain androgyny, Ellen's work in the realm of stand-up comedy demonstrated there was an audience for her socially awkward characterizations and offbeat humor. Ultimately, this would lead to her sitcom *These Friends of Mine* for ABC. The title was eventually changed to *Ellen* for fear that it would be confused with NBC's megahit *Friends* (1994–2004), which had premiered the same year.

On *Ellen* (1994–1998), DeGeneres's character went through that tried-and-true situation comedy cliché that relegated single characters to failed heterosexual dating experiences. DeGeneres, in the role of Ellen Morgan, was a neurotic but lovable bookstore owner living in Los Angeles who enjoyed a variety of quirky, devoted friends who bore witness to her dating woes. Among them was Adam Green, Ellen's roommate who secretly harbored a crush on her. The character of Adam, who was a photographer, left the show at the end of season 3, having revealed his affections only to learn that Ellen did not reciprocate them. Jeremy Piven joined the cast during season 3 playing Spence Kovak, Ellen's cousin from New York City, a well-meaning person with a violent streak. Spence dated Ellen's friend Paige, an acerbic, self-absorbed, and sexually motivated woman who held a job at a movie studio. There was also Joe, a sarcastic barista at the coffee shop in Ellen's bookstore. Clea Lewis played Audrey Penney, Ellen's overenthusiastic neighbor (and then coworker at the shop), who was Joe's polar opposite and a font of warm fuzzies and positivity (much to the annoyance of everyone around her).

Ellen DeGeneres and Laura Dern in *Ellen*. ABC/Photofest © ABC

By 1996, *Ellen* was a moderately popular sitcom, always performing in the top 30 of the Nielsen ratings (it was number 13 during its first season and at number 25 in its fourth season). It was at this point that DeGeneres began discussions with ABC about having her character come out of the closet as gay. Obviously, something so revolutionary had to be carefully vetted and planned. How would television audiences, who had grown comfortable with her character as a heterosexual (or at least had remained in denial of the four seasons of subtext), respond to such a shift? There were things to consider, such as sponsor backlash (the almighty dollar) and conservative/religious groups that might campaign against the character's epiphany. Hints of the character's coming out were being dropped in the episodes leading up to the big moment, which would finally happen on April 30, 1997.

It is important to acknowledge that while the lead-up to Ellen Morgan's coming out was in motion, DeGeneres was also orchestrating her own public coming out. Rumors were spreading all over the Hollywood tabloids and industry rags that either DeGeneres, her character, or both were going to come out of the closet. The gossip machine was in motion, helping to add an aura of mystery and intrigue around the rumored episode. Ellen DeGeneres officially came out publicly on *The Oprah Winfrey Show* on the afternoon of April 30, 1997, the same day that her character, Ellen Morgan, would come out on network television. Winfrey would be a guest star on that evening's episode.

Titled "The Puppy Episode," the coming-out installment was written by DeGeneres with Mark Driscoll, Tracy Newman, Dava Savel, and Jonathan Stark and was directed by Gil Junger. The title of the episode was an "in-joke." Disney executive Michael Eisner (Disney owns ABC), who was frustrated with the character of Ellen Morgan and her lack of interest in the common sitcom trope of dating, had sarcastically suggested that the character should get a puppy. Eisner was hoping that the successful show would find some direction. Essentially, Ellen's coming out would be that "new puppy" and refocus the show with a purpose and a story arc that would make it feel less scattered. In the short term, this was achieved but not without its drawbacks and consequences.

"The Puppy Episode" unfolded in the following manner. During a dinner with an old friend named Richard (Steven Eckholdt), who is a reporter, Ellen is introduced to his producer, Susan (Laura Dern), and the two women hit it off instantly. Back at Richard's hotel room, he puts the moves on Ellen, who is uncomfortable and leaves. As she departs, in the hallway she encounters Susan, who invites Ellen back to her room to continue their chat. Susan confesses that she is gay and assumes that Ellen is as well. Feeling that she is about to be seduced or recruited, Ellen puts up her usual walls. Susan is offended by the suggestion of "recruitment" and says she will have to call headquarters and let them know that Ellen got away, feigning disappointment over the toaster oven she will not receive as a bonus for sealing the deal. Ellen is clearly agitated by the recent events and, in an effort to prove her heterosexuality, returns to Richard's room, where she decides she is going to have sex with him.

The next day, Ellen shares with her friends that she had amazing sex the night before. At her therapist's office (Oprah Winfrey), she tells a different story. She never had sex with Richard, but she is longing to find someone she clicks with. Susan was that person. When Richard calls to tell her that he and Susan are departing town earlier than planned, Ellen rushes to the airport to find Susan and tell her how she feels. In a hilarious turn of events, Ellen finds her at the gate, where she tries to utter the words, but not until she accidentally leans over the intercom microphone does she say "I'm gay." The coming out reverberates throughout the terminal, where everyone stares. Susan warmly welcomes her to the world of self-acceptance and tells Ellen that her plans had changed and that she will be staying in town for a few more days.

Next we take a journey into Ellen's psyche as we witness a bizarre dream she has. Ellen is in a supermarket shopping and is offered a special lesbian discount on melons; the checkout lane says "10 lesbians or less," and her sexuality is announced over a speaker as if it is an in-store special. Once she is awake, Ellen shares the dream with her therapist, concluding that she has suppressed her sexuality for so long that she doesn't know if she can reconcile it. The therapist encourages her to talk to her friends about it, but Ellen is worried that she will not be accepted.

Ellen starts by telling her neighbor and close friend Peter (Patrick Bristow), an out gay man. He is thrilled and can't contain his excitement. When Ellen has her other friends over to the house to come out to them, Peter attends to lend her moral support. Before she can summon the words, Peter nearly bursts and tells everyone for her. It turns out that her friends are as good as she had hoped, and all show their support, though Paige, her closest female friend, appears somewhat uncomfortable at first.

The following day, Ellen tells Susan that she has feelings for her only to find out that Susan is in a long-term relationship and cannot reciprocate beyond friendship. Ellen appears crushed, but her gang of friends attempt to cheer her up by taking her to a lesbian coffeehouse where Paige, instead of Ellen, gets hit on by a waitress. The episode concludes with Susan taking Ellen to meet lesbian singer-songwriter Melissa Etheridge, who, after confirming with Ellen that she is indeed gay, bestows on Susan the coveted toaster oven.

That's it. There wasn't anything more to the episode than that, but for 1997, that was more than enough. The episode received quite a reaction from the television-viewing audience, drawing more than 42 million viewers. It performed extremely well in the ratings, and most LGBTQ groups were ecstatic over the landmark event. The Human Rights Campaign went so far as to send out party kits for those who wanted to celebrate the episode (they had requests for more than 3,000 of these kits). Unfortunately, some advertisers bowed to pressure from conservative and religious groups, with the likes of Wendy's, J.C. Penny, and Chrysler opting not to promote their products during their typical commercial time slots during *Ellen* episodes. Some ABC affiliates refused to air the episode, but that didn't stop LGBTQ organizations like Pride Birmingham in Birmingham, Alabama, from hosting a viewing party with the episode shown via satellite. More than 1,000 people attended.

"The Puppy Episode" was the highest-rated episode of *Ellen* in its five years on the air. It won an Emmy Award for Best Comedy Writing. It also won a Peabody Award and a GLAAD Media Award.

The episode that immediately followed "The Puppy Episode" was titled "Hello Muddah, Hello Faddah" and was, in many ways, even funnier and more poignant than its predecessor. In the episode, Ellen went through the steps of coming out to her parents, Harold and Lois Morgan (Steven Gilborn and Alice Hirson). Over a meal at a Chinese restaurant, we see the awkwardness unfold. Any child who ever had to muster the courage to tell their parents they were gay, quaking with the fear of their possible rejection, connected with Ellen Morgan that evening. Although there were many questions and concerns and a heart-wrenching sequence where Ellen's father first can't bring himself to accept her, Mr. and Mrs. Morgan eventually come around to showing love and support to their daughter.

Ellen was renewed for one final season, seeing a steep decline in its ratings during season 5. What had been intended as a means of giving the program a new focus had worked—but too well. Critics and audiences began to complain that the show was "too gay," that it had become so focused on Ellen's coming-out journey that everything else audiences liked about the show had gone by the wayside. ABC had received a large amount of backlash for what many perceived as an insistent gay agenda, and as executives will often do when money is concerned, the decision to cancel *Ellen* felt justified.

Until "The Puppy Episode," *Ellen* was a sitcom that was an agreeable diversion that rocked few boats. If the coming-out scenario hadn't come along, it is likely that the show would have faded into obscurity as an also-ran: warmly remembered but never groundbreaking. In courageously sharing her journey, both in real life and as her character Ellen Morgan, Ellen DeGeneres created a legacy for the show and for the LGBTQ movement that would evolve how television told the story of sexual orientation, leading to shows like *Will & Grace*, *Queer as Folk*, and *The L Word*.

All-American Girl
TOO ASIAN

Aired: September 14, 1994–March 15, 1995
Network: ABC
Created by: Gary Jacobs, based on the stand-up comedy of Margaret Cho
Cast: Margaret Cho (Margaret Kim), Jodi Long (Katherine Kim), Clyde Kusatsu (Benny Kim), B. D. Wong (Dr. Stuart Kim), J. B. Quon (Eric Kim), Amy Hill (Yung-hee "Grandma" Kim), Maddie Corman (Ruthie), Judy Gold (Gloria), Ashley Johnson (Casey Emerson)
Theme Song: "Theme to *All-American Girl*," by George Englund Jr., music by G.N.G./W Music (pilot)

Asian Americans have been notoriously underrepresented in all forms of entertainment, but the television sitcom may have been the most egregious at leaving them out of the conversation. There had been Asian characters here and there, most notably Miyoshi Umeki as the housekeeper Mrs. Livingston on *The Courtship of Eddie's Father*, Jack Soo as Detective Nick Yemena on *Barney Miller*, and the occasional episode of *M*A*S*H* that would occasionally employ Asian actors (in mostly bit parts and as extras). It wouldn't be until the advent of *Fresh Off the Boat* (2015–present) that television would produce a sitcom with mostly Asian characters that would prove successful. But *Fresh Off the Boat* wasn't the first attempt.

Stand-up comedian Margaret Cho had grown up in San Francisco in a traditional Korean American family. An audacious personality, Cho would become a favorite of the comedy circuit, with her stories of growing up American, under the strictures of her conservative Korean parents, in a city known for its large homosexual population (one of Cho's favorite subjects and one of her key demographics). Audiences loved her for her frank and often irreverent delivery.

Jodie Long, Margaret Cho, and Clyde Kusatsu in *All-American Girl*. *ABC/ Photofest © ABC*

Surely, Cho would be the perfect personality to take the lead in a sitcom that finally gave an Asian American family their first glimpse of the spotlight.

All-American Girl started out by achieving exactly what it set out to do. It told the story of the Kim family, based around their daughter Margaret, offering a perspective on how traditional Asian cultures reconcile their heritage in a modern, progressive city like San Francisco (where the show is set). Although the series is said to have been based on Cho's stand-up comedy, she has gone on record to refute that assertion, claiming that the producers told her that was the direction, but little of what the writers came up with bore any resemblance to her stand-up material. That aside, *All-American Girl* was giving Americans a glimpse at the first Asian American family at the center of a situation comedy. This is the one place where *All-American Girl* remains groundbreaking. The rest of the details surrounding the show are an embarrassing series of events that actually set television back a few notches both on and behind the scene.

From the beginning, Cho was put under a microscope about her weight. Neither an obese woman nor relatively thin, the producers of the show wouldn't go ahead with her casting unless she lost some weight. Cho herself would bring the details of her efforts to light and the body-shaming, self-esteem–shattering experience she had endured trying to meet the industry "standards" in her stand-up comedy special *I'm the One That I Want* (2000). She would joke about their concerns, one of them being that her face was too round. She mused about how it might have filled the screen. One has to wonder why it was relevant that a woman who had already proven herself to be a successful comedy personality had to be a certain weight to be considered pleasing to look at. It has always been the unfortunate reality of Hollywood that to be the lead, you are required to be thin. Only supporting performers could get away with some meat on their bones. The pressure to maintain an impossible weight led to medical problems for Cho, landing her in the hospital.

Equally as concerning was ABC's feedback that viewers were perceiving the program and Cho as "too Asian." Since the premise of *All-American Girl* was to tell the story of an Asian family, starring an almost entirely Asian cast and led by a comedic personality known for telling stories about the East-meets-West culture clashes she had experienced, how, exactly, were the powers that be hoping to make it all "less Asian"? The show was quickly retooled, and most of the cast was let go, save Cho and Amy Hill, who played her grandmother. Coaching was given to Cho to help her seem "more American." This translated into removing as many Asian references from the show as possible and turning *All-American Girl* into your typical run-of-the-mill sitcom.

In defense of the network and the producers, they were not necessarily wrong to be concerned. Not only was the average audience member unable (or unwilling) to relate to a show that immersed them in an unfamiliar culture, but Asian American viewers had their own reservations about it. Many felt that, as the show was initially rolled out, it was an offensive take on Asian American culture, playing into stereotypes. Others felt the show didn't go far enough or represented its subjects inaccurately. It seemed that no matter how hard everyone was trying, it was impossible to find an audience for *All-American Girl* in any incarnation.

In an interview, Margaret Cho offered these thoughts on *All-American Girl* as it was picked apart and analyzed by viewers and critics alike:

> When you're the first person to cross over this racial barrier, you're scrutinized for all these other things that have nothing to do with race, but they have everything to do with race—it's a very strange thing.[1]

Was race the factor that kept *All-American Girl* from igniting and taking off as a revolutionary (or successful) sitcom? Was America, as antediluvian as it sounds, just not ready to embrace a series that was about a family that didn't look like what they were used to? Time and time again, we have seen that, as a society, we are slow to embrace change and not always empathetic to or interested in anything outside of the status quo. Still, when a game-changing sitcom works, more often than not, it has found its way to an audience. Did the network try to retool *All-American Girl* too quickly, before an audience had spent enough time with the characters, to really get to know them? There seems to be some blame there.

All-American Girl was canceled after one season. Even for its short tenure, the series broke ground and gave Asian Americans their rightful place among the many stories to be told and cultures to be explored on television. It is interesting to note that on an episode of *Fresh Off the Boat*, an Asian character is watching *All-American Girl* and making fun of all of its inaccuracies. In a way, *Fresh Off the Boat* was paying homage to its ancestor: the series that pried open the door that would finally invite audiences in to have an experience with Asian characters. For a show that didn't run even 20 episodes, that was a pretty big legacy to hand off to an heir apparent.

Will & Grace

THE CLOSET DOOR IS OPEN

Aired: September 21, 1998–May 18, 2006, and September 28, 2017–present
Network: NBC
Created by: David Kohan and Max Mutchnick
Cast: Eric McCormack (Will Truman), Debra Messing (Grace Adler), Megan
  Mullally (Karen Walker), Sean Hayes (Jack McFarland), Shelley Morrison
  (Rosario Salazar)
Theme Song: "Theme to *Will & Grace*," composed by Jonathan Wolff

With all of the hoopla and negative backlash toward the coming-out episode
of the ABC series *Ellen* and its eventual spin into cancellation, it was unlikely
that a network would be quick to develop a new sitcom that focused on an out,
gay character as one of its leads. Why risk losing advertising dollars and raising
the ire of conservatives over telling the story of a minority? Not every network
thought this way, however, and thanks to Ellen DeGeneres's groundbreaking
move of having her character Ellen Morgan reveal herself as a lesbian simultaneously with her own coming out, the door had been opened for the possibility
of more gay characters in the world of sitcom television. So would there be any
takers?

Hot on the heels of *Ellen*'s cancellation in 1998, NBC would take such a
risk. Max Mutchnick and David Kohan created a pilot for a series titled *Will
& Grace*, which followed the close friendship between a gay man and straight
woman whose lives were tangled in a codependency, operating as if they were
married but without the sex. The character of Will Truman would be the first
out, gay male character as a lead role in a situation comedy. Although it appeared
to be an enormous chance for NBC to take, *Will & Grace* would be well worth
the gamble, becoming one of the network's top-performing shows for a better
part of the next decade.

Set in New York City in the late 1990s, *Will & Grace* touched on many topical issues of its day, even as it could be outlandishly crazy and far from the world of realism. At the show's start, Will Truman was a lawyer and a gay man who was overcoming a breakup with his long-term partner, his self-esteem crushed. Will came from an uptight Protestant family in Connecticut, a clan that defined every stereotype of the upper-middle-class WASP (white Anglo-Saxon Protestant). His best friend and former girlfriend Grace Adler was an interior designer, and she was the epitome of the unceremoniously dubbed "fag hag." Grace was a Jewish woman from Schenectady, New York, and had her own issues of neediness and a fear of commitment, but she was wholeheartedly devoted to Will. Will and Grace had met and dated during college, with Will's coming-out devastating Grace and crippling her self-worth for the decades to come. Throughout the series, the two would live together, then apart, and then together again, depending on what life's ups and downs brought them.

Rounding out the central characters on *Will & Grace* were Jack McFarland and Karen Walker. Jack was Will's "other" best friend, a flamboyantly gay and promiscuous man who was often critical of Will's life, appearance, and relationship with Grace. Jack was an aspiring performer with zero talent who held

Eric McCormack, Sean Hayes, and Debra Messing in *Will and Grace*. NBC/ Photofest © NBC

myriad jobs that never seemed to last very long, with the result that Jack tended to sponge off of others to get by. Later in the series, Jack would find out that he had a son, Elliot (Michael Angarano), the product of a sperm donation he had made for extra cash several years earlier. Karen was Grace's receptionist at her design firm. The wife of a zaftig millionaire, Karen didn't need the work, treated it like a hobby, never cashed her paychecks (she kept them in a box on her desk), and was completely inept at her job. Karen also suffered from alcohol and pill addiction, a scenario that was often treated as humorous and never led to anything dangerous other than Karen living in an alternate reality. Karen would disparage Grace for what she wore, for how she kept her hair, for the little "doodles" she made (her design renderings), and for her relationship with "Wilma" (as she referred to Will). Karen, however, could have a soft spot for Grace and would occasionally do something to help her employer and friend. Karen also had a maid named Rosario from El Salvador, an illegal alien with a degree in clinical psychology. Karen treated Rosario deplorably and often made ethnic slurs in reference to her, but it was always Rosario who stood by her side when things went wrong in Karen's life. Karen secretly could not live without her. As the series progressed, Jack and Karen also became close friends, usually conspiring against Will and Grace as a means of entertainment or getting into some ludicrous shenanigans from which Will and Grace would usually have to save them. *Will & Grace* would aspire to both broad comedy and more poignant episodes that proved all four leading players to be incredibly versatile and their characters to be deeper and more carefully rendered than what one would initially assume at face value.

Although it may seem to many like a small thing to address, it is significant that *Will & Grace* sought to explore the dynamic of a gay man and his best female friend who harbors romantic feelings for him. The idea of the fag hag has been around for as long as there have been gay men: that one person a homosexual male can trust to keep his secrets, be his beard for the senior prom, and emotionally support his coming-out journey. She also risks taking the emotional toll of investing her heart and energy in a man who will never love her back in the way that she needs. In the character of Grace Adler, the stories of these caring and essential allies of the gay community were given a voice, often a raw and unyielding one, that captured both the security and the pain at odds in these codependent friendships. No television show to date had addressed this in any depth, yet these women were so often a part of gay men's coming-out stories. But then, *Will & Grace* was one of the first TV sitcoms to address a realistic version of a gay man's story.

Will & Grace could also serve as a "how-to" and "how-not-to" manual for navigating the complicated world where rules were evolving and changing for both women and LGBTQ people. For example, how does a perpetually single woman and a gay man, both wanting to have a child, go about conceiving one? *Will & Grace* probed this conundrum on several occasions. First, an old high school friend of Will's approaches him and asks that he donate the sperm for her to have a child. Will considers it and wants to help his friend out, liking the idea of a piece of himself living on in the world. When Grace finds out, she is hurt to the core, telling Will that she has always considered his sperm to be her reserve in case she never finds someone to marry. Will assures her that she will eventually find love but also agrees not to donate to his friend out of loyalty toward Grace. Later, Grace decides she would like to have a baby of her own and wants Will to be the father. The two awkwardly try to have sex, an experiment that is an epic failure since neither can comfortably get naked in front of the other. With that option out of the way, they decide to let modern medicine intervene. Will is to donate his sperm at a fertility clinic, and Grace will be artificially inseminated. On the big day of fertilization, Grace is running late and has an accident while running through Central Park. She is knocked out, only to be revived by Dr. Leo Markus (Harry Connick Jr.) a dreamy, Jewish man of Grace's dreams. The fertilization is postponed as Grace explores a relationship with Leo, who ultimately proposes to her, and the two get married. The marriage of Grace to Leo then asked the question, How does the now-married former best friend of a gay man set aside that friendship in order to be devoted to her new husband? The brutal fact of the series was that Grace never could give herself entirely over to Leo, still relying on Will and thereby shunning her husband. Was it really Will's fault that she couldn't commit, or was it Grace all along who sought relationships where she knew commitment was never truly going happen?

The advent of *Will & Grace* would also give television an opportunity to explore some of the ongoing concerns of gay men and how they were perceived by society. In the late 1990s, attitudes toward homosexuality were shifting, with a higher percentage of the population more open to acceptance. It was not, however, an all-out love fest for the LGBTQ contingent. In episode 14 of season 2, titled "Acting Out," which aired in 2000, Jack is upset with his favorite NBC sitcom for cutting away from a gay kiss that had been promised on that episode. He is so frustrated about it, in fact, that it becomes an obsession. Will has Jack join him at an episode of the *Today* show, standing with the crowd in Rockefeller Center, hoping to get the attention of weatherman Al Roker. When Will is sure that the camera is focused on them, he plants a kiss on Jack's mouth, giving him (and us) television's first gay kiss between two men. Although the gesture didn't mean anything more than a friend giving a friend their wish with a quick peck on the mouth, it was a big step for television. A month later, a more passionate kiss would be shared between two men on an episode of the teen drama *Dawson's Creek*.

Where *Will & Grace* may arguably have had its greatest impact was in its depiction of a variety of homosexual personalities. Will was not the fashion-crazed, disco-dancing, show tune–singing, effeminate, man-hungry stereotype that entertainment had been painting for decades. Sure, he exhibited certain aspects of the stereotype, but he was genuinely concerned with being a successful lawyer, being a good friend, and searching for a committed relationship based in love. He eventually found a long-term companion in Vince D'Angelo (Bobby Cannavale), a gay cop whom he eventually married and had a child with. Jack McFarland, though, may have been a checklist of the aforementioned gay stereotypes, but as his character evolved over the series' 10 seasons, he proved a thoughtful father to his son Elliot and a loving friend to Will, Karen, Grace, and Rosario while masking a litany of insecurities with his outrageous behavior.

Will & Grace was a huge critical hit for NBC, winning an Emmy for Outstanding Comedy Series in 2000. All four of the leading performers won Emmys for their respective roles, and the show was also celebrated for its writing, directing, and a string of big-name guest stars, including Alec Baldwin, Leslie Jordan, Michael Douglas, Glenn Close, Cher, Matt Damon, Chita Rivera, Michelle Lee, Jeff Goldblum, Gregory Hines, Rosie O'Donnell, Gene Wilder, Molly Shannon, Eileen Brennan, Blythe Danner (as Will's mother), Veronica Cartwright, Victor Garber, James Earl Jones, and Debbie Reynolds (as Grace's mother). The show was a veritable "who's who" of the greatest talents of film, television, and theater. During its 10-season run, the show received just short of 100 Emmy nominations.

When *Will & Grace* ended its run after 10 seasons, it was with the titular characters at odds and no longer speaking, only to be reunited years later when their respective kids ended up living across the hall from one another in their college dorm. Putting their differences aside, the two realized how much they missed each other and began speaking again. The series concluded with each of them finally having found their own lives, separate from the other, but also giving the audience hope that they had finally found their way back to each other in a healthier, less dependent way. This would seemingly be where the story ended.

In the spring of 2017, it was announced that NBC would be bringing back *Will & Grace* after an absence of more than a decade. The series would throw out much of what had happened in the final episode, opting to continue the journey of Will Truman and Grace Adler as if children, marriage, and conflict had never torn their relationship apart. The reboot of the series would premiere in the fall of 2017, and it jumped right back into the topical issues that were dividing society. Since the show had last been on the air, gay marriage had been legalized, and a conservative wave of bigotry and fear had ensconced Donald Trump in the White House as one of America's most polarizing presidents. The new *Will & Grace* powerfully addressed the #MeToo movement: victims of sexual assault coming forward and sharing their stories. In a poignant episode, Grace sits her father down to tell him how his best friend had sexually assaulted her as a teenager. At first, her father doesn't want to believe it but then, devastated, outpours his shame for not being there to protect his little girl.

The reboot of *Will & Grace* made every effort to comment on the divided America of the 21st century. It also, however, skewed toward a liberal bias that depicted all conservatives as uncaring people who agreed wholeheartedly with where America was. The character of Karen Walker championed the presidency of Donald Trump and made dismissive and disparaging jokes about immigrants, the poor, and the societally oppressed. This was all done with a sense of hyperbole, a character designed to represent the most extreme cases of conservatism that were at the forefront of the current political climate, the vocal minority that had assumed the role of the seemingly vocal majority. But even Karen Walker had a heart, and she occasionally showed it. Her character's actions were a subtle call to conservatives to reconsider their complacency, to speak out against what many believed were the heartless and un-American actions of the Trump regime.

The return of *Will & Grace* also addressed another issue for gay men that had seldom been explored: aging. In the homosexual community, it is typical for youth and beauty to be celebrated, while getting old is something to be avoided at all cost. The problem is that it eventually happens. What does it look like to be gay and approach 50? What is it like to be a gay grandpa? Jack was faced with that rude awakening when his son Elliot shows up with his grandson and he had to assume the role of being a grandfather. In reality, gay men had always aged—it was just something that was kept locked away in the closet, where, it was hoped, it didn't have to be looked at. *Will & Grace* was always swinging that closet door open and dragging new and compelling stories of the gay experience out of it.

Modern Family

NOT YOUR TYPICAL SITCOM CLAN

Aired: September 23, 2009–present

Network: ABC

Created by: Christopher Lloyd and Steven Levitan

Cast: Ed O'Neill (Jay Pritchett), Sofía Vergara (Gloria Pritchett), Julie Bowen (Claire Dunphy), Ty Burrell (Phil Dunphy), Jesse Tyler Ferguson (Mitchell Pritchett), Eric Stonestreet (Cameron Tucker), Sarah Hyland (Haley Dunphy), Ariel Winter (Alex Dunphy), Nolan Gould (Luke Dunphy), Rico Rodriguez (Manny Delgado), Aubrey Anderson-Emmons (Lily Tucker-Pritchett in season 3 to present), Jaden and Ella Hiller (Lily Tucker-Pritchett, seasons 1 and 2), Jeremy Maguire (Joe Pritchett, season 5 to present), Rebecca and Sierra Mark (Joe Pritchett, season 4), Pierce Wallace (Joe Pritchett, seasons 5 and 6)

Theme Song: "Theme to *Modern Family*," composed by Gabriel Mann

The ever-evolving dynamic of the family unit is consistently one of the most fascinating questions answered by television throughout the decades. What makes up a family? By what rules do we define family? How do we navigate the relations that we may not like but are bound by genetics to love? The possible configurations of family are myriad, and the complexities are even more so. Television continues to find new and compelling ways to probe the possibilities of family. *Modern Family* was arguably the most unconventional of them all.

Or was it?

As a mock documentary, the series followed the Pritchett clan, representing three households: that of Jay Pritchett and those of his adult children Mitchell and Claire Dunphy. Each domestic scenario was composed of an atypical living situation (by sitcom standards) that's offered an interesting cross section of the American population.

Jesse Tyler Ferguson and Eric Stonestreet in *Modern Family*. ABC/Photofest © ABC

Jake was the patriarch of the family, divorced from his first wife, and on the brink of retirement from his business, Pritchett's Closets and Blinds. His second wife was Gloria Delgado Pritchett, a much younger woman from Colombia who happened to be the same age as Jay's adult children. Gloria was a passionate and sexy woman who spoke moderately comprehensible English. Although she made every effort to have positive relationships with Jay's kids, they were reluctant and judgmental of her in the beginning. When he married Gloria, Jay also gained a stepson, Manny Delgado, a sensitive and artistic boy with whom he shared little in common, though Jay found ways to eventually connect with the boy. As the series progressed, Gloria and Jay would give birth to a son, Joe.

Claire Dunphy's home was very different, as she was married to the whimsical, often childlike Phil, a real estate agent who was the polar opposite to Claire's controlling, domineering nature. Phil liked to play and was a gentle, accepting man (the opposite of Claire's father in almost every way). Claire was much like Jay and was her father's choice to take over the business when he retired. Phil and Claire had three kids: the ditzy, underachieving Haley; the practical, over-achieving Alex; and the goofy Luke, his father's constant companion in ridiculous shenanigans. The three siblings, all quite different from one another, were typically at odds but also looked out for and loved one another.

Then there was the home of Mitchell Pritchett, Jay's homosexual son, who lived with his partner (and eventual husband) Cameron. Mitchell was a lawyer, the practical one, and a control freak like his sister and father. Cam was a warm but melodramatic man, full of creativity and high expectations. In the show's first episode, Mitchell and Cam have just adopted an Asian baby, a little girl named Lily, whom Cam introduces to the family *Lion King* style, held on high above his head with "The Circle of Life" cued up on the CD player to underscore the moment. As Lily gets older, she reveals a caustic personality and soon becomes the de facto ruler of the roost. Jay and Mitchell have a strained relationship, Mitchell recalling a lifetime of his father trying to toughen him up and Jay clearly uncomfortable with his son's homosexuality. Cam, however, manages a congenial and often friendly relationship with his father-in-law.

In depicting three very different nuclear families as part of a larger extended family while also presenting them as very much a part of each other's lives, *Modern Family* is in many ways about as traditional as you can get. There was a time in this country when extended family was celebrated and revered, family taking care of each other, whether or not they shared the same roof. In recent decades, America has moved toward a more isolated approach, with immediate household members the chief (and often only) concern. The Pritchetts and the Dunphys don't just come together for the holidays. They are regularly seen on outings with each other, spending time at each other's homes, and more than just obligated to be a part of each other's worlds. They actually like each other. So, though their individual households don't look like the traditional family unit, they are traditional nonetheless. *Modern Family* helps viewers to see that families, despite their many differences, can still come together to be a part of a supportive unit. It is about the effort, not the people.

As of this writing, *Modern Family* has been renewed for its 11th (and allegedly final) season. The series has won 22 Emmy Awards, including Outstanding Comedy Series on four occasions. Although critics have nitpicked its direction (or lack thereof) in recent seasons, the show continues to be a strong audience draw for ABC. The show has proven infinitely relatable to anyone who has dealt with family conflict (haven't we all?) and has certainly shaped how we view family and what it can be.

Mom

A SOBERING SITCOM

Aired: September 23, 2013–present
Network: CBS
Created by: Chuck Lorre, Eddie Gorodetsk, and Gemma Baker
Cast: Anna Faris (Christy Jolene Plunkett), Allison Janney (Bonnie Plunkett), Sadie Calvano (Violet Plunkett), Nate Corddry (Gabriel), Matt L. Jones (Baxter), French Stewart (Chef Rudy), Spencer Daniels (Luke), Blake Garrett Rosenthal (Roscoe Plunkett), Mimi Kennedy (Marjorie Armstrong-Perugian), Jaime Pressly (Jill Kendall), Beth Hall (Wendy Harris), William Fichtner (Adam Janikowski), Kristen Johnston (Tammy Diffendorf)
Theme Song: "Overture" from *Ruslan and Lyudmila*, by Mikhail Glinka

Nearly 17 million adults suffer from alcohol addiction, and an estimated 88,000 die from alcoholism each year. The United States consumes 80 percent of the world's painkiller supply (the country making up only 5 percent of the world's population). Drug abuse has led to more than 2.5 million emergency room visits each year. One hundred people die every day from drug overdoses. This rate has tripled in the past 20 years. These are some daunting statistics about alcohol and drug abuse, yet the situation continues to be a growing problem in the United States. What statistics don't tell us in cut-and-dry numbers are the effects that addiction has on individuals, the day-to-day struggles of managing the cravings, or the way that this can eat into living happy, healthy, and productive lives. Recovery isn't easy. It's a one-step-at-a-time journey, plagued with pitfalls, temptations, and setbacks.

Sitcoms have looked at the challenges of the recovering alcoholic, but their journey is usually relegated to the periphery of the plot, where it only occasionally is addressed. The comedy *Cheers*, for example, featured Sam Malone as a recovering alcoholic who owns a Boston pub, and though his reasons for not drinking occasionally were brought up and though he was surrounded by a parade of alcoholics as part of his industry, the temptation of alcohol was seldom a part of his story arc. There was also the character of Grace Kelly in the sitcom *Grace under Fire*, who had been abused by her alcoholic husband and was trying to survive on her own and raise her kids away from that influence. Typically, sitcoms that tackled the problems of alcoholism did so as a "very special episode," as was the case with installments of *Family Ties* and *The Facts of Life*. That is not the case for the characters of Christy and Bonnie Plunkett in the sitcom *Mom*.

Set in California's Napa Valley, formerly estranged daughter and mother duo Christy and Bonnie Plunkett are both recovering alcohol and substance abusers who are trying to start over fresh, getting their lives on track while rebuilding their relationship. Bonnie had given birth to Christy when she was just 17, the father disappearing soon after. Living together now, Bonnie and Christy attend regular Alcoholics Anonymous (AA) meetings in an effort to manage the disease. At AA, Marjorie Armstrong-Perugian serves as Christy's and Bonnie's sponsor. She's blunt and direct, a survivor of breast cancer but still struggling with her own addictions. There is also Jill Kendall, whom Christy sponsors, and Wendy Harris, a nurse who cries and who is seldom listened to at meetings. These five ladies create the central core of the program's often sobering tales about remaining sober.

Emily Osment, Allison Janney, and Anna Faris in *Mom*. CBS/Photofest © CBS

Christy also has a teenage daughter Violet, whom she gave birth to at age 17, and a son, Roscoe, by her ex-husband, Baxter, a deadbeat dad. She is trying to get her life together as an example for her kids. She doesn't want them to repeat her mistakes. Working as a waitress and also navigating a gambling addiction, Christy is working to regain the trust of Violet, who reveals to her in the show's pilot that she is pregnant (at age 17). The family demons appear poised to continue repeating themselves, but Violet chooses to give her baby up for adoption, hopefully breaking the family curse. Violet and Christy have their own conflicts, resulting in the daughter and mother having an on-again/off-again relationship.

Mom is a sitcom that is outrageously funny while simultaneously taking a serious look at alcohol and substance addiction. No sitcom has ever spent so much time exploring the motivation and genetics behind the disease, nor has any series ever so bluntly demonstrated the consequences that addiction has on the day-to-day life of an addict. Media and entertainment, more often than not, have painted recovering addicts as monsters who made bad choices. *Mom* depicts them as human beings who are trying, growing, changing, and sometimes failing, helping us to see a piece of ourselves in their circumstances.

The series, which was created by Chuck Lorre, Eddie Gorodetsky, and Gemma Baker, has received mostly praise. It has been critically lauded for its sincere attempts to tell the story of addiction within the confines of a situation comedy. Allison Janney has won two Emmy Awards for her no-holds-barred and caustic portrayal of Bonnie, and Faris has been nominated in the same category. More than anything, *Mom*, through its laughter and its uncompromising story lines, is delivering information to the masses, giving our society a better understanding of the dangers of drugs and alcohol. It also gives those of us who do not understand addiction a way to empathize with the real struggles these people live with every day of their lives.

Black-ish

THINGS AREN'T ALWAYS BLACK AND WHITE

Aired: September 24, 2014–present
Network: ABC
Created by: Kenya Barris
Cast: Anthony Anderson (Andre "Dre" Johnson), Tracee Ellis Ross (Dr. Rainbow Johnson), Yara Shahidi (Zoey Johnson), Marcus Scribner (Andre "Junior" Johnson), Miles Brown (Jack Johnson), Marsai Martin (Diane Johnson), Deon Cole (Charles Telphy), Jenifer Lewis (Ruby Johnson), Jeff Meachum (Josh Oppenhol), Pater Mackenzie (Leslie Stevens)

The evolving story of the African American family and the black experience in America in general have been ongoing themes in television storytelling practically since the medium started. From *Amos 'n' Andy* to *Good Times* and *The Jeffersons* through *The Cosby Show*, *Family Matters*, and *Everybody Hates Chris*, the sitcom continues to reinvent itself with new and more authentic perspectives for capturing their stories as well as for representing the challenges presented by being a minority in the United States. The latest series to tackle this subject matter is the popular, contemporary sitcom *Black-ish*.

Black-ish, which was created by Kenya Barris, tells the story of the upper-middle-class, African American family the Johnsons. Andre "Dre" Johnson Sr. is an advertising executive married to his wife Rainbow, a successful anesthesiologist, the daughter of a mixed-race, hippie marriage. Together, the two are raising their children, trying to maintain pieces of their own background and culture while their disinterested offspring couldn't care less. Their oldest, Zoey, is a shallow teenager concerned mostly with being popular. The character of Zoey would be spun off into her own sitcom called *Grown-ish*. The next child is the teenage Andre Jr., the awkward nerd of the family who often is an embarrassment to his

185

more socially savvy and popularity-driven father and siblings. He is followed by Jack and Diane, fraternal twins, the former the more affable and laid back of the pair, the latter the more aggressive and driven.

Outside of the Johnson family, *Black-ish* includes a handful of other character regulars, including Charlie Telphy, Dre's best friend and off-the-beam coworker. Then there is Dre's mother, Ruby; Josh Oppenhol, another of Dre's coworkers; and Leslie Stevens, Dre's boss. The series also features a diverse parade of recurring guest stars, including Laurence Fishburne, Marla Gibbs, Raven-Symoné, Tyra Banks, Nicole Sullivan, Wanda Sykes, Regina Hall, Daveed Diggs, Faizon Love, Catherine Reitman, Anna Deveare Smith, and Beau Bridges.

Black-ish, despite the fact that it trades primarily in broad situation comedy, has never shied away from delving into controversial issues, particularly those that affect contemporary minorities in America. From the outset, the series' writers have skillfully kept in tandem with current events and made them a part of *Black-ish*'s overarching themes. Racial inequality, racial sensitivity, and the current political climate all play into the show's deft depictions of our nation's reality, egregious disparity, and bigotry softened and served through comedy.

Marcus Scribner, Yara Shahidi, Tracee Ellis Ross, Anthony Anderson, Miles Brown, Marsai Martin, Laurence Fishburne, and Jenifer Lewis in *Black-ish*. ABC/Photofest © ABC

In episode 12 of season 3, titled "The Lemons," the series addressed the shock that had fallen over our country with the 2016 presidential election. A conservative wave had swept the nation, leaving many Americans confused, depressed, and off balance. The episode took us into Dre's workplace, where, despite eight weeks having passed since the election, nothing was getting done. It reflected a time in our country when many people, particularly liberals, felt uncertainty about their future and afraid to move ahead into what came next.

In season 4, episode 2, *Black-ish* went down a road that sitcoms rarely travel with "Mother Nature." Dre and Bow have just welcomed a new child into the world, the little DeVante. Bow is struggling after the pregnancy and having a hard time adjusting, overwhelmed by the experience. We soon learn that she is suffering from postpartum depression. In a somewhat uncharacteristic moment for the typically self-absorbed Dre, he stands by her side, offers support, and helps her get the care she needs. An estimated 10 to 15 percent of women suffer from postpartum depression, yet it has seldom been addressed on situation comedies when new babies arrive as part of the story line. *Black-ish* shed a light on the phenomenon for many viewers and helped many new mothers understand that they were not alone in these feelings of anxiety, panic, and melancholy. It also offered hope by presenting options of treatment and helped point spouses in the right direction, demonstrating how to be supportive.

Black-ish carefully explored the day-to-day experience of the African American living in a Caucasian-centric world. Episode 10 of season 1, "Black Santa/White Christmas," found Dre, who is worried that his kids are losing touch with their racial culture, arguing for a black Santa at the office Christmas party (a role he himself ends up filling). In the episode "ToysRn'tUs" (season 3, episode 17), Bow goes in search of a black doll for Diane and is frustrated by the lack of options, the doll market catering mostly to whites. This is where *Black-ish* arguably shines the most: in drawing attention to the day-to-day issues that many of us, particularly white Americans, aren't aware of with regard to minority and racially diverse populations.

"Hope" (season 2, episode 16) was arguably the most politically and racially charged episode to date. Dre and Rainbow find themselves fielding questions from their kids about police brutality. A highly publicized court case over the treatment of an African American teenager by law enforcement (resulting in his death) has the Johnson kids wondering what this could mean for them. How could the system be so rigged and racially biased that the boy ended up in this position in the first place? The parents are divided over how they should talk to their kids about this, with Dre wanting to take a more realistic approach and Rainbow opting for a more optimistic one. The episode was directly probing the concerns that minorities in the United States are having with regard to their often unfair treatment by the law.

A particular episode of *Black-ish* met with controversy and was pulled before it ever aired: "Please, Baby, Please," which was set to air on February 27, 2018. The episode proposed to address social and political issues in the United States, including the debates surrounding professional athletes who kneel during the "Star-Spangled Banner" in protest of police brutality and to draw attention to racial inequality. Creative differences between the show's creator and the network ended without resolution, and "Please, Baby, Please" never aired. A definitive reason for pulling the episode was never given, but the scenario does point to the fact that *Black-ish* was tackling a subject that has proven polarizing in America. In a March 11, 2018, *New York Times* article by Andrew R. Chow, this episode was discussed. "One of the things that has always made *Black-ish* so special is how it deftly examines delicate social issues in a way that simultaneously entertains and educates, however, on this episode there were creative differences we were unable to resolve."[1]

Additionally, and perhaps with even greater impact, the series also addressed how African Americans look at, view, and treat each other. Episode 1 of season 2 started off with a bang. Titled "THE Word," this installment of the show addressed the use of the "N" word, a historically disparaging moniker for the African American, by African Americans. Jack says the word at school, quoting a lyric from a Kanye West song, and faces repercussions. Dre must decide whether the reclaiming of the word is an action of empowerment or a further degradation of his race and then figure out how to talk to his son about it. In episode 8 of season 3, "Being Bow-Racial," Bow finds herself at odds with her feelings about her biracial identity when Junior introduces his white girlfriend to the family. She tries to deny that she is bothered by the girl's race but ultimately has to admit that, though she has a black mother and a white father, she lives the life of a black woman and has a hard time identifying with the Caucasian part of herself.

"Black Like Us," the title of the season 5, episode 10, installment of *Black-ish*, brought up a topic that many Americans had never thought to consider. Dre and Rainbow become upset when, during a school picture, Diane isn't properly lit. In the episode, the parents speak to the school principal to address racial sensitivity where photographing a variety of complexions is concerned. The incident brought up a stirring debate within the family over the difference of being a light-skinned black or a dark-skinned black. Junior claims that there is a disparity within their own household and how different members of the family are treated.

Black-ish has proven to be a popular and issue-charged series about the contemporary African American experience in the United States. More important, the program has incorporated a culturally diverse cast of characters, providing a wide range of perspectives that address current cultural issues from various points of view. *Black-ish* has been hailed by critics for its social relevancy and its willingness to tackle the current, divided political climate. The series just completed (as of this writing) its fifth season. It remains uncertain what *Black-ish*'s long-term impact will be, but it will be interesting to sit back and see if it takes on the iconic status of the groundbreaking shows that came before it.

One Day at a Time

WE'LL JUST TAKE IT LIKE IT COMES

Aired: January 6, 2017–present

Network: Netflix

Created by: Gloria Calderon Kellett and Mike Royce, based on the original CBS
   television series *One Day at a Time*, by Whitney Blake and Allan Manings

Cast: Justina Machado (Penelope Alvarez), Todd Grinnell (Schneider), Isabella
   Gomez (Elena Alvarez), Marcel Ruiz (Alex Alvarez), Stephen Tobolowsky
   (Dr. Leslie Berkowitz), Rita Moreno (Lydia Margarita del Carmen Inclán
   Maribona Leyte-Vidal de Riera)

Theme Song: "This Is It," by Jeff Barry and Nancy Barry (performed by Gloria
   Estefan)

The themes of the classic sitcom *One Day at a Time* may seem tethered to the
1970s, but the idea of a single woman raising her family with minimal help from
the father has carried over the decades. The sitcom would ultimately be given
a reboot that shared many similarities with the original but also packed its own
punch when delving into contemporary issues. In 2017, Norman Lear would
again be involved as producer, and the show was reimagined by Gloria Calderon
Kellett and Mike Royce for the online streaming platform Netflix. *One Day at a
Time* proved an audience and critic favorite in its new life.

For this version, the story followed Penelope Alvarez, a Cuban American
woman raising her two kids while living in a small Los Angeles apartment (that
was cleverly reminiscent of Ann Romano's dwelling in the original). Penelope
was a veteran of the U.S. Army Nurse Corps, having served in the Middle
East. Penelope suffered from depression and anxiety and participated in group
therapy sessions. Her former husband, Victor (James Martinez), suffers from
posttraumatic stress disorder, and his use of alcohol as a means of coping led
to both their separation and his inability to regularly participate in the lives of

his kids. Penelope's career involves working as a nurse in the office of Dr. Leslie Berkowitz, a kindly but awkward physician. Her two kids are both warm and supportive. Her daughter Elena is a strong-willed, independent-minded teenager who supports many social causes but is also puzzled by her own unclear sexuality (she's pretty sure she likes women but is not one to subscribe to labels). Her son Alex is concerned with establishing popularity and wearing fashionable brand clothing and exhibits a growing interest in girls. As the only male in the household, he struggles to understand what becoming a man means yet is loving and supportive to all the females who surround him. Both children have a hard time reconciling their father's inconsistent efforts to be a part of their lives.

Also living in their apartment is their grandmother and Penelope's mother Lydia, a Cuban-born woman who immigrated to America when she was young. Living in a curtained-off alcove of the apartment's living area, Lydia is a constant reminder of Cuban and Catholic tradition, often troubled by her family's less devoted views. Lydia develops a romantic relationship with Dr. Berkowitz but has never truly recovered from the loss of her husband Berto (Tony Plana). The building landlord and superintendent Dwayne Schneider rounds out the central cast. Schneider finds himself drawn to the Alvarez household, often participating

Isabella Gomez, Todd Grinnell, Marcel Ruiz, Justina Machado, and Rita Moreno in *One Day at a Time*. Netflix/Photofest © Netflix

as one of the family. The womanizing goof regularly serves as a surrogate father to the kids, stepping in when Penelope needs some extra help.

The reboot of *One Day at a Time* was undaunted in its immediate embrace of current event issues. Nowhere was it more unyielding than in its discussion of immigration and deportation. During the first season, Elena is good friends with a girl of Mexican descent named Carmen (Ariela Barer). In an episode titled "Strays," it is revealed that Carmen's parents are illegal immigrants and are being deported. Elena begs her mother to let Carmen stay with them, but Penelope recognizes the importance of being with family, operating within the law whether or not we like it, and the more practical considerations of their already cramped living situation. With a great deal of heartbreak, Penelope has to turn her daughter and her friend down, and Carmen is shipped off to Texas to stay with one of her relatives in Austin. The episode came hot on the heels of the many contested immigration policies and the often divisive rhetoric surrounding them. The episode took a serious look at America's policies on illegal aliens while simultaneously humanizing those most impacted by their harsh repercussions.

Arguably, the most affecting episode came as Elena's quinceañera arrived at the end of season 1. The family came together to plan the coming-of-age ritual, complete with a big party and an atypical dress converted by her *abuelita* to suit Elena's more gender-fluid sensibility. Elena is looking forward to her father being in attendance to dance the traditional father–daughter dance. At the rehearsal, Elena chooses the moment to tell her dad about her sexuality, something he adamantly disagrees with. The next day at the party, he does not show up to have his special dance with his little girl. Mom to the rescue. Penelope takes to the floor and scoops her daughter up in her arms, dancing in her father's place. One by one, the other family members and close family friends move in around her, embracing the girl in love and support. Never has television's depiction of a parent rejecting their child over their sexuality been so potent and heart-wrenching.

In its third season (which launched in February 2019), *One Day at a Time* has shown no signs of playing it safe or settling in for more traditional sitcom tropes. Topics such as toxic masculinity, sexual consent, and the #MeToo movement were addressed with an unyielding fervor. "Outside," the title of episode 2 of season 3, finds Penelope taking a look at Alex's phone only to discover a private Instagram account where she finds pictures of her son groping a girl's breast as well as other repugnant behaviors fueled by his notion of how boys act. When confronted by his mother, Alex reveals that it was his grandmother who told him to pursue the girl aggressively, that he "shouldn't take no for an answer." But it is also likely that Alex learned much of his behavior from his father, inheriting a machismo that has been passed down through centuries of a male-dominated culture. Instead of excusing his behaviors with a "boys will be boys" mentality, the show used this scenario as an opportunity to educate Alex (and society as a whole), his mother and sister stepping up to school the boy on what is and is not appropriate treatment of women. Despite messages to the contrary (including a school rape prevention day that told girls not to dress provocatively and not to walk alone), they make it clear that it is not a woman's responsibility to endure or avoid these behaviors from men but that it is the duty of boys to learn how to treat girls with respect. The women also share their stories of sexual harassment, something that has a profound effect on the boy when the behaviors he exhibited were aimed at people he loved. To Alex's credit, he seemed to get the message and apologized for his actions.

In season 3, episode 7, "The First Time," Elena and her now steady girlfriend Syd (Sheridan Pierce) plan a night in a hotel where they plan their first sexual experience. They have a long conversation in which they discuss the implications of the experience they are about to embark on, exchanging verbal consent before their actions commence. In having the discussion, the inexperienced Elena learns that Syd has already had her first sexual experience, something she thought they would be sharing together.

At this writing, the new *One Day at a Time* is both a critical and an audience darling. What its long-term impact will be, only time can tell, but for now, it is delving into some important territory where topical events are concerned.

Conclusion

Television has come a long way since families gathered around their little 10-inch screens to watch their favorite situation comedies. Each decade has brought change and evolution in the medium. As programming has matured, the utilization of humor has been one of the key ingredients for presenting thoughtful story lines that open our eyes to societal issues, creating a place for dialogue through the common ground of laughter.

Reaching a mass audience, television offers us one of our greatest opportunities to consider subjects that might be foreign to us. The influence it has demonstrated in breaking down barriers over race, gender, sexual orientation, and a multitude of other divisive topics by simply giving them faces with which we can empathize and story lines that afford us the chance to walk in someone else's shoes should not be underestimated.

I think back to when I was a child living in upstate New York. There were no African American families that I was aware of. I had no idea what their lives were like and had really no frame of reference to figure that out other than what I saw on television. Shows like *Good Times*, *The Jeffersons*, and *The Cosby Show* helped me know a little bit more about their stories than what I would have otherwise encountered. Through the decades, I have been grateful for the exposure that television brought me. Although it may not have always been an accurate depiction, it did make me aware, a cognizance that I would not otherwise have been privy to. It prepared me for when I would go to college and then live in different geographical locations where I would learn that there were so many stories to encounter. TV gave me that. TV gives us that.

I continually think about how some little gay boy grew up in the 1990s and encountered *Will & Grace* and felt a little less lonely by finding commonality with Will and Jack or about the little lesbian girls who watched that groundbreaking episode of *Ellen* earlier that decade and saw a piece of themselves there.

And then there are the parents of gay kids watching *Modern Family* who realize through Jay Pritchett that moms and dads can work at (and achieve) a loving relationship with their gay children. TV can be a beautiful tool for making connections and eradicating our feelings of being alone in the world.

TV still has a long way to go in telling the stories of all the cross sections of American life. Indeed, will that goal ever truly be achieved? Situation comedies have recently begun exploring bisexuality and transgender story lines. They have touched on the struggles of illegal immigrants. Sitcoms have delved into topics as diverse as infertility, aging, substance abuse, the #MeToo movement, and the ongoing struggle for equal pay for women. They continue to tell the stories of minorities and their struggles to have a voice in the policies that repress them. There is a whole world full of people out there whose stories are waiting to be told through the one common bond we all seem to share: our need to laugh.

Appendix: The Series That Tried and the Series That Might

Over the years, there have been many TV sitcoms that had the potential to make a difference, open minds on social issues, and create a dialogue over divisive topics, but because the shows didn't catch on with the viewing public or the networks didn't give them enough of a chance to build an audience, they never realized that potential. Here are some of the titles that could have had an impact but departed too early:

The Series That Tried

HOT L BALTIMORE (JANUARY 24–APRIL 25, 1975)

Producer Norman Lear, despite his iconic output in television production, couldn't have a hit every time out. *Hot L Baltimore*, adapted from the play by Lanford Wilson, was one of those shows that just didn't ignite. The show took place in the residential Hotel Baltimore (The letter "E" had burned out on the sign) and followed the stories of its residents, including prostitutes, an illegal immigrant, and one of television's first gay couples. The series ran on ABC in the spring of 1975 and starred the likes of James Cromwell, Richard Masur, Conchata Ferrell, Al Freeman Jr., and Charlotte Rae. It ran for a total of 13 episodes and was Lear's first failure after such monumental successes as *All in the Family*, *Maude*, *The Jeffersons*, and *Good Times*.

THE POWERS THAT BE (MARCH 7, 1992–JANUARY 16, 1993)

Another sitcom from the pioneering Norman Lear, *The Powers That Be* was a sitcom that aired on NBC. The series was created by David Crane and Marta Kauffman (who would later create *Friends*), and Lear served as executive producer. With a cast featuring John Forsythe, Holland Taylor, David Hyde Pierce, Eve Gordon, Joseph Gordon-Levitt, Valerie Mahaffey, Peter MacNicol, Elizabeth Berridge, and Robin Bartlett, the series followed U.S. Senator William Powers and his eccentric family with more problems than any clan should ever have to deal with. *The Powers That Be* was a political satire, commenting on the corrupt politics of the day.

WOMEN OF THE HOUSE (JANUARY 4–SEPTEMBER 8, 1995)

A spin-off of the popular (and consistently socially relevant) *Designing Women*, *Women of the House* saw the character of Suzanne Sugarbaker (Delta Burke) enter politics as a newly appointed member of the U.S. House of Representatives. As she had done for *Designing Women*, Linda Bloodworth-Thomason created and wrote the episodes of *Women of the House* with the hope that juxtaposing the often uninformed beauty queen with an eccentric life against the world of D.C. politics and the day's socially relevant issues would strike comedic gold. It didn't. The show, which also starred Teri Garr, Patricia Heaton, Valerie Mahaffey, Lisa Rieffel, and William Newman, lasted for 13 episodes on CBS in 1995.

THE NEW NORMAL (AUGUST 29, 2012–APRIL 2, 2013)

The New Normal represented a new shift in LGBTQ storytelling, centering on a wealthy gay couple who are trying to have a baby. The series follows them as they secure a surrogate, move her into their home (with her nine-year-old daughter) and begin to plan for the arrival of their new child. Starring Justin Bartha, Andrew Rannells, Georgia King, Bebe Wood, NeNe Leakes, Jayson Blair, and Ellen Barkin, the series ran for one season on NBC and was abruptly canceled. It had faced criticism from affiliate stations such KSL-TV in Salt Lake City, Utah, owned by the Church of Jesus Christ of Latter-day Saints. They would not carry *The New Normal*, claiming the show contained messages and content they believed to be inappropriate for broadcast during prime-time television. The series was created by Ryan Murphy (*Glee*, *Nip/Tuck*, *American Horror Story*) and Allison Adler (*Supergirl*).

THE REAL O'NEALS (MARCH 2, 2016–MARCH 14, 2017)

Reconciling one's faith with one's sexuality, particularly if you are a gay teenager, can be a challenging obstacle of adolescence. In *The Real O'Neals*, Kenny O'Neal (Noah Galvin) is a teenager in a Catholic family where their reputation in the Chicago community is of paramount importance to his mother, Eileen (Martha Plimpton). When Kenny comes out of the closet, Eileen struggles to deal with how her son's homosexuality will be perceived, not so much about how it will look in the eyes of God but in the eyes of their congregation. Meanwhile, her own marriage is heading toward divorce, and that, in her eyes, is the unforgivable sin. The series also starred Jay R. Ferguson, Matthew Shively, Bebe Wood, and Mary Hollis Inboden. Created by Joshua Sternin and Jennifer Ventimilia and based on an idea by Dan Savage, *The Real O'Neals* played on ABC for two seasons.

The Series That Might

Just as there are series that tried to offer discussion of social issues, there are series that are still too new to determine what their impact will be. Here are some sitcoms that have the potential to change the face of television with their daring, out-of-the-box story lines and characters:

FRESH OFF THE BOAT (FEBRUARY 4, 2015–)

Having come a long way since the troubled run of *All-American Girl* in the 1990s, *Fresh Off the Boat* has definitely overcome the networks' concerns that a culturally Asian American family would not play successfully to the masses. It had been two decades since America had witnessed an Asian clan at the center of a television sitcom. This time around, audiences seem to have embraced the idea. As of this writing, *Fresh Off the Boat* has enjoyed five seasons on ABC. The story follows the Taiwanese Huang family, who have relocated from Chinatown in Washington, D.C., to Orlando, Florida, where they are an anomaly in their white suburban neighborhood. Created by Nahnatchka Khan, *Fresh Off the Boat* stars Randall Park, Constance Wu, Hudson Yang, and Ian Chen.

THE COOL KIDS (SEPTEMBER 28, 2018–)

Running on the Fox network, *The Cool Kids* seems to be picking up where *The Golden Girls* left off. Set in the Shady Meadows Retirement Community in

Arizona, four neighbors and dining partners (played by David Alan Grier, Martin Mull, Leslie Jordan, and Vicki Lawrence) prove that age is irrelevant where living happily is concerned. Although the show brims with shenanigans that are akin to a sitcom about high schoolers, it serves to point out that we are never too old for fun, sex, love, and adventure. The show also delves into the daunting prospect of our own mortality, as the characters realize that they have only so much time left to live life. Charlie Day and Paul Fruchborn created the show.

ALEXA AND KATIE (MARCH 23, 2018)

A surprisingly delightful sitcom aimed at tweens and teens popped up on Netflix in 2018. *Alexa and Katie* is about the friendship between two teenage girls, Alexa (Paris Berelc), who is going through treatment for cancer, and Katie (Isabel May), her supportive best friend who stands by her side through it all. The series, though lighthearted and aimed at a younger crowd, is helping to give kids an understanding of the challenges of being sick with something as devastating as cancer. Particularly poignant was Katie's supportive move of shaving her head when Alexis begins to lose her hair during treatment. The show, created by Heather Wordham, also stars Tiffani Thiessen, Eddie Shinn, Jolie Jenkins, Emery Kelly, and Finn Carr.

Notes

Mary Kay and Johnny

1. *Billboard*, March 6, 1948.

Amos 'n' Andy

1. J. Fred MacDonald, *Blacks and White TV: African Americans in Television since 1948* (Belmont, CA: Wadsworth, 1992).
2. "Why the *Amos 'n' Andy* Show should be Taken Off the Air." *NAACP Bulletin*, July 1951.
3. MacDonald, *Blacks and White TV*.

That Girl

1. Herbie J. Pilato, "*That Girl*: The One Who Changed Everything," Academy of Television Arts and Sciences, April 4, 2016.
2. Pilato, "*That Girl*."

Julia

1. Richard Warren Lewis, "The Importance of Being Julia," *TV Guide*, December 14, 1968.
2. "Breaking Barriers: African American Visibility in *Julia*," season 4, episode 3, *Pioneers of Television*, PBS, April 29, 2014.

3. Alice George, "Was the 1968 TV Show *Julia* a Milestone or a Millstone for Diversity?," Smithsonian.com, September 6, 2018.

The Mary Tyler Moore Show

1. Hans Peter Dreitzel, ed., *Recent Sociology No. 4: Family, Marriage, and the Struggle of the Sexes* (New York: Macmillan, 1972), 201–16.
2. Peabody Awards Committee, *The Mary Tyler Moore Show*, http://www.peabody-awards.com/award-profile/the-mary-tyler-moore-show.

Maude

1. Music by Dave Grusin; lyrics by Marilyn and Alan Bergman, "And Then There's Maude," 1972.

Bridget Loves Bernie

1. "Jewish Group Scores New TV Show for Intermarriage Theme," *Jewish Telegraphic Agency Daily Bulletin*, no. 204, October 24, 1972, 2.

M*A*S*H

1. Larry Gelbart, *Laughing Matters: On Writing M*A*S*H, Tootsie, Oh, God!, and a Few Other Funny Things* (New York: Random House, 1998).

Good Times

1. Music by Dave Grusin; lyrics by Alan and Marilyn Bergman, "Good Times," 1974.
2. Louie Robinson, "Bad Times on the *Good Times* Set," *Ebony*, September 1975.
3. Robinson, "Bad Times on the *Good Times* Set."

Laverne & Shirley

1. Norman Gimbel and Charles Fox, "Making Our Dreams Come True," 1976.

Soap

1. Harry F. Waters, "99 and 44/100% Impure," *Newsweek*, June 13, 1977.

Diff'rent Strokes

1. Alan Thicke, Al Burton, and Gloria Loring, "It Takes Diff'rent Strokes," 1978.

The Cosby Show

1. Katherine Schulten, "What Television Shows Have Mattered to You?" *New York Times,* September 25, 2014.
2. NewsOne staff, "Celebrating the 30th Anniversary of *The Cosby Show*," NewsOne, September 21, 2014.
3. Jake Flanagin, "Why *The Cosby Show* Still Matters," *New York Times*, September 24, 2014.

Head of the Class

1. Luaine Lee for Scripps-Howard News Service, "Hesseman Gives 'Head of the Class' a Low Grade," *Chicago Tribune*, August 16, 1989.

All-American Girl

1. *Finding Your Roots with Henry Louis Gates, Jr.*, featuring Sanjay Gupta, Margaret Cho, and Martha Stewart, season 1, episode 8, PBS, May 6, 2012.

Black-ish

1. Andrew R. Chow, "ABC Pulls 'black-ish' Episode over 'Creative Differences,'" *New York Times*, March 11, 2018.

Bibliography

Adamo, Gregory. *African Americans in Television: Behind the Scenes*. Bern: Peter Lang, 2010.

Adler, Richard. *All in the Family: A Critical Appraisal*. New York: Praeger, 1979.

Alley, Robert S. *Love Is All Around: The Making of The Mary Tyler Moore Show*. Crystal Lake, IL: Delta, 1989.

Armstrong, Jennifer Keishin. *Mary and Lou and Rhoda and Ted: And All the Brilliant Minds Who Made the Mary Tyler Moore Show a Classic*. New York: Simon & Schuster, 2013.

Ball, Lucy. *Love, Lucy*. New York: Putnam Adult, 1996.

Barlow, Aaron, and Laura Westengard. *The 25 Sitcoms That Changed Television*. Santa Barbara, CA: Praeger, 2017.

Barr, Roseanne. *My Lives*. New York: Ballantine, 1994.

Becker, Ron. *Gay TV and Straight America*. New Brunswick, NJ: Rutgers University Press, 2006.

Bergen, Candice. *A Fine Romance*. New York: Simon & Schuster, 2016.

Berman, A. S. *Soap! The Inside Story of the Sitcom That Broke All the Rules*. Albany, GA: BearManor Media, 2013.

Braxton, Greg. "It's All in the (Ground-Breaking) Family: Television: As a Sitcom Centered on Asian Americans, 'All-American Girl' Is Being Monitored by Advocacy Groups Concerned about Racial Stereotypes. Welcome to the Pressure Cooker." *Los Angeles Times*, September 14, 1994. http://articles.latimes.com/1994-09-14/entertainment/ca-38522_1_asian-americans.

Bridges, Todd. *Killing Willis: From Diff'rent Strokes to the Mean Streets to the Life I Always Wanted*. New York: Touchstone, 2010.

Burns-Ardolino, Wendy. *TV Female Foursomes and Their Fans*. Jefferson, NC: McFarland, 2015.

Campbell, Sean. *The Sitcoms of Norman Lear*. Jefferson, NC: McFarland, 2006.

Carroll, Diahann. *The Legs Are the Last to Go: Aging, Acting, Marrying, and Other Things I Learned the Hard Way*. New York: Amistad, 2008.

Cheers, Imani. *The Evolution of Black Women on Television: Mammies, Matriarchs and Mistresses*. New York: Routledge, 2017.

Clarkson, Wensley. *John Travolta: Back in Character*. New York: Overlook Press, 1996.

Cole, Stephen. *That Book about That Girl*. Amazon Digital Services, 2017.

Colucci, Jim. *Golden Girls Forever: An Unauthorized Look behind the Lanai*. New York: Harper Design, 2016.

———. *Will & Grace: Fabulously Uncensored*. New York: Time Home Entertainment, 2004.

Correll, Charles J., and Freeman F. Gosden, eds. *All about Amos 'n' Andy and Their Creators Correll and Gosden*. Chicago: Rand McNally, 1929.

Crowe, Allen. *The Q Guide to Designing Women*. New York: Alyson Books, 2007.

DeGeneres, Ellen. *Seriously . . . I'm Kidding*. New York: Grand Central Publishing, 2012.

Edelstein, Andrew H., and Frank Lovece. *The Brady Bunch Book*. New York: Warner Books, 1990.

Edwards, Elisabeth. *I Love Lucy: Celebrating 50 Years of Love and Laughter*. Philadelphia: Running Press, 2010.

Eleftheria, Kalogeras, and Jopi Nyman, eds. *Racial and Ethnic Identities in the Media*. Basingstoke: Palgrave Macmillan, 2016.

Ely, Melvin Patrick. *The Adventures of Amos 'n' Andy: A Social History of an American Phenomenon*. New York: Free Press, 1991.

Fields. Kim. *Blessed Life*. New York: Faith Words, 2017.

Fuller, Linda K. *The Cosby Show: Audiences, Impact, and Implications*. Westport, CT: Greenwood, 1992.

Gelbart, Larry. *Laughing Matters: On Writing M*A*S*H, Tootsie, Oh, God!, and a Few Other Funny Things*. New York: Random House, 1998.

Guillaume, Robert. *Guillaume: A Life*. Columbia: University of Missouri Press, 2017.

Harper, Valerie. *I, Rhoda*. New York: Gallery Books, 2013.

Irvin, Richard. *The Early Shows: A Reference Guide to Network and Syndicated Prime-Time Television Series from 1944 to 1949*. Albany, GA: BearManor Media, 2018.

Jhally, Sut. *Enlightened Racism: The Cosby Show, Audiences, and the Myth of the American Dream*. London: Routledge, 1992.

Jung, E. Alex. "All-American Girl at 20: The Evolution of Asian Americans on TV." *Los Angeles Review of Books*, November 9, 2014. https://lareviewofbooks.org/article/american-girl-20-evolution-asian-americans-tv#!.

Kalter, Suzy, and Larry Gelbart. *The Complete Book of M*A*S*H*. New York: Harry N. Abrams, 1988.

Klein, Allison. *What Would Murphy Brown Do? How the Women of Prime Time Changed Our Lives*. New York: Seal Press, 2006.

Lear, Norman. *Even This I Get to Experience*. New York: Penguin, 2014.

Leonard, David J., and Lisa Guerrero. *African Americans on Television: Race-ing for Ratings*. Santa Barbara, CA: Praeger, 2013.

Levin, Elana. *Wallowing in Sex: The New Sexual Culture of 1970s Television*. Durham, NC: Duke University Press, 2007.

Mann, Chris. *Come and Knock on Our Door: A Hers and Hers and His Guide to Three's Company.* New York: St. Martin's Griffin, 1998.

Marshall, Garry. *My Happy Days in Hollywood: A Memoir.* New York: Crown Archetype, 2012.

Marshall, Penny. *My Mother Was Nuts: A Memoir.* Boston: New Harvest, 2014.

McCrohan, Donna. *Archie & Edith, Mike & Gloria: The Tumultuous History of All in the Family.* New York: Workman, 1988.

Moody, David L., and Rob Prince Obey. *The Complexity and Progression of Black Representation in Film and Television.* Lanham, MD: Lexington Books, 2017.

Oppenheimer, Jess, with Gregg Oppenheimer. *I Love Lucy: The Untold Story.* Gregg Oppenheimer, 2012.

Pearl, Jonathan, and Judith Pearl. *The Chosen Image: Television's Portrayal of Jewish Themes and Characters.* Jefferson, NC: McFarland, 1999.

Phillips, Mackenzie. *High on Arrival.* New York: Gallery Books, 2011.

Pilato, Herbie. *Mary: The Mary Tyler Moore Story.* Clarksville, TN: Jacobs Brown Press, 2019.

Press, Andrea L., and Elizabeth R. Cole. *Speaking of Abortion: Television and Authority in the Lives of Women.* Chicago: University of Chicago Press, 1999.

Rae, Charlotte, and Larry Strauss. *The Facts of My Life.* Albany, GA: BearManor Media, 2015.

Reiss, David S. *M*A*S*H: The Exclusive, Inside Story of TV's Most-Popular Show.* London: Macmillan, 1983.

Ross, Shavar. *On the Set of Diff'rent Strokes.* Pasadena, CA: Tri-Seven Entertainment, 2010.

Saget, Bob. *Dirty Daddy: The Chronicles of a Family Man Turned Filthy Comedian.* New York: It Books, 2014.

Schwartz, Sherwood, and Lloyd J. Schwartz. *Brady, Brady, Brady: The Complete Story of The Brady Bunch as Told by the Father/Son Team Who Really Know.* New York: Running Press, 2010.

Spangler, Lynn. *From Mary Kay and Johnny to Murphy Brown: Fifty Years of Sitcoms and Feminism.* Westport, CT: Greenwood, 2003.

Starr, Michael Seth. *Black and Blue: The Redd Foxx Story.* Milwaukee, WI: Applause Books, 2011.

Storey, T. R. *Full House: Behind the Series.* Lake Oswego, OR: Troll, 1993.

Sweetin, Jodie. *UnSweetined: A Memoir.* New York: Gallery Books, 2010.

Thomas, Marlo. *Growing Up Laughing.* New York: Hyperion, 2010.

Van Dyke, Dick. *Dick Van Dyke: My Lucky Life in and out of Show Business.* New York: Crown Archetype, 2011.

Varady, David P. *Desegregating the City: Ghettos, Enclaves, and Inequality.* Albany: State University of New York Press, 2006.

Waldron, Vince. *Classic Sitcoms: A Celebration of the Best in Prime-Time Comedy.* Los Angeles: Sillman James, 1998.

———. *The Official Dick Van Dyke Show Book: The Definitive History of Television's Most Enduring Comedy.* Chicago: Chicago Review Press, 2011.

Weitzman, Elizabeth, and Austen Claire Clements. *Renegade Women in Film & TV*. New York: Clarkson Potter, 2019.

White, Betty. *If You Ask Me (and of Course You Won't)*. New York: Berkley, 2011.

Williams, Barry, and Chris Kreski. *Growing Up Brady*. New York: HarperCollins, 1992.

Williams, Cindy. *Shirley, I Jest! A Storied Life*. Guilford, CT: Lyons Press, 2017.

Index

About the Author

Mark Robinson is a graduate of the State University of New York in Cortland with a degree in speech/theater. He has taught high school theater and writing and regularly directs youth and professional theater productions. A resident of upstate New York, he has been honored by the New York State Legislature for his work bringing arts education to underprivileged youth in economically depressed areas. A featured writer for several theater websites, including BroadwayDirect.com, ShowTickets.com, and Playbill.com, he has spent the past 15 years researching and writing about theater, film, and television. He is also a travel and tourism writer for a variety of e-commerce platforms. He is the author of the books *The Disney Song Encyclopedia* (with Thomas S. Hischak), *The Encyclopedia of Television Theme Songs*, and the two-volume reference series *The World of Musicals*.